Management for Professionals

The Springer series "Management for Professionals" comprises high-level business and management books for executives, MBA students, and practice-oriented business researchers. The topics cover all themes relevant to businesses and the business ecosystem. The authors are experienced business professionals and renowned professors who combine scientific backgrounds, best practices, and entrepreneurial vision to provide powerful insights into achieving business excellence.

The Series is SCOPUS-indexed.

Jianrong Wang

ESG Strategies and Financial Markets

Antecedents, Corporate Decision-Making, and Real Effects

Springer

Jianrong Wang
Asia Europe Business School, Shanghai
International School of Chief Technology
Officer
East China Normal University
Shanghai, China

ISSN 2192-8096 ISSN 2192-810X (electronic)
Management for Professionals
ISBN 978-981-95-5619-9 ISBN 978-981-95-5620-5 (eBook)
https://doi.org/10.1007/978-981-95-5620-5

This Springer imprint is published by the registered company Springer Nature Singapore Pte Ltd.
The registered company address is: 152 Beach Road, #21-01/04 Gateway East, Singapore 189721, Singapore

Preface

This book offers an integrated, theory-grounded and evidence-based analysis of Environmental, Social, and Governance (ESG) strategy and its interaction with financial markets. We begin by situating the rise of ESG within debates on sustainability, corporate purpose, and financial performance. We trace the evolution from corporate social responsibility (CSR) to ESG, document the diffusion of practices across industries, and assemble the conceptual foundations needed to explain how ESG initiatives originate, scale, and alter corporate outcomes.

We then examine the antecedents of ESG adoption. Internal drivers include managerial incentives, leadership vision, governance design, and organizational routines. External forces—social capital, stakeholder expectations, regulatory frameworks, and policy regimes—shape firms' incentives and constraints. By analyzing how these forces interact, the book explains cross-firm differences in ESG strategy and the prioritization across environmental, social, and governance dimensions under resource and compliance limits.

The analysis proceeds to financial-market consequences. We study how ESG affects risk-taking, resilience, and long-term competitiveness, and how it maps into financing outcomes, including the cost of equity and debt, access to capital, and capital allocation. We also examine how markets process ESG information—through disclosures, third-party ratings, and controversies—and how this information changes price informativeness, liquidity, and investor decision-making.

The concluding chapters synthesize results and clarify contributions to finance, corporate governance, and sustainability research. We identify measurement and identification challenges, outline limitations in current evidence, and chart directions for future work in data, methods, and theory. By integrating conceptual foundations, adoption drivers, and market effects in a single framework, the book advances ESG as both a strategic corporate choice and a determinant of financial outcomes. We intend the analysis to be useful to scholars, investors, policymakers, and managers seeking decision-relevant insights.

We hope this book stimulates rigorous research on ESG strategy, encourages the development of richer data and methods, and informs policy design. We also hope it offers practical guidance to managers and investors on implementing ESG initiatives that are material, auditable, and value-creating. Our aim is that years of accumulated work in this field contribute useful knowledge to academic inquiry and managerial practice.

Shanghai, China Jianrong Wang

Acknowledgments This book is the result of years of research and the support of many individuals and organizations. It builds on the work of scholars whose ideas have shaped the questions, theory, and methods presented here. Any remaining errors are my own.

I am indebted to my co-authors for sustained collaboration across projects, drafts, and data work. Their discipline in research design, coding, and interpretation set a high standard throughout. I am grateful to mentors and senior colleagues who challenged early versions of the arguments and pressed for sharper identification and clearer mechanisms.

Anonymous reviewers and journal editors provided rigorous critique on related articles. Their comments on construct validity, variable measurement, instrument strength, and robustness checks informed multiple revisions and improved the quality of the work. I also benefited from discussions at the Academy of Management and Financial Management Association conferences, as well as from seminar participants at host institutions.

I thank Springer Nature for the opportunity to publish this book and for professional guidance from proposal through production. I appreciate the editorial, production, and marketing teams for their clear timelines, careful editing, and steady coordination.

I am especially grateful to my Ph.D. advisor, Haizhi Wang. He opened my mind and introduced me to the wider world of academia. His encouragement, guidance, and confidence in me have been unwavering. My deepest thanks go to my family for their steadfast support throughout this project.

Jianrong Wang

Competing Interests The author has no competing interests to declare that are relevant to the content of this manuscript.

Contents

Part III Discussions and Conclusions

About the Author

Jianrong Wang is an Assistant Professor at East China Normal University. She holds a Ph.D. in Finance from Illinois Institute of Technology. Her research focuses on corporate finance, innovation, and ESG. Her work appears in journals including the *Journal of Business Research*, *Applied Economics*, *Managerial Finance*, and the *International Journal of Financial Studies*. She has also presented at the Academy of Management and Financial Management Association annual meetings.

List of Figures

List of Tables

Part I

Foundations of ESG and Corporate Strategy

Introduction to ESG and Its Growing Importance

1

1.1 From Shareholder Value to Stakeholder Value

The traditional foundation of corporate finance rests on the principle that the primary objective of a firm is to maximize shareholder wealth. This principle has guided financial theory and practice since the mid-twentieth century. The logic is rooted in agency theory and the assumption that shareholders, as residual claimants, bear the ultimate risks of corporate activity. Thus, the value of a firm should be maximized by aligning managerial decisions with shareholder interests. Classic models in corporate finance reinforced the centrality of shareholder value. The feature of the corporation posits that corporate managers act as agents whose task is to deliver financial returns to shareholders.

Experience revealed material limits to strict shareholder value maximization. First, firms operate in dense networks of incomplete, multi-period contracts with employees, customers, suppliers, and communities. Value creation relies on firm-specific human capital, tacit knowledge, and supply-chain reliability that are not perfectly priced or contractible ex ante. Second, externalities—environmental damage, data privacy harms, systemic risk—alter social welfare without entering private cash flows unless priced or regulated. Third, principal–agent problems extend beyond "shareholders vs managers" to principal–principal conflicts among equity holders, debt holders, and other financiers with different payoff convexities and horizons. Finally, reputational capital and license-to-operate are now salient assets; shocks to these intangibles can rapidly erase market value even when near-term cash flows look intact.

The concept of the stakeholder emerged to capture this broader range of interests. Freeman (1984) defined stakeholders as "any group or individual who can affect or is affected by the achievement of an organization's objectives." Stakeholder theory argues that corporate purpose should reflect responsibilities to these parties. Descriptively, it maps how real firms negotiate claims. Stakeholder theory challenged the narrow focus on shareholders by arguing that long-term corporate

J. Wang, *ESG Strategies and Financial Markets*, Management for Professionals,
https://doi.org/10.1007/978-981-95-5620-5_1

success depends on balancing the interests of multiple constituencies. Firms that ignore stakeholder concerns may face reputational damage, regulatory backlash, or operational disruptions.

Stakeholder theory comprises three strands—descriptive, instrumental, and normative—that differ in purpose yet inform one another.

Descriptive stakeholder theory explains how firms actually behave in environments populated by many claimants. It observes that corporations build and manage networks of relationships with employees, customers, suppliers, creditors, communities, and regulators. These relationships shape strategy, execution, and performance under incomplete contracts. Descriptive work maps who the stakeholders are, how salient they become, and how managers interact with them. Salience depends on power, legitimacy, and urgency, which together determine who receives attention and resources in practice. This strand documents routines of engagement, crisis response, and coalition building. It does not prescribe goals. It characterizes governance as it is.

Instrumental stakeholder theory links stakeholder management to measurable economic outcomes. It asks a positive question: if managers invest in relationships with material stakeholders, what happens to cash flows, growth, risk, and the cost of capital. The mechanisms are operational. Better employee relations raise productivity and lower turnover. Strong supplier ties reduce input volatility and quality failures. Customer trust supports margins and repeat business. Community acceptance and regulatory credibility protect growth options and shorten adoption lags. Credible management of environmental and conduct risks can reduce credit spreads and equity risk premia when such risks are priced. Robust processes lessen the frequency and severity of fines, boycotts, and operational shutdowns, which compresses left-tail risk. The empirical literature tests whether stronger stakeholder or social performance predicts stronger financial performance, whether effects concentrate in issues that are financially material by industry, and whether stakeholder capital improves crisis resilience. The results guide design. Managers translate stakeholder priorities into validated operating metrics, tie incentives to those metrics with horizon-matching deferral, and disclose decision-useful data so capital markets can price what matters. Instrumental theory is conditional. Benefits arise when the issues are material to the business model, when metrics are reliable, when investments are efficient, and when claims are credible rather than symbolic.

Normative stakeholder theory provides the ethical ground. It argues that firms owe duties to stakeholders because these parties make firm-specific investments, bear risk, and possess rights that deserve respect independent of immediate financial payoff. Directors in this view steward a cooperative enterprise, not only an equity contract. The board mediates among contributors to protect the joint surplus from opportunistic appropriation. This strand informs legal and governance arrangements that recognize broader purposes, such as constituency statutes and co-determination. It sets a floor for acceptable conduct even when markets do not yet price an externality.

1.2 CSR as Bridge to ESG

1.2.1 The Rise of Corporate Social Responsibility (CSR)

Corporate Social Responsibility (CSR) is a firm's voluntary integration of social and environmental concerns into its business operations and stakeholder interactions. Modern CSR was articulated in the United States in the 1950s with Bowen's call for business leaders to pursue policies desirable to society. Quaker industrialists such as Cadbury and Rowntree built model villages, set worker-welfare norms, and tied product quality to civic obligations. Those experiments gave CSR visible institutional form long before the vocabulary stabilized. In the postwar United States, civil-rights, consumer-protection, and environmental movements pressed firms to address product safety, workplace standards, and pollution. The debate sharpened with Friedman's 1970 claim that the social responsibility of business is to increase profits within the rules, which forced clearer definitions of what responsibility covered and what counted as "the rules." Through the 1980s and 1990s, stakeholder theory reframed the firm as a nexus of relationships, and CSR shifted from peripheral philanthropy to a managerial agenda linked to strategy, operations, and supply chains. Reporting frameworks and voluntary standards followed, making claims observable and comparable.

To understand CSR's content, it helps to anchor on Carroll's formulation, which Dahlsrud identified as the most widely accepted because it specifies the substance of corporate obligations rather than only their motivations. Carroll argued that a definition covering all obligations a company owes to society must incorporate economic, legal, ethical, and philanthropic facets of performance. In 1991 he organized these into a pyramid that clarified sequence and interdependence (see Fig. 1.1).

Economic responsibility forms the base because sustained profitability finances every other obligation. Legal responsibility sits above it, since firms must pursue profit within the law and comply with codified rules. Ethical responsibility extends

Fig. 1.1 Pyramid of CSR

beyond statutes to what is fair and just when regulation is silent or lagging. Philanthropic responsibility crowns the structure and encompasses voluntary actions that improve the quality of life for employees, local communities, and society at large, including charitable donations, school support, and sponsorship of cultural or sporting events. The pyramid did not pretend that firms climb steps in a clean order. Its use was pragmatic: it gave managers, boards, and regulators a shared language to map decisions, trade-offs, and disclosures.

Institutionalization accelerated once firms could disclose and verify what they were doing. Environmental management systems such as ISO 14001, labor and accountability frameworks such as SA8000 and AA1000, the Global Reporting Initiative's guidelines, and the UN Global Compact offered process discipline and comparability. In the 2000s and 2010s, globalization of supply chains and the diffusion of social media reduced information frictions. Misconduct surfaced faster. Credible remediation mattered more. Europe moved early on mandatory sustainability reporting and human-rights due diligence. Denmark required large companies to report on CSR policies and outcomes well before most jurisdictions, and Nordic boards integrated climate and labor oversight into mainstream risk management rather than treating them as side projects. The United States remained the wellspring of CSR scholarship and many reporting innovations, while Britain's earlier industrial paternalism provided concrete precedents. Today, the best firm-level execution is widely associated with Nordic economies, notably Denmark and Sweden, where disclosure quality, stakeholder engagement, and supply-chain due diligence are embedded in governance and supported by policy. No single jurisdiction dominates every metric, but the Nordic pattern of early, integrated practice sets a benchmark.

The economic logic of CSR is not a slogan about "doing well by doing good." It is a set of channels that connect specific policies to cash flows and discount rates. Where CSR targets financially material issues for a given industry, firms can reduce regulatory, legal, and reputational tail risks and avoid costly disruptions. Resource-efficiency programs yield operating savings with short paybacks and predictable variance reduction. Credible disclosure and third-party assurance can broaden the investor base, lower information asymmetry, and tighten credit spreads. Human-capital practices that raise workplace quality, safety, inclusion, and purpose help recruit and retain scarce talent and raise productivity. For differentiated products, provenance, safety, and low carbon intensity bolster pricing power and customer loyalty. Community engagement and transparent permitting lower policy and project-delay risk. Supplier auditing, capacity building, and multi-sourcing raise resilience to labor, safety, and geopolitical shocks. None of these payoffs are automatic. They depend on materiality, execution, and time horizon, and they can fail when firms make symbolic commitments that are not backed by incentives, data, and controls.

Well-known cases trace the arc from crisis response to strategic integration. In the 1990s, Nike faced sustained criticism over labor conditions at supplier factories. Initial defensiveness damaged credibility and brand equity. The firm changed course by disclosing supplier lists, adopting independent audits, creating grievance and remediation channels, and integrating sustainability into design and materials choices. Over time Nike recovered legitimacy and converted lessons into product and process innovation. Unilever made CSR strategic through the Sustainable Living plan, tying brand growth to health, hygiene, and lower environmental intensity. Targets were embedded in procurement and R&D, which simplified narratives for consumers and investors and supported long-horizon brand strength. Patagonia institutionalized repair and resale, invested in supply-chain traceability, and placed ownership into a perpetual purpose trust aligned with ecological objectives. Circular design and governance commitments increased customer stickiness and reduced exposure to future regulation. These cases differ in sector and governance, but each shows the same pattern: transparency, measurable targets, and operating integration turn CSR from a reputational shield into a capability.

1.2.2 CSR to ESG Interconnection

CSR also has credible critiques. Vague, voluntary programs enable decoupling between talk and action and raise greenwashing risk. Rating dispersion across data vendors reflects measurement noise, coverage gaps, and different materiality maps. Some initiatives impose near-term costs that managers struggle to defend without clear metrics and board-level sponsorship. There are trade-offs among stakeholders that cannot be reconciled by aspiration alone. These limits motivate the move from CSR to ESG, where the goal is decision-useful information for investors and creditors.

CSR laid the normative and managerial groundwork. ESG provides the measurement and capital-allocation layer. The shift adds an "outside-in" lens that asks how environmental, social, and governance exposures change firm cash flows and the cost of capital. Industry-specific standards translate high-level aims into comparable indicators. Climate risk disclosure frames transition and physical risks in financial terms. Integrated reporting links sustainability to value creation, and assurance lowers the cost of trust. Governance is the hinge. Boards need domain expertise, clear oversight of material E and S risks, incentive plans aligned with measurable outcomes, and internal control systems that can withstand audit. When these elements are in place, ESG becomes a practical extension of CSR: the same responsibilities, rendered in metrics that inform capital budgeting, credit analysis, stewardship, and regulation.

Geography and history together explain the current landscape. Britain undertook the earliest recognizable CSR practice at scale in the industrial era, and the United States produced the core academic articulation and many of the managerial tools. Today Nordic economies—especially Denmark and Sweden—offer the most consistent record of firm-level execution, with early laws on reporting, rigorous supply-chain oversight, and boards that treat sustainability as standard risk management. The direction of travel is clear across jurisdictions. CSR began as ethics and philanthropy, matured into governance and systems, and now underpins ESG's quantified, investor-facing architecture, where credible practice is defined by materiality, measurement, and assurance. In that progression, Carroll's pyramid remains useful: profitability finances obligations, law constrains means, ethics guides conduct where law is incomplete, and philanthropy strengthens the social fabric on which markets depend. Dahlsrud's reminder is still apt. Without clear dimensions and definitions, CSR drifts. With them, it becomes a workable part of corporate finance.

1.3 The Rise of ESG

1.3.1 What is ESG?

ESG entered mainstream corporate finance when a series of structural shifts made non-financial factors impossible to ignore. Climate volatility exposed physical and transition risks that balance sheets did not capture. Governance failures and data breaches wiped out equity value overnight. Social expectations hardened into regulation and procurement rules. Meanwhile, digitization increased transparency, allowing investors, lenders, and customers to observe operational practices in real time. As these forces compounded, markets began to price not only what a firm earns today, but how robust those earnings are to environmental, social, and governance shocks. ESG emerged as a practical response: a way to organize decision-useful information about exposures and capabilities that traditional accounting only partially reflects.

At its core, ESG is an information framework. It expands the set of variables managers and investors use to forecast cash flows, choose discount rates, and assess tail risks. It is not a moral doctrine, a public-relations exercise, or a promise of excess returns. Properly scoped, ESG supplies structured, comparable, and auditable data about how a firm's operations interact with its regulatory, physical, human, and institutional environment. Two materiality lenses guide what enters the framework. Financial (single) materiality considers only those sustainability factors that affect enterprise value. Double materiality adds the firm's significant impacts on the environment and society on the view that these impacts can feed back through law, norms, customer behavior, and supply-chain dynamics. Firms operate under both lenses to differing degrees depending on jurisdiction and stakeholder demands, but the organizing principle is the same: identify what moves value and measure it consistently.

1.3.2 Why Do Companies Pay Attention?

Capital markets now condition access and pricing on ESG readiness. Banks embed climate and conduct risk in covenants and offer pricing step-downs when verified targets are met. Bond investors expect credible use-of-proceeds and external reviews. Equity investors use ESG data to reduce information asymmetry, refine stewardship, and lower the risk premia they demand for agency and controversy risk. Insurers price hazard exposure and operational controls. Large customers impose supplier standards on labor, safety, and emissions as a prerequisite to participation in global value chains. Regulators and listing venues standardize disclosures and enforce claims. In each channel, ESG acts as a passport: without a baseline of controls, data, and governance, firms face higher capital costs, narrower investor bases, and shrinking commercial opportunity.

ESG also improves managerial decision quality inside the firm. By mapping salient sustainability topics into enterprise risk management, companies can quantify exposures that were previously treated as narrative—location-specific climate hazards, cybersecurity posture, supply-chain labor compliance, product safety regimes—and link them to budgets, hurdle rates, and contingency plans. Scenario analysis translates long-horizon uncertainties into today's capital allocation. Clear ownership and incentive design convert broad aspirations into a small set of measurable targets tied to accountable managers. The result is fewer surprises, faster recovery from shocks, and better identification of profitable opportunities such as resource-efficient processes, trusted products, and more reliable supplier networks.

Reporting is the mechanism that makes ESG credible. High-quality ESG reporting reduces information risk for external capital providers and aligns internal actors on definitions, baselines, and trajectories. It turns qualitative claims into audit-ready metrics with documented scope, methods, and controls. Consistent reporting supports comparability across peers and over time, allowing markets to distinguish execution from rhetoric and to reward operational improvements rather than marketing. It also lowers litigation and enforcement risk by ensuring that public statements are substantiated and that boundary choices—what parts of the value chain are included, which methodologies are applied—are explicit and defensible. For management, the discipline of reporting forces data governance: firms must locate source systems, reconcile conflicting figures, establish change control, and commission assurance where credibility and financing depend on accuracy. Over time, this infrastructure pays for itself by shortening diligence cycles, unlocking sustainability-linked financing, and enabling rapid, evidence-based responses to stakeholder scrutiny.

1.3.3 The Three Pillars

1.3.3.1 Environmental Pillar

Environmental factors measure how a company manages its resource use, emissions, and physical footprint across its full value chain. From wildfires to floods, the catastrophic impacts of climate change threaten to outpace our global ability to adapt, reinforcing the importance of companies and people doing all they can to reduce their carbon emissions. Microsoft, for example, was an early adopter of an internal carbon fee, first implemented in 2012, that charges each business unit for its direct and indirect greenhouse gas emissions. This fee is not symbolic; it generates real costs and revenues that are reinvested in emissions reduction and removal projects. Microsoft's ambition is to remove from the environment all the carbon the company has emitted since it was founded by 2050.

Walmart has set a global example through Project Gigaton, an initiative that works with its vast supplier network to avoid 1 billion metric tons of emissions in the company's collective value chains by 2030.[1] This project embeds climate targets directly into procurement and logistics, requiring suppliers to measure, report, and actively reduce their own emissions. By 2024, Walmart announced it was on track to meet this target ahead of schedule, illustrating how supply-chain collaboration can yield measurable climate impact and operational savings.In heavy industry and logistics, Maersk is moving the needle on transition risk by ordering methanol-fueled vessels and building a green fuel ecosystem. These choices signal a capital allocation strategy aligned with decarbonization, supporting Maersk's target to achieve net-zero emissions by 2040.[2]

In all cases, metrics such as absolute and intensity emissions, renewable energy share, internal carbon price, and climate value-at-risk analysis are wired into investment decisions and performance reviews, ensuring that environmental commitments are material to the business.

1.3.3.2 Social Pillar

The social dimension covers a firm's approach to its workforce, customers, suppliers, and broader community. Effective management is strongly linked to productivity, risk, and market access. Salesforce provides a notable example: it conducts an annual company-wide equal pay assessment and publicly reports the results, adjusting compensation where disparities are found. This practice reduces legal and reputational risk, supports retention and engagement, and sets a measurable standard for inclusion.

Apple operates one of the world's largest supply chain audit programs, conducting regular labor and safety checks across thousands of supplier sites. Results are published annually, including pass rates and corrective actions, and the company escalates or terminates suppliers who persistently fail to meet standards. This approach directly impacts supply continuity, product quality, and brand trust.

Unilever takes a data-driven approach to workplace safety, tracking incidents through metrics across all facilities. These actions inform continuous improvement processes and are linked to management evaluation, reducing downtime and improving morale.

Across these firms, social indicators such as injury rates, employee turnover, pay equity dispersion, supplier audit outcomes, and customer complaint resolution times are systematically tracked and managed. The result is a more stable, productive, and resilient organization, better equipped to anticipate and respond to stakeholder expectations.

[1] https://corporate.walmart.com/news/2019/05/08/walmart-on-track-to-reduce-1-billion-metric-tons-of-emissions-from-global-supply-chains-by-2030.

[2] https://www.maersk.com/sustainability/all-the-way-to-net-zero.

1.3.3.3 Governance Pillar

Governance relates to the systems, controls, and leadership structures that direct corporate behavior and ensure accountability. Wells Fargo's experience after its sales-practice scandal is instructive: in the aftermath, the board took unprecedented action by clawing back over $180 million in executive compensation, implementing new risk controls, and increasing board oversight of management. These governance reforms were not optional; they were demanded by investors, regulators, and the public, and were essential to restoring the bank's market standing and regulatory compliance.

On a broader scale, the U.S. Securities and Exchange Commission has mandated, via Rule 10D-1, that all listed companies adopt clawback policies for incentive compensation in the event of financial restatements, signaling a system-wide expectation for recovery of ill-gotten rewards. Meanwhile, Siemens, after a major corruption scandal in the late 2000s, overhauled its compliance systems, introduced strict anti-corruption controls, and launched ongoing internal training and auditing. This reset not only limited regulatory and legal risk but also restored trust with business partners and investors.

Governance metrics that matter include board independence and diversity, quality of internal controls, executive compensation alignment, anti-corruption enforcement, and transparency in related-party transactions and tax strategies. These features are priced into a company's cost of capital and resilience to crisis, directly affecting shareholder and stakeholder value.

In summary, the three pillars of ESG are not abstract categories—they are operational levers with concrete business examples across industries. Leading firms make these factors visible, measurable, and material to strategy and performance, setting new standards for value creation in the process.

1.3.4 Measurement and Rating Divergence

Environmental, social, and governance (ESG) measures have become increasingly central to both industry practice and academic research on corporate social responsibility (CSR). The environmental dimension continues to emphasize carbon emissions across scopes 1 to 3, energy and water usage, waste management, local pollution, and biodiversity footprint, but recent developments have extended attention to climate stress testing, nature and biodiversity loss, and supply-chain emissions, often drawing on life-cycle analyses and satellite or remote sensing data. On the social side, long-standing concerns with labor practices, workplace safety, discrimination, and community relations are now joined by a stronger focus on diversity, equity, and inclusion beyond surface metrics, mental health, modern slavery in supply chains, and the social implications of data privacy and artificial intelligence. Governance measures remain rooted in board composition, executive compensation, shareholder rights, and anti-corruption safeguards, but they now increasingly incorporate oversight of ESG risk itself, executive pay linked to ESG outcomes, cyber-security and data governance, and regulatory compliance under evolving disclosure regimes. Collectively, these shifts indicate that ESG is no longer limited to backward-looking performance indicators but is expanding into forward-looking assessments of risk and resilience.

The measurement of these dimensions is dominated by rating agencies that apply different methodological lenses. MSCI ESG Ratings, one of the most influential providers, assesses more than 17,000 issuers worldwide using a rules-based, industry-specific methodology and assigns relative ratings from AAA to CCC, drawing on both corporate disclosures and alternative data. Sustainalytics adopts a distinct risk-oriented framework, evaluating how exposed a firm is to ESG challenges and how effectively it manages them, which has made it a favored tool for investors screening portfolio risk. Other prominent providers include Refinitiv, ISS-ESG, S&P Global's Trucost, and Moody's, each combining policy assessments with performance outcomes and varying in emphasis on forward-looking scenarios. KLD, which originated as the Domini 400 Social Index and is now incorporated into MSCI's ESG index family, remains a touchstone in both practice and research for its role in benchmarking socially conscious investment portfolios. In academia, these ratings have been scrutinized for their divergence, as studies consistently find that different agencies apply distinct weighting schemes, materiality assumptions, and data sources, which often leads to sharply different scores for the same firm.

This divergence has generated a series of concerns that define the current ESG debate. Methodological inconsistency undermines comparability and creates noise for investors, while opaque disclosure of weighting schemes reduces transparency. Much of the available data remains backward-looking, raising questions about whether ESG ratings can anticipate forward risks such as climate regulation, social unrest, or technological disruption. Regulatory bodies, particularly in the European Union and India, are responding with rules that require greater disclosure and standardization from both corporations and rating providers.

At the same time, advances in alternative data and computational methods are reshaping the landscape: large language models and other machine learning techniques are being used to analyze annual reports, news, and social media, while satellite imagery offers independent measures of environmental performance. Academic research has taken up these issues, evaluating whether ratings add predictive value for risk and return, how ratings influence corporate disclosure behavior, and whether ESG integration can systematically enhance financial performance. The consensus emerging is that ESG measures are valuable but fragmented, reflecting not only the complexity of sustainability but also the contested terrain of what constitutes responsible corporate behavior. This evolving landscape ensures that ESG and CSR ratings remain both an indispensable tool for practitioners and a fertile ground for scholarly inquiry.

1.4 Government Attitudes and the Policy–Regulatory Landscape

1.4.1 China

China's official stance on ESG is framed by the overarching vision of "ecological civilization" and the pursuit of high-quality development, with carbon peaking before 2030 and carbon neutrality by 2060 as central policy anchors. A wide range of instruments has been introduced to support these objectives, including mandatory ESG disclosure guidance issued by stock exchanges, green-bond catalogues that specify eligible use-of-proceeds, sector-level rules to cap energy intensity and emissions, and the gradual expansion of pilot carbon markets toward a unified national trading scheme. State-owned enterprises are subject to strong directives not only on environmental compliance but also on governance, anti-corruption, and transparency, reflecting the state's role in aligning corporate conduct with policy priorities. Financial regulators encourage green lending, transition finance, and clean-technology innovation. Listed firms face growing requirements to provide quantitative, third-party-assured reporting rather than relying solely on narrative disclosure.

Despite this comprehensive policy architecture, the emphasis remains heavily weighted toward the environmental pillar, especially carbon reduction initiatives. China's carbon-neutrality roadmap and associated measures, while ambitious and globally significant, risk crowding out systematic attention to the social and governance dimensions of ESG. Issues such as labor standards, community engagement, board independence, minority shareholder protection, and anti-bribery practices often receive less policy visibility compared to carbon emission reduction. As a result, the country's ESG trajectory demonstrates a strong environmental orientation, with progress on carbon neutrality and green finance at the forefront, but with social and governance considerations still lagging behind in regulatory focus and market practice.

1.4.2 United States

The U.S. approach to ESG remains primarily market-driven, shaped by contested federal rulemaking and strong influence from institutional investors. Federal initiatives, most visibly through the Securities and Exchange Commission (SEC), emphasize climate-related and financially material sustainability disclosures, aligning ESG with the narrow lens of investor-relevant risk and return. Large asset managers and proxy advisors exert significant stewardship pressure, while state-level policies diverge—some promoting ESG integration and others restricting its application. Rules governing labor and retirement plans permit ESG considerations only insofar as they are financially material, reinforcing the primacy of shareholder-focused objectives. Instruments such as sustainability-linked loans and green bonds have grown, driven by lender covenants and investor demand, but political polarization has intensified litigation, compliance risk, and accusations of greenwashing. This environment has pushed firms to concentrate heavily on environmental metrics, particularly carbon risk, while often overlooking social and governance dimensions such as workforce equity, board accountability, and anti-corruption practices. The result is an ESG regime where environmental disclosure advances steadily, but the broader balance across the three pillars remains uneven.

1.4.3 Europe

Europe has established itself as the global leader in mandatory sustainability reporting and sustainable-finance infrastructure, underpinned by an expansive regulatory framework. Corporate sustainability reporting rules enforce the principle of double materiality, requiring firms to account not only for financial impacts but also for their external effects on society and the environment. Reports are subject to digital tagging and independent assurance to ensure comparability and reliability. Financial intermediaries face product-level disclosure and labeling obligations under the Sustainable Finance Disclosure Regulation (SFDR), while the EU Taxonomy provides a detailed classification of environmentally sustainable activities. Supervisory authorities integrate climate and biodiversity risks into stress testing and scenario analysis, embedding ESG into the prudential oversight of banks and insurers. Europe's prescriptive design is intended to curb greenwashing and set a global benchmark that influences non-EU multinationals with material operations in the European market. Nevertheless, the system remains heavily oriented toward environmental sustainability, with detailed frameworks on carbon emissions, energy transition, and biodiversity. By contrast, social and governance aspects—such as labor rights, diversity, and corporate accountability—receive comparatively less regulatory depth, leaving the European model highly advanced in environmental standardization but still underdeveloped in fully integrating the other ESG pillars.

1.4.4 Implications for Multinationals

ESG matters to multinational companies because it has become a core determinant of regulatory compliance, capital access, operational resilience, and corporate legitimacy across markets. For global firms, environmental issues such as carbon emissions, energy intensity, and climate risks now directly influence cost structures, supply chain stability, and access to green finance. Governments in major economies—including the EU with its Corporate Sustainability Reporting Directive and taxonomy, the U.S. with SEC climate disclosure proposals, and China with its carbon-neutrality agenda—are embedding ESG requirements into financial and corporate law. Compliance is no longer optional, and failure to meet reporting and performance standards can restrict market entry, raise financing costs, or trigger sanctions.

Investors and lenders likewise integrate ESG into decision-making, using ratings from MSCI, Sustainalytics, and others to benchmark risk exposure. Multinationals that demonstrate strong ESG performance benefit from lower capital costs, inclusion in ESG indexes, and greater access to sustainability-linked loans and green bonds. Conversely, poor ESG scores can increase scrutiny from asset managers, raise the risk of shareholder activism, and limit participation in institutional portfolios.

Operationally, ESG practices strengthen supply chain resilience and stakeholder trust. Multinationals face exposure to environmental risks such as floods, droughts, and extreme weather, as well as social pressures linked to labor standards, diversity, and community impact across jurisdictions. Effective ESG management helps mitigate these risks, improves employee retention, and reduces reputational vulnerabilities. In governance, transparent reporting, strong board oversight, and alignment of executive incentives with ESG outcomes help reduce compliance and litigation risk across diverse regulatory environments.

Finally, ESG contributes to corporate legitimacy in an era of heightened scrutiny. Consumers, employees, and civil society groups expect multinationals to demonstrate responsibility not only in financial terms but also in environmental stewardship, social equity, and ethical governance. Firms that fall short face reputational damage and market exclusion, while those that lead in ESG can differentiate themselves globally, shaping brand value and long-term competitiveness. Put simply, ESG is not peripheral; for multinationals it is now a decisive factor in strategy, finance, and survival across interconnected economies.

1.5 Corporate Postures Toward ESG: Compliance, Strategy, Insurance, and Misrepresentation

Firms confront the same external demands yet act differently because their cash-flow engines, data systems, and legal settings differ. Treat ESG as a continuum of strategies. Compliance is the legal floor. Value-creation uses ESG to change unit economics. Risk insurance compresses the downside tail when upside is uncertain. Misrepresentation sits outside the continuum and can erase gains from any other action.

1.5.1 Compliance Minimum

At the minimum level, firms fulfill disclosure and policy obligations with the least possible resource outlay. Reports are dominated by narrative, with limited quantitative indicators; scope and reporting periods are loosely defined; accountability is housed within legal or corporate affairs departments; budgets are constrained; supplier oversight depends on self-declarations rather than formal audits; board review is infrequent and focused on past activities. This approach is rational in contexts where profit margins are slim, data systems are underdeveloped, and trading partners have not embedded verified ESG outcomes into commercial terms or pricing.

The main drawback is informational. Stakeholders—including investors, customers, and regulators—are shifting expectations from simple reporting to providing decision-useful, externally assured information. When buyers, lenders, or supervisors begin conditioning terms on verifiable, objective outcomes—such as injury frequency, greenhouse gas emissions across Scopes 1–3, audit results, or remediation timelines—firms with minimalist practices must scramble to retrofit measurement, traceability, and assurance capabilities. Before the introduction of more robust assurance requirements in the EU, many multinational firms produced lengthy, policy-driven reports that satisfied non-financial disclosure guidance but neglected supply-chain depth. These firms upgraded their systems only after retailers and financial institutions began linking shelf space, financing, or pricing to independently validated performance measures. The broader lesson is clear: regulatory compliance may avoid penalties for non-reporting, but it does not protect against market disadvantages arising from lack of comparability.

The practical progression involves building in sequence: first, define precise scope boundaries across the full value chain; second, establish measurement and traceability systems that generate auditable data series; third, obtain limited assurance on the most material indicators; and fourth, embed these measures into core planning, budgeting, and incentive systems. Disclosure becomes meaningful only when measurement actively informs capital allocation and operational choices, moving beyond surface-level compliance.

1.5.2 ESG as Strategy

Moving up the spectrum, firms use ESG to reshape cash-flow level, variance, and duration. The mechanisms operate on three fronts. First, cost: lower resource intensity and waste reduce unit cost and volatility. Second, demand: safety, health, and privacy features open premium segments and extend customer lifetime value. Third, policy and supply: alignment with transition policy and resilient sourcing stabilizes input risk and secures contracted revenues. Governance completes the loop through board-level oversight, incentive links, hurdle rates that price externalities, time-bound targets, and independent assurance.

Consider four well-documented trajectories. Ørsted pivoted from fossil generation to offshore wind, compounding construction and O&M know-how under policy tailwinds and long-dated offtake contracts; cash flows became more predictable and the cost of capital fell with transition risk. Microsoft instituted an internal carbon fee that hits business-unit P&Ls, converting a diffuse externality into an explicit budget constraint; the fee funds efficiency, clean power, and carbon-removal procurement while disciplining vendor choice. Apple embedded privacy and device-side security into product architecture and branding, foregoing some data-monetization income to build durable trust and hardware differentiation.

Unilever used life-cycle analysis to steer innovation and M&A screens, coordinating with retailers that face Scope 3 targets; shelf space and brand equity moved together as intensity fell.

Across cases, the order of operations is consistent: redesign operations and capital allocation first, let reporting document the economics after. In corporate-finance terms, strategy-grade ESG raises NPV by lifting expected cash flow, shortening payback through efficiency gains, extending asset life through regulatory fit, and compressing cash-flow volatility through resilient supply. The technical inflection is the hurdle-rate adjustment that internalizes priced externalities; once embedded, ESG moves from cost center to capital-budget rule.

1.5.3 ESG as Insurance

ESG serves an insurance function for firms. By integrating ESG strategies into operations and governance, a company can build stronger relationships with stakeholders—including employees, customers, suppliers, investors, and the broader community. These relationships can provide practical support and flexibility when the firm faces adverse events or external shocks. During periods of stress, such as regulatory scrutiny, supply chain disruptions, or reputational crises, firms with credible ESG practices are more likely to receive assistance, tolerance, or partnership from their networks. This capacity to draw support in challenging times reduces downside risk and can help the firm recover more quickly, making ESG not only a value-creation tool but also a source of resilience.

For example, consider the experience of Johnson & Johnson during the Tylenol crisis in 1982. Decades before ESG became a mainstream term, the company's culture emphasized stakeholder responsibility and ethical conduct. When cyanide-laced capsules caused fatalities and triggered a nationwide scare, Johnson & Johnson's rapid, transparent response—prioritizing consumer safety over short-term profit—preserved public trust. Retailers, regulators, and the media rallied behind the company's efforts, allowing Tylenol to quickly regain market share after the crisis. This episode illustrates how long-term commitment to social responsibility can mobilize external support, buffer reputational damage, and speed recovery when unpredictable events strike.

Similarly, Unilever's longstanding investment in sustainable sourcing, fair labor practices, and climate initiatives paid off during the COVID-19 pandemic. Unilever's supplier relationships, built on mutual accountability and transparent standards, enabled the company to secure critical inputs and maintain operational continuity while many competitors faced shortages. The company's public commitments to workforce health and job security also reinforced employee loyalty and minimized disruptions. As a result, Unilever experienced less volatility in supply chains and labor costs, preserving both productivity and brand reputation under stress.

Another example is Starbucks, which has made social and environmental stewardship central to its business model. In the aftermath of Hurricane Katrina and subsequent supply disruptions, Starbucks leveraged its community partnerships and ethical sourcing networks to reroute coffee shipments and support affected suppliers. The company's established relationships with local NGOs and farmer cooperatives provided critical information and coordination, ensuring a faster operational rebound and deepening loyalty among its partners.

Empirical research further supports the insurance-like effect of ESG. Studies have shown that firms with higher ESG ratings or stronger stakeholder engagement experience smaller stock price declines and faster recovery during market crises, such as the 2008 financial downturn and the COVID-19 shock. These firms are less likely to face regulatory penalties, litigation, or activist pressure, and are more likely to receive favorable terms from lenders and investors during periods of heightened uncertainty.

In sum, by embedding ESG principles into strategy and operations, firms create networks of support that act as informal insurance during adverse events. Stakeholders are more willing to grant concessions, collaborate on solutions, and defend the firm's reputation when crises occur. This collective resilience reduces downside risk, supports operational continuity, and enhances the firm's long-term value in volatile environments.

1.5.4 Greenwashing and Misrepresentation

Truthfulness is a non-negotiable requirement for all levels of ESG engagement. Misrepresentation takes many forms, such as presenting only selective or favorable information, exaggerating the real-world effects of ESG initiatives, setting ambiguous or shifting targets, misusing certification labels, and transferring environmental or social harms down the supply chain rather than addressing them directly. As regulatory scrutiny intensifies, enforcement mechanisms have evolved from issuing guidance and recommendations to imposing substantial financial and reputational penalties. Modern advertising and securities regulations now focus on the net impression left by corporate communications, holding firms accountable for partial truths or omissions that may mislead stakeholders even if technically accurate.

Real-world cases demonstrate the escalating consequences of failing to meet truthfulness standards. Volkswagen's diesel emissions scandal is a cautionary tale: the company's efforts to market its vehicles as environmentally responsible were undermined by deliberate software manipulation that concealed excessive emissions. This deception led to billions of dollars in fines, massive recalls, criminal proceedings against executives, and enduring brand damage—far outweighing any initial cost savings from noncompliance. In the investment sector, several asset managers have incurred regulatory penalties for overstating the extent to which ESG criteria influenced their portfolios. When auditors and regulators reviewed actual investment decisions and internal controls, they found gaps between promotional materials and underlying evidence, resulting in fines, client losses, and public censure. Advertising authorities have also pulled corporate campaigns that showcased green initiatives while omitting significant, high-emission activities within other business units. In each case, incomplete or misleading communication has proven costly in both direct sanctions and lasting trust erosion.

To uphold truthfulness, firms must build robust internal controls and approval processes into their ESG reporting and communications. The first step is to precisely define the scope of claims, explicitly covering all material impacts across the full value chain, including indirect and supplier-related activities. Statements and reports must be anchored to quantifiable, time-bound outcomes that are independently assured and aligned with recognized frameworks or standards. Promotional materials and prospectuses must be tightly linked to underlying operational data and verified processes, ensuring consistency between public claims and internal records. Before any ESG-related communication is released, it should pass through a structured workflow involving legal, compliance, risk management, and independent assurance functions. When discrepancies or errors are identified, rapid escalation and remediation protocols must be enacted to address the issue transparently and correct the public record.

Ultimately, the safest and most credible claims are those that can be fully supported by present, verifiable evidence. Firms that prioritize accuracy and transparency build resilience against regulatory action, litigation risk, and reputational harm. In an environment of rising stakeholder expectations and stricter enforcement, credible reporting is not merely a compliance task but a strategic necessity that supports sustainable value creation and market trust.

1.5.5 Why Firms Differ: Incentives, Constraints, and Regulatory Geography

Persistent heterogeneity follows directly from incentives and constraints. Managerial horizons push short-tenure leaders toward compliance unless boards hard-wire longer-dated metrics into pay. Ownership and control affect tolerance for upfront spend; controlled firms may accept longer paybacks if family or state owners prize resilience. Industry economics matter: capital-intensive, high-hazard sectors gain most from insurance; brand-sensitive consumer and platform firms monetize trust and inclusion; regulated utilities move at the cadence allowed by rate cases. Data systems and supplier leverage are binding: without metering, traceability, and audit rights, even willing firms cannot set credible targets or secure assurance. Regulatory geography interacts with all of the above; identical rules yield different choices because internal frictions and strategic options vary.

Decision frame. Map financially material ESG items by business line. For each, specify the primary value channel: cost, demand, or risk. Calibrate hurdle-rate adders or cash-flow haircuts accordingly. If counterparties do not yet price verified performance and margins are thin, compliance can be efficient while you build data plumbing. If tail events dominate enterprise value, prioritize insurance to compress the left tail. If policy and technology open new profit pools or protect existing ones, push to strategy and scale early. In all cases, install the anti-greenwashing controls; trust once lost is expensive to repurchase in spreads and multiples.

Research and practice implications. For scholars and practitioners, posture functions as an estimable latent variable with observable markers: the breadth and depth of assurance, the detail and benchmarking of reported measures, adjustments to investment hurdle rates based on identified risks, frequency of crisis-management exercises, and patterns in enforcement or regulatory outcomes. Analyzing transitions between compliance, insurance, and strategic postures helps explain variation in cash-flow volatility, downside risk, and capital costs across firms. For boards, the most effective intervention is to embed ESG into the firm's internal frameworks for capital allocation and risk management, so that external reports simply reflect the discipline already present in operational and financial decisions.

1.6 Synthesis and Preview of the Book

This chapter moved from shareholder primacy to stakeholder value and explained how CSR opened the path to ESG. It defined the E, S, and G pillars and their value channels, set out why ratings diverge, and described the disclosure architecture shaping practice. It categorized corporate postures as compliance minimum, strategy, and insurance, highlighted greenwashing risks, and detailed financial implications for performance, risk, capital costs, financing access, and market informativeness. It also outlined research design principles and an implementation playbook. Subsequent chapters deepen topic-level analysis, develop sector-specific measurement, and examine transition strategies that link targets to capital allocation and verified outcomes.

Designing and Implementing ESG Strategies: Current Status (Anecdotal Evidence)

2

2.1 Introduction: The Growing Importance and Contribution of ESG Strategy for the Firm

ESG now alters firm cash flows, risk, and access to capital. Boards allocate budgets, build data systems, and assign executive ownership because ESG programs change operating variance, regulatory exposure, and the option value of future growth. Lenders and investors integrate ESG into underwriting and stewardship. Pricing grids in sustainability-linked financing, index inclusion, and voting policies feed back into incentives and the cost of debt and equity. The result is deliberate resource reallocation toward initiatives with demonstrable business cases and auditable metrics, not broad slogans.

By ESG strategy this book means the systematic integration of environmental, social, and governance considerations into corporate purpose, capital budgeting, operating routines, and performance measurement. Materiality anchors scope so attention flows to issues that move cash flows or discount rates. Governance supplies decision rights and accountability so targets convert into funded work and verifiable outputs. Data and assurance enable learning by turning noisy operational signals into decision-useful indicators. Heterogeneity is expected. A blast furnace, a nationwide retailer, and a cloud platform face different externalities, technologies, and stakeholder claims.

Environmental initiatives show how technology, contracting, and process control reshape unit economics and tail risk. Internal carbon pricing hard-wires a shadow cost of emissions into project screening and tilts capital toward efficiency, electrification, and long-term renewable power purchase agreements. Supplier and logistics programs that reduce fuel, packaging, and waste lower variable costs, shrink exposure to carbon border adjustments, and cut insurance premia where catastrophe and transition risks are priced. Fleet and asset choices that enable lower-carbon fuels preserve market access as product- or route-level constraints tighten. Payoffs materialize in lower energy intensity, reduced input volatility,

J. Wang, *ESG Strategies and Financial Markets*, Management for Professionals,
https://doi.org/10.1007/978-981-95-5620-5_2

fewer compliance events, and revenue from carbon-sensitive customers. Apple's supplier clean-energy program operationalizes this logic by embedding renewable electricity commitments and recycled-materials targets into procurement and manufacturing. Long-dated PPAs, recycled content thresholds, and air-freight substitution are contractable levers that move Scope 2 and upstream Scope 3 while stabilizing input costs and reducing regulatory exposure in carbon-priced markets.

Social investments operate through human-capital and stakeholder channels that affect throughput, quality, and continuity. High-wage, high-tenure models reduce shrink, error rates, and hiring frictions, which raises store- and line-level productivity despite higher hourly pay. Education and career-path programs widen applicant pools, compress ramp time, and improve internal promotion rates, lowering turnover and vacancy risk. In supply chains, moving from audit-only regimes to capability building with strategic vendors reduces stoppages and quality drift, improving on-time-in-full delivery and inventory turns. Customer-facing safety and privacy controls lessen legal risk and churn and raise lifetime value. Starbucks demonstrates these mechanisms: wage design, education benefits, and advancement paths link directly to retention and service quality; reusable-cup and waste-reduction programs adjust customer behavior and materials intensity. The economics are realized through workforce stability and customer lifetime value rather than short-run payroll ratios.

Governance is the execution spine that determines whether environmental and social intentions convert to durable performance. Board structure, independence, domain expertise, and committee charters shape information flow and decision rights. Simplified legal structures increase agility in portfolio moves and reduce agency frictions in capital deployment. Incentive design that ties a bounded share of variable pay to verified climate, safety, or data-quality metrics reduces misreporting and aligns operating targets with financing terms, including sustainability-linked pricing ratchets. Strong internal controls, independent assurance, and high-quality disclosure reduce the left tail of fines, restatements, and catastrophic failures and support lower required returns. Current governance debates show the stakes. Tesla's CEO compensation litigation and shareholder votes place incentive design, board independence, and disclosure discipline at the center of investor risk assessment, with implications for control systems and capital stewardship. Apple's proxy architecture illustrates pay-for-performance calibration, related-party controls, and audit rigor that support capital deployment and compliance. Starbucks has iterated the mapping between executive pay and ESG-relevant metrics to clarify scopes, assurance, and links to operating outcomes, aligning non-financial targets with financial performance. Across these examples the mechanism is incentive compatibility and verifiability.

ESG is not free. It requires upfront spend, management attention, and data infrastructure. Rational managers and investors ask two questions: What is the net effect on value, and which dimensions matter most here and now? The answer is conditional on technology, regulation, market structure, and organizational capability. Environmental projects often pay through efficiency, regulatory hedging, supply-chain resilience, and access to green demand or cheaper capital. Social projects pay through productivity, safety, and retention that stabilize service quality and reduce disruption. Governance pays by lowering agency costs and improving decision quality in investment, risk, and control. The empirical problem is attribution under selection, time-varying regulation, and concurrent transformations. The portfolio problem is prioritization under budget and bandwidth constraints. A workable solution is to target a short list of high-materiality levers, specify causal mechanisms and leading indicators, hard-wire ownership and audit, and retire efforts that fail verification.

This chapter's empirical focal point is governance. The paper introduced here examines affiliated banker directors—bank executives or partners who sit on corporate boards—and their impact on mergers and acquisitions. The study tests whether such affiliations change deal incidence, pricing, financing structure, completion, and post-merger performance. Two mechanisms compete. Information and financing advantages may raise screening quality, reduce funding frictions, and improve integration outcomes. Conflicts of interest may bias boards toward transactions that generate advisory or lending revenue for the affiliated bank, weakening selection and terms. By exploiting variation in director–bank ties and transaction timing, the paper estimates the net effect of this governance feature on M&A outcomes. This isolates a concrete governance lever—board composition with financial-intermediary affiliations—and evaluates whether it improves or degrades one of the highest-stakes corporate decisions.

2.2 Affiliated Banker Directors and Firm Mergers and Acquisitions

Abstract

Corporate boards play an important role during the process of mergers and acquisitions (M&As). In this study, we empirically investigate the effects of affiliated banker directors (ABDs) on firm acquisition activities. We find that acquiring firms with ABDs experience higher announcement returns and exhibit superior post-merger market and operating performance. The positive effect of ABDs on announcement returns is stronger in M&A deals with higher levels of information asymmetry and complexity. Additionally, we document evidence on the mechanisms through which ABDs enhance acquisition performance. Our results indicate that ABDs positively affect acquisition outcomes by leveraging their information advantage, improving corporate governance, and favoring diversifying M&A deals that reduce the acquiring firm's risk exposure.

2.2.1 Introduction

In today's rapidly evolving economic environment, firms actively engage in acquisitions to maintain their competitive advantages, adapt to technological advancements, expand market share, and achieve synergy gains (Alexandridis et al., 2017; Cefis & Marsili, 2015; Cornaggia & Li, 2019). In 2022, U.S. acquisitions surpassed \$1.73 trillion, highlighting M&As as crucial corporate investment strategies for fostering growth. However, the success of M&As is far from guaranteed, with many transactions failing to achieve the anticipated benefits (Dos Santos et al., 2008; Gigante & Rubinacci, 2023). Existing research (e.g. Gada et al., 2021) highlights the important governance role played by corporate boards of acquiring firms in the success of M&As. In particular, an emerging line of research on the compositions of corporate boards explores the influence of board directors' background and expertise on various firm financial and operational decisions (Adams et al., 2010; Huang et al., 2014; Wang et al., 2015).

In this paper, we focus on a special type of corporate board director, namely affiliated banker directors (ABDs). An affiliated banker director is a board member who is also sitting in the board of a commercial bank that maintains a lending relationship with the firm (Erkens et al., 2014). With access to inside information from the borrowing firms and their expertise, ABDs are not only delegated monitors and representatives from lending banks (Diamond, 1984), but also part of the governance mechanisms to safeguard the interests of shareholders and influence various firm decisions. Existing literature documents that ABDs are associated with reduced tax avoidance (Song et al., 2024), improved environmental management (Zhao et al., 2021), and lower conservative accounting (Erkens et al., 2014). In our study, we intend to extend this line of research, and empirically investigate whether and to what extent ABDs may affect firm decisions on M&As and their associated outcomes.

Using a sample of 6951 acquisitions in U.S. announced between 2000 and 2016, our study reveals that acquiring firms with ABDs experience significantly higher abnormal returns around the acquisition announcements. In the post-acquisition period, acquirers with ABDs experience better stock market performance and accounting performance. We employ the instrumental variables approach and Heckman correction method (1979) to address the potential endogeneity problem, and report consistent results. Furthermore, we find that board representation of ABDs is associated with better announcement returns for acquiring firms operating in high information asymmetry environment, supporting the informational advantage held by ABDs. We report that the positive effect of ABDs on announcement returns is more pronounced for firms with lower scores of managerial ability and higher institutional turnover rate. We document evidence that acquiring firms with ABDs are more likely to undertake diversifying M&A deals, which is in line with the notion that creditors may induce greater propensity of firms to engage in risk-reducing activities (Acharya et al., 2011).

We believe that our research contributes to the literature in several important ways. First, our study provides new insights into the influence of bank lenders on borrowing firms' acquisition performance through their board representations. We thus extend the line of research investigating the relation between creditor rights and firm M&As (Acharya et al., 2011; Becher et al., 2022; Bharadwaj & Shivdasani, 2003; Ivashina et al., 2009; Nini et al., 2012). Second, our analysis adds to a large literature on corporate governance by focusing on the effects of board composition and the identity of board members on firm acquisition performance (Byrd & Hickman, 1992; Masulis & Zhang, 2019; Moeller, 2005; Masulis et al., 2007). Lastly, our paper highlights the dual roles of ABDs as both representatives of bank lenders (i.e., delegated monitors) and fiduciaries acting on behalf of the shareholders (Erkens et al., 2014; Kang & Kim, 2017; Kang et al., 2020; Kroszner & Strahan, 2001; Sisli-Ciamarra, 2012).

2.2.2 Literature Review

2.2.2.1 Board of Directors and M&A Performance

The success of mergers and acquisitions (M&A) has been widely studied, with various determinants influencing the likelihood of achieving desired outcomes. Key factors include strategic alignment (Bauer & Matzler, 2014), due diligence (Wangerin, 2019), and effective integration processes (Birkinshaw et al., 2000).

Corporate governance is a crucial determinant of M&A performance (Masulis et al., 2007). The board of directors, as the foundation of a firm's governance structure, plays an important role in monitoring and advising top management (Adams & Ferreira, 2007; Harris & Raviv, 2008). Effective board oversight in mergers and acquisitions hinges on access to and processing of information. Prior studies document that active engagement of firm directors in the M&A process results in a better deal performance (Demirtaş, 2017). Moreover, board reforms (Ahmad et al., 2024), board connections (Cai & Sevilir, 2012), board independency (Teti et al., 2017), board overconfidence (Twardawski & Kind, 2023) affects the M&A performance through information and monitoring channel.

2.2.2.2 ABDs and Mergers and Acquisitions

Boards with professional backgrounds and industry experience are highly valued because they are able to provide effective monitoring and advising on various firm decision (Qiao et al., 2018). In particular, affiliated banker directors may exert unique influence on corporate management because of their dual roles (Cai & Sevilir, 2012; Erkens et al., 2014; Sisli-Ciamarra, 2012; Song et al., 2024; Zhao et al., 2021). In other words, ABDs hold positions on a firm's board while concurrently being employed by a commercial bank with lending relationship with the borrowing firms (Ghosh, 2016).

Existing literature has explored how debtholders may affect firm M&A decisions. For instance, Becher et al. (2022) find that creditors use contractual rights and the renegotiation process to limit value-destroying acquisitions. Huang et al. (2022) demonstrate that bank-financed deals have higher acquirer's cumulative abnormal returns relative to other cash M&A deals. Acharya et al. (2011) show that stronger creditor rights induce greater propensity of firms to engage in diversifying acquisitions. Despite this, limited attention has been given to the influence of creditors who also sit on acquiring firms' boards on the M&A performance.

Building on the existing literature, we posit that acquiring firms with ABDs experience better acquisition performance. Moreover, we propose two potential mechanisms through which ABDs may affect the acquisition performance. First, ABDs may use their informational advantages to influence the M&A strategy and the corresponding outcomes. Banks are insiders to a firm and are able to obtain private information through their lending relationships with borrowing firms (Fama, 1985; James, 1987). ABDs may leverage their expertise and their inside information to evaluate the potential targets and provide financial advising. Second, ABDs, as representatives of the lending banks, have incentive to monitor M&A deals to mitigate the possibility of overvaluation and excessive risk-taking (e.g., Erkens et al., 2014).

2.2.3 Sample, Variables, and Methodology

2.2.3.1 Data and Sample

We use Thompson Financials SDC Platinum Mergers and Acquisitions database (SDC) to retrieve M&A deals announced and completed by U.S. public acquirers between 2000 and 2016. Our criteria include a minimum deal value of $1 million and a requirement that the acquisitions represent at least 5% of the acquirer's market value. Additionally, acquiring firms must be available in Compustat for the year preceding the deal announcement and have stock return data accessible from CRSP for the 180 trading days prior to the announcement through 5 trading days afterward. We also require that the acquirer controls less than 50% of the target's shares before the announcement and owns 100% of the target afterward. Furthermore, the target firm must be domiciled in the United States. We follow the literature to exclude acquiring firms that are financial firms (SIC codes 6000–6999) and utilities (SIC codes 4000–4999).

We obtain director information from BoardEx database. To identify banker directors, we employ text-matching algorithms by matching the employer's names of firm directors reported in BoardEx with bank names collected from the Consolidated Reports of Condition and Income ("Call Reports") and the Commercial Bank Database of the Federal Reserve Bank of Chicago. Following Güner et al. (2008) and Kang et al. (2020), we use DealScan database to classify firm directors with commercial bank background as ABDs if they are also the directors of the banks who have provided loans to the firms over the previous five years.

We complement our sample with accounting and financial information from Compustat and stock information from Research in Security Prices (CRSP). Our sampling procedure yields a sample of 6951 acquisitions by 2442 unique firms, with some acquirers having multiple acquisitions during the 17-year sample period.

2.2.3.2 Measures

To measure abnormal returns on the M&A announcements, we calculate cumulative abnormal returns (CARs) using the standard event study methodology over a five-day (−2, +2) event window centered on the announcement date (Tunyi, 2021).

In the regression analysis, we construct an indicator of ABDs which equals one if the acquirer has at least one affiliated banker director, and zero otherwise. In addition, we include a set of control variables to capture acquiring firms' characteristics and deal characteristics including firm size, leverage, market-to-book ratio, cash ratio, an indicator of public target, an indicator of tender offer, relative deal size, stock price run up, and payment methods (Field & Mkrtchyan, 2017; Jovanovic & Braguinsky, 2004; Moeller et al., 2004). Previous studies document the effect of board characteristics on acquisition performance. Therefore, we also include a set of controls for corporate governance including board size, board independency, and financial expertise on board (Chen et al., 2020; Hauser, 2018; Wang et al., 2015; Yermack, 1996). Additionally, we include 2-digit-SIC industry and year fixed effects in the regression model. To mitigate the effect of outliers, all continuous variables are winsorized at the 1% and 99% levels. Appendix Table A1 presents detailed variable definitions.

2.2.3.3 Summary Statistics

Panel A of Table 2.1 presents the distribution of M&A deals by year along with information on deal value, acquirers' market capitalization, and relative size between targets and acquirers. The highest frequency of acquisition occurs between 2005 and 2007, and the number of M&A deals drops significantly following the 2007–2009 financial crisis. The average deal has a transaction value of $463 million, which is about 5% of the average acquirer's pre-acquisition market capitalization (i.e., $10 billion). Panel B reports summary statistics of the variables used in the regression analyses. The average CAR during the five-day window is 1%. Approximately, 4% of our sample has at least one ABD on board, which is consistent with those reported in the prior literature (Güner et al., 2008; Kang & Kim, 2017; Kang et al., 2020). Other firm characteristics and deal characteristics are generally consistent with prior studies (Cai & Sevilir, 2012).

2.2.4 Empirical Results

2.2.4.1 Affiliated Banker Directors and Announcement Effects

We posit that acquirers with ABDs make better acquisitions. Therefore, we model the acquirer's announcement returns as a function of ABDs and other control variables as follows:

$$CAR_{it} = \alpha_0 + \beta_1 \cdot ABD_{it} + \gamma \cdot X_{it} + \mu_i + \upsilon_t + \varepsilon_{it} \tag{2.1}$$

where the dependent variable is the acquirer's CAR in the five-day (−2,2) window around the announcement. The main explanatory variable, ABD_{it}, is an indicator variable that equals to one if acquirer i has at least one ABD sitting on board in year t and zero otherwise. X_{it} is a set of controls for the acquirer's firm, board, and deal characteristics in year t, and μ_i and υ_t are industry and year fixed effects, respectively. Heteroskedasticity-robust standard errors clustered by acquirers are reported in parentheses.

Table 2.1 Descriptive statistic

Year	Number of deals	Deal value (in $million)	Acquirer's MVE (in $million)
Panel A: Distribution of M&A deals by year			
2000	354	786.02	20,174.03
2001	299	472.61	14,570.9
2002	330	252.75	7863.14
2003	407	204.07	6738.94
2004	544	251.19	7007
2005	580	429.6	8923.09
2006	584	327.53	8785.19
2007	562	323.73	8588.63
2008	385	335.68	5211
2009	304	494.9	10,288.38
2010	360	466	11,448.27
2011	327	370.14	6396.54
2012	385	448.14	11,002.26
2013	331	510.51	10,193.67
2014	404	609.48	11,311.19
2015	429	937.36	10,654.31
2016	366	866.63	14,975.9
Total	6951		

Variable	N	Mean	Std Dev	Median
Panel B: Summary statistics				
CAR [−2,2]	6951	0.01	0.11	0
BHAR (0,3)	5500	−0.04	0.77	−0.14
Change in ROA (−1, 3)	6682	−0.02	0.14	−0.02
ABD	6951	0.04	0.21	0
Firm size	6951	7.07	1.87	6.99
Leverage	6951	0.23	0.2	0.21
M/B	6951	2.07	1.25	1.7
Cash ratio	6951	0.42	0.21	0.4
Board size	6951	8.47	2.23	8
Board independence	6951	0.69	0.15	0.71
%board financial expertise	6951	0.36	0.18	0.33
Relative deal size	6951	0.22	0.42	0.07
Public target	6951	0.18	0.38	0

(continued)

Table 2.1 (continued)

Variable	N	Mean	Std Dev	Median
Panel B: Summary statistics				
Tender	6951	0.04	0.19	0
Stock price run-up	6951	0.14	0.53	0.04
Cash deal	6951	0.51	0.5	1
Stock deal	6951	0.09	0.28	0
Diversify	6592	0.39	0.49	0
Vertical relatedness	3766	0.64	0.48	1

Table 2.2 presents the main results. Column (1) shows a significantly positive relation between ABDs and the announcement returns. In addition, the estimated coefficients of other control variables are in line with our expectation. We document that acquirers with higher growth companies and higher leverage have better announcement returns (Field & Mkrtchyan, 2017). Large acquirers and public targets are associated with lower announcement returns (e.g., Huang et al., 2014).

The positive relation between ABDs and acquirer announcement returns may be subject to endogeneity problem due to the fact that the board composition is not randomly assigned (Adams et al., 2010; Hermalin & Weisbach, 1998). We address this concern with an instrumental variable (IV) approach. Specifically, following David H. Erkens et al. (2014), we use three instrumental variables that capture the likelihood of having a banker director on the board of a particular firm. The first measure is *the geographic proximity of lead lender within a 50-mile radius*, as a closer physical distance increases the chance for the banker to serve on board to provide better monitoring. We thereby include an indicator which equals to one when the lead lenders' headquarters is within a 50-mile radius of the firm's headquarters, and zero otherwise. We use *the number of commercial banks that have a headquarters within a 50-mile radius of the acquirer's headquarters* as our second instrument. Following Dass and Massa (2011), we measure *the concentration of the commercial bank market* by calculating a Herfindahl Index (ranging between 0 to 1) based on the deposits of all the banks in the county where the acquirer's headquarters is located.

Column (2) of Table 2.2 presents the second-stage estimation of IV approach and reports a significant positive relation between ABDs and acquirer announcement returns. To ensure the robustness of our results, we also conduct several post-estimation diagnostic tests. The result of Durbin-Wu-Hausman test indicates that the endogenous variable necessitates the instrumental variable approach. The J-statistic indicates that instrument variables are valid and uncorrelated with the error terms. The Kleibergen-Paaprk LM statistic suggests that our estimation is not subject the weak instrument problem. Therefore, we conclude that our results remain unchanged after addressing the endogeneity concern.

Table 2.2 ABDs and acquirer's announcement returns

Independent variables	Dependent variables	
	CAR [−2,2]	
	(1)	(2)
ABD	0.015*** (0.005)	0.258** (0.131)
Firm size	−0.003** (0.001)	−0.008** (0.003)
Leverage	0.035** (0.014)	0.060** (0.026)
M/B	0.004** (0.002)	0.006** (0.003)
Cash ratio	0.019 (0.012)	0.025 (0.016)
Board size	−0.000 (0.001)	−0.002 (0.002)
Board independence	0.004 (0.011)	0.030 (0.022)
Public target	−0.036*** (0.004)	−0.036*** (0.010)
Tender	0.024*** (0.006)	0.006 (0.012)
Relative deal size	0.044*** (0.012)	0.058*** (0.018)
Stock price run-up	−0.017*** (0.005)	−0.023*** (0.009)
Stock deal	−0.004 (0.007)	−0.007 (0.013)
Cash deal	0.000 (0.004)	0.004 (0.004)
%board financial expertise	−0.002 (0.013)	−0.019 (0.016)
Constant	−0.017 (0.017)	0.016 (0.030)
Industry FE	Yes	Yes
Year FE	Yes	Yes
Observations	6951	3,479
R-squared	0.069	0.065
Durbin-Wu-Hausman test		3.81
(Endogeneity test)		($p < 0.05$)
Kleibergen-Paap rk LM statistic		19.992
(Underidentification test)		($p<0.01$)
Kleibergen-Paap rk Wald F statistic		10.23

(continued)

Table 2.2 (continued)

Independent variables	Dependent variables	
	CAR [−2,2]	
	(1)	(2)
(Weak identification test)		($p < 0.1$)
Hansen J statistic		0.436
(Overidentification test)		($p = 0.804$)

2.2.4.2 Affiliated Banker Directors and Long-Term Performance

We further examine whether the presence of ABDs improves the acquiring firms' performance after the acquisitions. We measure long-term market-based performance using the post-merger stock returns of the acquirer over a 3-year period following the year of acquisition. Specifically, BHAR (0,3) is defined as the difference between the buy-and-hold returns of an acquiring firm over the three-year period after deal completion and that of the market portfolio proxied by the value-weighted CRSP index returns. In Column (1) of Table 2.3, we document that the presence of ABDs is positively and significantly associated with post-merger long-run deal performance.

Following Custódio and Metzger (2013), we use the change in industry-adjusted return on assets (ROA) to measure the long-term accounting-based performance of acquirers. The dependent variable is the average ROA for both the three-year periods preceding the acquisitions and the period following deal completion, adjusted for the industry average during the same intervals. Our results are robust when we measure the change in ROA at (−1,3) and (0,3) performance window (Chen et al., 2007). Column (2) of Table 2.3 shows that the coefficient of presence of ABDs is positive, suggesting that acquirers with ABDs experience better operational performance due to synergy gains (Dutordoir et al., 2014).

2.2.4.3 How Does the Presence of ABDs Affect M&A Performance?

In this section, we further explore how ABDs influence acquisition activities. ABDs can utilize their informational advantage to improve acquisition performance, and play a more important role when the acquiring firms are associated with greater information asymmetry (Chen et al., 2020). We therefore use the firm's R&D intensity, measured as the ratio of the acquirer's R&D expenses to sales, as a proxy for the acquirers' information asymmetry (Honoré et al., 2015). In addition, we measure the acquirer's industry R&D intensity to capture the complexity and opacity of the acquisitions (Chemmanur et al., 2019). We interact our measures of information asymmetry with the indicator of ABDs, and report the results in Table 2.4. We find that the positive relation between ABDs and acquisition performance is stronger for deals that are subject to higher information asymmetry. This evidence aligns with our expectation that ABDs' expertise and informational advantages are more valuable in M&A transactions with higher levels of information asymmetry and complexity.

Table 2.3 ABDs and long-term performance

Independent variables	Dependent variables	
	BHAR (0,3)	Change in industry adjusted ROA (−1, 3)
	(1)	(2)
ABD	0.067* (0.035)	0.016*** (0.006)
Firm size	0.004 (0.016)	−0.006** (0.002)
Leverage	0.195* (0.104)	0.004 (0.015)
M/B	0.061*** (0.013)	0.004 (0.003)
Cash ratio	0.030 (0.101)	−0.009 (0.016)
Board size	−0.012 (0.008)	0.001 (0.001)
Board independence	0.217* (0.105)	−0.017 (0.015)
Public target	0.049 (0.042)	−0.013* (0.008)
Tender	−0.069 (0.048)	−0.006 (0.009)
Relative deal size	0.020 (0.035)	0.021** (0.010)
Stock price run-up	−0.123** (0.045)	0.001 (0.006)
Stock deal	−0.133*** (0.039)	0.029** (0.014)
Cash deal	0.060** (0.022)	0.008* (0.004)
%board financial expertise	0.056 (0.081)	0.015 (0.013)
Constant	−0.050 (0.268)	0.022 (0.033)
Industry FE	Yes	Yes
Year FE	Yes	Yes
Observations	5500	6682
R-squared	0.046	0.055

Table 2.4 ABDs, information asymmetry, and acquirer's announcement returns

Independent variables	Dependent variables			
	CAR [−2, 2]			
	(1)	(2)	(3)	(4)
ABD	0.014** (0.005)	0.057*** (0.014)	0.014*** (0.005)	0.067*** (0.012)
R&D intensity (firm)	−0.000 (0.000)	0.005*** (0.002)		
ABD × R&D intensity (firm)		0.131*** (0.043)		
R&D intensity (industry)			0.001*** (0.000)	0.009*** (0.002)
ABD × R&D intensity (industry)				0.189*** (0.047)
Firm size	−0.003** (0.001)	−0.003** (0.001)	−0.002* (0.001)	−0.002* (0.001)
Leverage	0.036** (0.013)	0.036** (0.013)	0.035** (0.014)	0.035** (0.014)
M/B	0.004** (0.002)	0.004** (0.002)	0.004** (0.002)	0.004** (0.002)
Cash ratio	0.014 (0.011)	0.014 (0.011)	0.020 (0.012)	0.020 (0.012)
Board size	−0.000 (0.001)	−0.000 (0.001)	−0.000 (0.001)	−0.000 (0.001)
Board independence	0.002 (0.011)	0.002 (0.011)	0.004 (0.011)	0.004 (0.011)
Public target	0.035*** (0.006)	0.035*** (0.006)	0.036*** (0.004)	0.036*** (0.004)
Tender	0.023** (0.009)	0.022** (0.009)	0.023*** (0.006)	0.023*** (0.006)
Relative deal size	0.042*** (0.012)	0.042*** (0.012)	0.044*** (0.012)	0.044*** (0.012)
Stock price run-up	−0.018** (0.006)	−0.018** (0.006)	−0.016*** (0.005)	−0.016*** (0.005)
Stock deal	−0.004 (0.010)	−0.004 (0.010)	−0.005 (0.007)	−0.005 (0.007)
Cash deal	−0.000 (0.003)	−0.000 (0.003)	0.000 (0.004)	0.000 (0.004)
%board financial expertise	−0.002 (0.012)	−0.002 (0.012)	−0.002 (0.013)	−0.003 (0.013)
Constant	−0.014 (0.032)	−0.011 (0.032)	−0.020 (0.017)	−0.017 (0.017)
Industry FE	Yes	Yes	Yes	Yes

(continued)

Table 2.4 (continued)

Independent variables	Dependent variables			
	CAR [−2, 2]			
	(1)	(2)	(3)	(4)
Year FE	Yes	Yes	Yes	Yes
Observations	6,925	6,925	6,951	6,951
R-squared	0.068	0.069	0.070	0.070

Next, we examine whether ABDs' prior knowledge in the target industry affects acquirer's announcement returns.[1] An affiliated bank can gain access to the financial and operational details of a particular industry through screening and monitoring borrowers in that industry. In our study, we use the average of the industry expertise measures to proxy an ABD's informational advantage in the target's industry. Following Jiang and Li (2022), we use two measures to gauge an affiliated bank's expertise in the target's industry by focusing on its loan portfolio. Specifically, we define the industry expertise of affiliated bank$m$ in industry i as:

$$\text{Industry expertise}_{\text{m}}(\text{N}) = \frac{\text{Loan number to industry i by bank m in last 5 years}}{\text{Total loan number by bank m in last 5 years}} \tag{2.2}$$

$$\text{Industry expertise}_{\text{m}}(\text{Exposure}) = \frac{\text{Outstanding loans to industry i by bank m in last year}}{\text{Total outstanding loans by bank m in last year}} \tag{2.3}$$

We further utilize Heckman two-stage sample selection model to address the selection bias (Heckman, 1979) because ABDs are not randomly assigned to our sample. In the first stage, we use a probit model to estimate the likelihood of having ABDs as a function of various firm characteristics including firm size, leverage, cash holding, market-to-book ratio, capital structure, board size (Ferreira & Matos, 2012). In the second stage, we estimate the CARs as a function of ABDs' expertise in the target industries with the inclusion of an inverse Mill's ratio estimated from the first-stage regression result.

Panel A of Table 2.5 presents the probit regression results, and report that firm size, short-term debt, R&D intensity, MTB ratio, and board size are the determinants of the presence of ABDs on an acquirer's board. This is consistent with previous findings that the ABDs are more likely to sit on boards of larger and more matured firms and firms with higher debt ratio and information asymmetry (Byrd & Mizruchi, 2005; Kroszner & Strahan, 2001; Sisli-Ciamarra, 2012). Panel B reports the second-stage regression results relating ABD's target firm's industry

[1] In untabulated analyses, we test the effect of ABD industry expertise regarding the acquirer's industry on deal performance and find insignificant results. Results are available upon request.

expertise to acquisition announcement returns. The coefficients of ABD's target industry expertise measures are significantly positive in both model specifications, supporting the notion that affiliated bank's information advantage in the target industry matters for the acquisition performance.

Board of directors provides valuable advice for firm decisions (Stiles, 2001), and managers with strong managerial skills are better able to utilize the informational advantages of ABDs. Therefore, we posit that the positive relation between ABDs and acquisition performance is more pronounced for firms with strong managerial ability. Our proxy for acquirer's managerial ability is the *MA_Score* developed by Demerjian et al. (2012), which is widely adopted by existing literature to capture firm's managerial ability (Bonsall et al., 2016; Doukas & Zhang, 2021). Furthermore, banks have incentives to monitor borrowing firms because creditor may bear the consequences of inefficient investment decisions due to managerial discretion (Chava et al., 2010). We posit that the effects of ABDs on acquisition performance are more pronounced among acquiring firms that lack strong mechanisms to discipline managers. Following Gaspar et al. (2005), we use institutional investor turnover as a proxy for governance quality, with higher turnover rates indicating weaker governance.

We further interact the ABD indicator with the managerial ability scores and institutional investor turnover rates, respectively, and report the regression results in Table 2.6. The coefficients of ABD indicators and two interaction terms are positive and statistically significant, indicating that ABDs are positively associated with acquisition performance, and the positive relation is more pronounced for acquirers with stronger managerial ability and weaker governance from institutional investors.

ABDs possess a dual advantage in terms of combining their information advantages and expertise in risk management to influence lending firms' risk taking (John et al., 2008). We posit that ABDs are more inclined towards favoring diversifying acquisitions to reduce the risk exposure of acquiring firms. Diversifying deals are typically complex and rely heavily on acquirers' knowledge of the targets. For example, Fang et al. (2015) demonstrate that acquirers with pre-acquisition alliance partnerships benefit from learning about their partner's industry, with information spillover from these alliances proving valuable in diversifying acquisitions. Similarly, a bank's knowledge of the target industry can assist acquirers in better identifying and managing diversifying deals that create shareholder wealth. Diversifying acquisitions are defined as those deals in which the acquirers and targets do not belong to the same two-digit SIC industry (Gokkaya et al., 2023). We also adopt Fan and Goyal (2006) approach to use U.S. BEA input–output data to construct the vertical relatedness coefficient, and code a deal as a vertical acquisition if the vertical relatedness coefficient between the acquirer and target surpasses 5%.[2] Accordingly, our second measure is an indicator that equals one for acquirer-target pairs without horizontal or vertical relatedness, and zero otherwise. We regress the

[2] Our results are robust when we use the 1% and 10% cutoff of vertical relatedness coefficient.

Table 2.5 Heckman's selection model relating affiliated bank's information about target industry to acquirer announcement returns

Panel A: Stage one- Probit regression predicting firm with ABDs		
Independent variables	Dependent variables	
	ABDs	
	(1)	(2)
Firm size	0.247*** (0.033)	0.245*** (0.033)
Leverage	−0.799 (1.217)	−0.711 (1.155)
Short-term debt	4.622*** (1.183)	4.286*** (1.162)
Cash ratio	−0.517* (0.302)	−0.296 (0.290)
MTB	−0.144** (0.062)	−0.160*** (0.062)
R&D intensity	3.231*** (1.029)	2.909*** (1.020)
ROA	1.121 (0.768)	1.090 (0.758)
Sales growth	−0.218 (0.342)	−0.240 (0.331)
Capital structure	0.090 (1.256)	0.158 (1.174)
Board size	1.190*** (0.256)	1.253*** (0.251)
Constant	−6.291*** (0.526)	−6.446*** (0.520)
Observations	5023	5023
Pseudo-R squared	0.262	0.259
Panel B: Stage two - Heckman outcome equation		
Independent variables	Dependent variables	
	CAR [−2,2]	
	(1)	(2)
Industry expertise (Loan number)	0.014** (0.007)	
Industry expertise (Exposure)		0.091** (0.042)
Firm size	−0.032*** (0.007)	−0.018*** (0.006)
Leverage	−0.107** (0.045)	−0.086** (0.034)
M/B	0.003 (0.007)	0.003 (0.006)

(continued)

Table 2.5 (continued)

Panel B: Stage two - Heckman outcome equation		
Independent variables	Dependent variables	
	CAR [−2,2]	
	(1)	(2)
Cash ratio	0.065 (0.050)	−0.013 (0.046)
Board size	−0.003 (0.003)	−0.002 (0.003)
Board independence	0.111*** (0.039)	−0.007 (0.032)
Public target	0.007 (0.009)	0.006 (0.008)
Tender	−0.005 (0.014)	−0.011 (0.013)
Relative deal size	0.098*** (0.016)	0.053*** (0.014)
Stock price run-up	−0.014 (0.017)	−0.031** (0.015)
Stock deal	0.004 (0.015)	−0.018 (0.014)
Cash deal	0.014* (0.008)	0.015** (0.008)
%board financial expertise	0.043 (0.029)	0.056** (0.027)
Inverse mills ratio	−0.055** (0.022)	−0.042* (0.021)
Constant	0.352*** (0.120)	0.288** (0.112)
Industry FE	Yes	Yes
Year FE	Yes	Yes
Observations	212	203
R-squared	0.581	0.502

diversifying deal dummy on the presence of ABDs using logit estimation, with the results reported in Table 2.7. The results show that both coefficients of ABD indicator are significantly positive at 1% level, indicating that the presence of ABDs is associated with a higher likelihood of conducting diversifying acquisitions.

We also examine the possibility that the superior M&A performance may be attributed to access to cheaper bank financing through relationship banks. However, the results presented in an tabulated table are insignificant. Consequently, our findings suggest that ABDs positively influence acquisition outcomes by leveraging their information advantage, enhancing corporate governance, and promoting diversifying M&A deals that reduce the acquiring firm's risk exposure.

Table 2.6 ABDs, corporate governance, and acquirer's announcement returns

Independent variables	Dependent variables			
	CAR [−2,2]			
	(1)	(2)	(3)	(4)
ABD	0.014** (0.006)	0.010* (0.006)	0.014** (0.005)	0.017*** (0.006)
Management score	−0.009 (0.012)	−0.012 (0.011)		
ABD × Management score		0.048** (0.018)		
Institutional investor turnover			−0.001 (0.052)	0.004 (0.051)
ABD × Institutional investor turnover				0.196** (0.081)
Firm size	−0.002** (0.001)	−0.002** (0.001)	−0.003** (0.001)	−0.003** (0.001)
Leverage	0.040*** (0.013)	0.040*** (0.013)	0.037** (0.014)	0.037** (0.014)
M/B	0.004*** (0.001)	0.004*** (0.001)	0.004** (0.002)	0.004** (0.002)
Cash ratio	0.014 (0.011)	0.014 (0.011)	0.015 (0.011)	0.015 (0.011)
Board size	−0.000 (0.001)	−0.000 (0.001)	−0.001 (0.001)	−0.001 (0.001)
Board independence	0.009 (0.010)	0.009 (0.010)	−0.001 (0.009)	−0.001 (0.009)
Public target	−0.035*** (0.006)	−0.035*** (0.006)	−0.035*** (0.007)	−0.035*** (0.007)
Tender	0.023** (0.009)	0.023** (0.009)	0.023** (0.009)	0.023** (0.009)
Relative deal size	0.041*** (0.012)	0.041*** (0.012)	0.044*** (0.012)	0.044*** (0.012)
Stock price run-up	−0.018** (0.006)	−0.018** (0.006)	−0.018** (0.006)	−0.018** (0.007)
Stock deal	−0.004 (0.010)	−0.004 (0.010)	−0.005 (0.010)	−0.005 (0.010)
Cash deal	−0.001 (0.003)	−0.001 (0.003)	0.000 (0.003)	0.000 (0.003)
%board financial expertise	−0.002 (0.012)	−0.002 (0.012)	−0.002 (0.013)	−0.002 (0.013)
Constant	−0.023 (0.035)	−0.023 (0.035)	−0.014 (0.037)	−0.014 (0.034)
Industry FE	Yes	Yes	Yes	Yes
Year FE	Yes	Yes	Yes	Yes
Observations	6,766	6,766	6,558	6,558
R-squared	0.070	0.070	0.070	0.070

Table 2.7 ABDs and deal diversification

Independent variables	Dependent variables: Diversifying Deal Dummy	
	(1)	(2)
ABD	0.311** (0.152)	0.436** (0.177)
Firm size	−0.053*** (0.019)	0.016 (0.031)
Leverage	0.254 (0.192)	−0.152 (0.279)
M/B	−0.052 (0.032)	0.047 (0.043)
Cash ratio	0.068 (0.207)	−0.112 (0.272)
Board size	0.077*** (0.012)	−0.003 (0.029)
Board independence	−0.159 (0.195)	−0.089 (0.229)
Public target	−0.050 (0.131)	0.085 (0.085)
Tender	−0.034 (0.203)	−0.063 (0.147)
Relative deal size	−0.398*** (0.062)	0.091 (0.126)
Stock price run-up	0.049 (0.068)	0.030 (0.079)
Stock deal	0.005 (0.078)	−0.104 (0.135)
Cash deal	0.037 (0.128)	−0.093 (0.203)
%board financial expertise	−0.088 (0.178)	0.546*** (0.189)
Constant	2.047* (1.057)	0.975** (0.380)
Industry FE	Yes	Yes
Year FE	Yes	Yes
Observations	6570	4779
Pseudo-R squared	0.078	0.116

2.2.5 Conclusion and Discussion

A growing body of literature underscores creditors' influence on borrowers' M&A transactions through deal financing, lending contracts, and loan renegotiation (Acharya et al., 2011; Becher et al., 2022; Bharadwaj & Shivdasani, 2003; Ivashina et al., 2009; Nini et al., 2012). Our paper extends this line of research by examining whether and how ABDs affect firm acquisitions. Using a unique dataset linking ABDs to acquisition deals, we report that ABDs significantly influence both short-term and long-term acquisition performance. This study provides further evidence that creditors play an active role in borrowing firms' M&A decisions, especially when the acquirers operate in complex and opaque industries and lack sufficient corporate governance. Furthermore, our study reveals that firms with ABDs are more inclined to pursue diversifying acquisitions. Our results highlight the positive influence of ABDs on firm M&A decisions due to their informational advantages, governance role, and risk-averse incentives. Nonetheless, our study is not without limitations. For example, this study focuses exclusively on U.S. listed acquiring firms, which may restrict the generalizability of our findings to other markets with different economic, regulatory, and technological landscapes. For another instance, we focus exclusively on acquiring firms but not the target firms. It is equally important and meaningful to explore the effects of ABDs on the target firms in acquisitions in future research.

Acknowledgements This chapter is based on the article previously published as: Wang, J., Li, H., Jia, V., & Wang, H. (2025). Affiliated banker directors and firm mergers and acquisitions. *Applied Economics*, 1–14. https://doi.org/https://doi.org/10.1080/00036846.2025.2491793.

Reprinted by permission of the publisher (Taylor & Francis Ltd, http://www.tandfonline.com).

References

Acharya, V. V., Amihud, Y., & Litov, L. (2011). Creditor rights and corporate risk-taking. *Journal of Financial Economics, 102*(1), 150–166.

Adams, R. B., & Ferreira, D. (2007). A theory of friendly boards. *The Journal of Finance, 62*(1), 217–250.

Adams, R. B., Hermalin, B. E., & Weisbach, M. S. (2010). The role of boards of directors in corporate governance: A conceptual framework and survey. *Journal of Economic Literature, 48*(1), 58–107.

Ahmad, M. F., Aktas, N., Cumming, D., & Xu, G. (2024). Board reforms and M&A performance: international evidence. *Journal of International Business Studies*, 1–22.

Alexandridis, G., Antypas, N., & Travlos, N. (2017). Value creation from M&As: New evidence. *Journal of Corporate Finance, 45*, 632–650.

Bauer, F., & Matzler, K. (2014). Antecedents of M&A success: The role of strategic complementarity, cultural fit, and degree and speed of integration. *Strategic Management Journal, 35*(2), 269–291.

Becher, D. A., Griffin, T. P., & Nini, G. (2022). Creditor control of corporate acquisitions. *The Review of Financial Studies, 35*(4).

Bharadwaj, A., & Shivdasani, A. (2003). Valuation effects of bank financing in acquisitions. *Journal of Financial Economics, 67*(1), 113–148.

Birkinshaw, J., Bresman, H., & Hakanson, L. (2000). Managing the post-acquisition integration process: How the human integration and task integration processes interact to foster value creation. *Journal of Management Studies, 37*(3), 395–425.

Bonsall, S. B., Holzman, E. R., & Miller, B. P. (2016). Managerial ability and credit risk assessment. *Management Science, 63*(5), 1425–1449.

Byrd, D. T., & Mizruchi, M. S. (2005). Bankers on the board and the debt ratio of firms. *Journal of Corporate Finance, 11*(1), 129–173.

Byrd, J. W., & Hickman, K. A. (1992). Do outside directors monitor managers?: Evidence from tender offer bids. *Journal of Financial Economics, 32*(2), 195–221.

Cai, Y., & Sevilir, M. (2012). Board connections and M&A transactions. *Journal of Financial Economics, 103*(2), 327–349.

Cefis, E., & Marsili, O. (2015). Crossing the innovation threshold through mergers and acquisitions. *Research Policy, 44*(3), 698–710.

Chava, S., Kumar, P., & Warga, A. (2010). Managerial agency and bond covenants. *The Review of Financial Studies, 23*(3), 1120–1148.

Chemmanur, T. J., Ertugrul, M., & Krishnan, K. (2019). Is it the investment bank or the investment banker? A study of the role of investment banker human capital in acquisitions. *Journal of Financial and Quantitative Analysis, 54*(2), 587–627.

Chen, S.-S., Chen, Y.-S., Kang, J.-K., & Peng, S.-C. (2020). Board structure, director expertise, and advisory role of outside directors. *Journal of Financial Economics, 138*(2), 483–503.

Chen, X., Harford, J., & Li, K. (2007). Monitoring: Which institutions matter? *Journal of Financial Economics, 86*(2), 279–305.

Cornaggia, J., & Li, J. Y. (2019). The value of access to finance: Evidence from M&As. *Journal of Financial Economics, 131*(1), 232–250.

Custódio, C., & Metzger, D. (2013). How do CEOs matter? The effect of industry expertise on acquisition returns. *The Review of Financial Studies, 26*(8), 2008–2047.

Dass, N., & Massa, M. (2011). The impact of a strong bank-firm relationship on the borrowing firm. *The Review of Financial Studies, 24*(4), 1204–1260.

Demerjian, P., Lev, B., & McVay, S. (2012). Quantifying managerial ability: A new measure and validity tests. *Management Science, 58*(7), 1229–1248.

Demirtaş, G. (2017). Board involvement in the M&A negotiation process. *International Review of Financial Analysis, 50*, 27–43.

Diamond, D. W. (1984). Financial intermediation and delegated monitoring. *The Review of Economic Studies, 51*(3), 393–414.

Dos Santos, M. B., Errunza, V. R., & Miller, D. P. (2008). Does corporate international diversification destroy value? Evidence from cross-border mergers and acquisitions. *Journal of Banking & Finance, 32*(12), 2716–2724.

Doukas, J. A., & Zhang, R. (2021). Managerial ability, corporate social culture, and M&As. *Journal of Corporate Finance, 68*, Article 101942.

Dutordoir, M., Roosenboom, P., & Vasconcelos, M. (2014). Synergy disclosures in mergers and acquisitions. *International Review of Financial Analysis, 31*, 88–100.

Erkens, D. H., Subramanyam, K., & Zhang, J. (2014). Affiliated banker on board and conservative accounting. *The Accounting Review, 89*(5), 1703–1728.

Fama, E. F. (1985). What's different about banks? *Journal of Monetary Economics, 15*(1), 29–39.

Fan, J. P. H., & Goyal, V. K. (2006). On the patterns and wealth effects of vertical mergers. *The Journal of Business, 79*(2), 877–902.

Fang, Y., Jin, D., Sun, X., & Wang, H. (2015). New evidence on alliance experience and acquisition performance: Short-run pain, long-run gain? *Studies in Economics and Finance, 32*(1), 53–73.

Ferreira, M. A., & Matos, P. (2012). Universal banks and corporate control: Evidence from the global syndicated loan market. *The Review of Financial Studies, 25*(9), 2703–2744.

Field, L. C., & Mkrtchyan, A. (2017). The effect of director experience on acquisition performance. *Journal of Financial Economics, 123*(3), 488–511.

Gada, V. P., Popli, M., & Malhotra, S. (2021). Time to complete the due diligence phase in mergers and acquisitions: Impact of CEO psychological characteristics. *Applied Economics, 53*(50), 5812–5825.

Gaspar, J.-M., Massa, M., & Matos, P. (2005). Shareholder investment horizons and the market for corporate control. *Journal of Financial Economics, 76*(1), 135–165.

Ghosh, S. (2016). Banker on board and innovative activity. *Journal of Business Research, 69*(10), 4205–4214.

Gigante, G., & Rubinacci, F. (2023). Explaining M&A performance: A configurational approach. *Applied Economics, 55*(5), 487–503.
Gokkaya, S., Liu, X., & Stulz, R. M. (2023). Do firms with specialized M&A staff make better acquisitions? *Journal of Financial Economics, 147*(1), 75–105.
Güner, A. B., Malmendier, U., & Tate, G. (2008). Financial expertise of directors. *Journal of Financial Economics, 88*(2), 323–354.
Hansen, L. P. (1982). Large sample properties of generalized method of moments estimators. *Econometrica, 50*(4), 1029–1054.
Harris, M., & Raviv, A. (2008). A theory of board control and size. *The Review of Financial Studies, 21*(4), 1797–1832.
Hauser, R. (2018). Busy directors and firm performance: Evidence from mergers. *Journal of Financial Economics, 128*(1), 16–37.
Heckman, J. J. (1979). Sample selection bias as a specification error. *Econometrica, 47*(1), 153–161.
Hermalin, B. E., & Weisbach, M. S. (1998). Endogenously chosen boards of directors and their monitoring of the CEO. *The American Economic Review, 88*(1), 96–118.
Honoré, F., Munari, F., & de La Potterie, B. V. P. (2015). Corporate governance practices and companies' R&D intensity: Evidence from European countries. *Research Policy, 44*(2), 533–543.
Huang, Q., Jiang, F., Lie, E., & Yang, K. (2014). The role of investment banker directors in M&A. *Journal of Financial Economics, 112*(2), 269–286.
Huang, S., Lu, R., & Srinivasan, A. (2022). Bank dependence and bank financing in corporate M&A. *Management Science, 68*(3), 2250–2283.
Ivashina, V., Nair, V. B., Saunders, A., Massoud, N., & Stover, R. (2009). Bank debt and corporate governance. *The Review of Financial Studies, 22*(1), 41–77.
James, C. (1987). Some evidence on the uniqueness of bank loans. *Journal of Financial Economics, 19*(2), 217–235.
Jiang, S., & Li, J. Y. (2022). He who lends knows. *Journal of Banking & Finance, 138*, Article 106412.
John, K., Litov, L., & Yeung, B. (2008). Corporate governance and risk-taking. *The Journal of Finance, 63*(4), 1679–1728.
Jovanovic, B., & Braguinsky, S. (2004). Bidder discounts and target premia in takeovers. *American Economic Review, 94*(1), 46–56.
Kang, M. J., & Kim, A. (2017). Bankers on the board and CEO incentives. *European Financial Management, 23*(2), 292–324.
Kang, M. J., Kim, Y. H., & Liao, Q. (2020). Do bankers on the board reduce crash risk? *European Financial Management, 26*(3), 684–723.
Kroszner, R. S., & Strahan, P. E. (2001). Bankers on boards: Monitoring, conflicts of interest, and lender liability. *Journal of Financial Economics, 62*(3), 415–452.
Masulis, R. W., Wang, C., & Xie, F. (2007). Corporate governance and acquirer returns. *The Journal of Finance, 62*(4), 1851–1889.
Masulis, R. W., & Zhang, E. J. (2019). How valuable are independent directors? Evidence from external distractions. *Journal of Financial Economics, 132*(3), 226–256.
Moeller, S. B., Schlingemann, F. P., & Stulz, R. M. (2004). Firm size and the gains from acquisitions. *Journal of Financial Economics, 73*(2), 201–228.
Moeller, T. (2005). Let's make a deal! How shareholder control impacts merger payoffs. *Journal of Financial Economics, 76*(1), 167–190.
Nini, G., Smith, D. C., & Sufi, A. (2012). Creditor control rights, corporate governance, and firm value. *The Review of Financial Studies, 25*(6), 1713–1761.
Qiao, Z., Chen, K. Y., & Hung, S. (2018). Professionals inside the board room: Accounting expertise of directors and dividend policy. *Applied Economics, 50*, 6100–6111.
Sisli-Ciamarra, E. (2012). Monitoring by affiliated bankers on board of directors: Evidence from corporate financing outcomes. *Financial Management, 41*(3), 665–702.
Song, Q., Ding, W., Hasan, I., & Wang, Q. (2024). Banker directors on board and corporate tax avoidance. *Journal of Empirical Finance*, 101551.

Stiles, P. (2001). The impact of the board on strategy: An empirical examination. *Journal of Management Studies, 38*(5), 627–650.

Teti, E., Dell'Acqua, A., Etro, L., & Volpe, M. (2017). The impact of board independency, CEO duality and CEO fixed compensation on M&A performance. *Corporate Governance: The International Journal of Business in Society, 17*(5), 947–971.

Tunyi, A. A. (2021). Revisiting acquirer returns: Evidence from unanticipated deals. *Journal of Corporate Finance, 66*, Article 101789.

Twardawski, T., & Kind, A. (2023). Board overconfidence in mergers and acquisitions. *Journal of Business Research, 165*, Article 114026.

Wang, C., Xie, F., & Zhu, M. (2015). Industry expertise of independent directors and board monitoring. *The Journal of Financial and Quantitative Analysis, 50*(5), 929–962.

Wangerin, D. (2019). M&A due diligence, post-acquisition performance, and financial reporting for business combinations. *Contemporary Accounting Research, 36*(4), 2344–2378.

Yermack, D. (1996). Higher market valuation of companies with a small board of directors. *Journal of Financial Economics, 40*(2), 185–211.

Zhao, H., Jin, D., Li, H., & Wang, H. (2021). Affiliated bankers on board and firm environmental management: US evidence. *Journal of Financial Stability, 57*, Article 100951.

3 Theoretical Foundations of ESG Strategy

3.1 Introduction: From Profit Logic to Sustainable Value

Corporate finance began with a single objective: maximize shareholder wealth (Jensen & Meckling, 1976). Agency theory, contract design, and market discipline provided the tools (Fama, 1980; Hart & Moore, 1990). The logic remains necessary but incomplete when externalities, systemic risk, and stakeholder interdependence feed back into cash flows and discount rates (Coase, 1960; Freeman, 1984; Williamson, 1985). ESG strategy does not replace profit maximization; it operationalizes it under modern constraints by expanding the set of priced risks, relevant assets, and enforceable contracts (Khan et al., 2016; Pastor et al., 2022).

Definition and scope. ESG strategy is the systematic integration of environmental, social, and governance considerations into corporate purpose, resource allocation, operating routines, and performance measurement. Materiality anchors scope so attention flows to issues that move expected cash flows or the cost of capital (Khan et al., 2016). Governance supplies decision rights and accountability so targets convert into funded work and verifiable outputs (Holmström & Milgrom, 1991). Measurement and assurance transform noisy signals into decision-useful indicators for managers and markets (Christensen et al., 2021; Simnett et al., 2009).

Why, when, and how. ESG can create value through cash-flow improvement, discount-rate reduction, and real-options flexibility (El Ghoul et al., 2011; Trigeorgis, 1996). Payoffs are highest when issues are financially material, capabilities fit the task, markets validate signals, and initiatives complement core strategy (Barney, 1991; Khan et al., 2016; Teece et al., 1997).

J. Wang, *ESG Strategies and Financial Markets*, Management for Professionals,
https://doi.org/10.1007/978-981-95-5620-5_3

3.2 Conceptual Foundations of ESG

CSR emphasizes corporate obligations and community engagement; sustainability stresses biophysical limits and intergenerational constraints; "responsible business" centers on ethics beyond compliance; ESG targets investor-relevant, decision-useful metrics tied to risk, return, and governance (Eccles & Krzus, 2018). Distinguish disclosure from performance: disclosure improves transparency by creating signals and comparability; operating practices change cash flows and risk (Healy & Palepu, 2001; Verrecchia, 2001). Conflation impairs inference and weakens incentives, especially given rating divergence (Berg et al., 2022).

Levels of analysis. Macro institutions and regulation set incentives (Scott, 2013). Meso industry structure and supply-chain networks transmit shocks and norms (DiMaggio & Powell, 1983; Williamson, 1985). Micro firm choices allocate capital, contract with stakeholders, and execute processes (Grossman & Hart, 1986).

Value-creation logics. Risk mitigation, efficiency, innovation, and legitimacy interact rather than substitute (Lins, Servaes, & Tamayo, 2017; Kramer & Porter, 2011; Russo & Fouts, 1997; Suchman, 1995).

3.3 Economic Theories Informing ESG

Agency and governance. ESG assigns clear decision rights for environmental and social risks. Boards translate diffuse exposures into mandates, limits, and escalation paths (Hart & Moore, 1990; Jensen & Meckling, 1976). Capital requests for ESG initiatives are evaluated using the same hurdle rates as other investments. Incentive structures are based on risk-adjusted, objectively measured outcomes rather than simple output totals (Holmström & Milgrom, 1991).

Stakeholder and relational contracting. Specific investments by employees, suppliers, customers, communities, and financiers create quasi-rents that are vulnerable under incomplete contracts (Freeman, 1984; Mitchell et al., 1997). ESG policies stabilize these relationships by allocating surplus to preserve cooperation and reduce hold-up (Baker et al., 2002). Multi-year supplier development with shared savings. Safety and wage floors tied to productivity gain-sharing. Customer SLAs with reliability bonuses. Community-benefit agreements to cut permitting delays. Transition-finance covenants that phase capital with milestone tests. Grievance channels and remediation funds lower renegotiation costs. Human-capital investments raise retention and reduce defect risk.

Transaction-cost economics. Make-or-buy choices shift when environmental and social hazards raise ex post bargaining costs (Klein et al., 1978; Williamson, 1985). Firms internalize activities with high measurement difficulty or large externalities. Otherwise they craft hybrids that harden terms.Contract features include audit rights, unannounced inspections, warranties tied to safety and defect metrics, data-sharing standards, traceability, and liquidated damages. In high physical risk nodes, dual sourcing with minimum volumes hedges exposure while preserving incentives. Joint monitoring with tier-1 suppliers extends credible oversight into deeper tiers. Certification and common protocols reduce search and enforcement costs across networks.

Information economics and signaling. When quality is hidden, only costly and verifiable signals separate types (Spence, 1973; Verrecchia, 2001). In ESG these include third-party assurance, science-based targets with interim checks, internal carbon prices applied in capital budgeting, and product-level chain-of-custody evidence (Dhaliwal et al., 2011; Simnett et al., 2009).Signal precision depends on data lineage, control testing, and assurance scope. Market reaction scales with financial materiality. Pricing grids in loans and supply contracts translate signal quality into cash terms. Better signals shrink adverse selection and monitoring costs for outside financiers and counterparties.

Financing frictions and sequencing. With information gaps firms prefer internal funds, then debt, then equity (Myers & Majluf, 1984). ESG projects with short paybacks are financed first. Examples include energy efficiency, yield and scrap reduction, and safety process controls. Long-dated transition bets are staged to create decision points. Firms update continuation as technology costs, policy paths, and customer demand become clearer (Christensen et al., 2021).External financing improves as validation rises. Covenants tied to objective performance measures, independent assurance, and structured offtake or procurement contracts help reduce issuance costs. Sustainability-linked instruments use features such as pricing adjustments to align incentives, share execution risk, and discourage inefficient expansion.

Public-economics interface. Private bargaining fails when rights are diffuse or transaction costs are high (Coase, 1960). Regulation then prices externalities and sets minimum process controls. Instruments differ in information needs and dynamic incentives. Taxes and trading align marginal abatement costs. Standards address measurement difficulty. Disclosure mandates cut information frictions and enable private ordering (Christensen et al., 2021). Policy credibility governs response. Clear, durable, and enforced rules lower uncertainty and support investment in capabilities. Anticipated tightening raises the option value of early measurement and control systems. Unstable rules raise hurdle rates and favor reversible pilots over irreversible reconfiguration. Enforcement design matters. Predictable penalties and audit probability support compliance investment. Sporadic enforcement invites cosmetic disclosure.

3.4 Strategic-Management Perspectives

Resource-based view. ESG capabilities confer advantage when they are valuable, rare, inimitable, and non-substitutable (Barney, 1991; Hart, 1995). Value arises through lower unit cost, higher reliability, or premium willingness-to-pay. Rarity stems from proprietary data, supplier access, or hard-won tacit know-how. Inimitability follows from causal ambiguity, path dependence, and co-specialized assets. Non-substitutability holds when rivals cannot replicate performance with cheaper inputs. Concrete assets include product-level footprint and traceability systems, supplier remediation routines with rapid closure cycles, inclusive talent pipelines that reduce error rates and hiring time, and incident-response playbooks that shorten mean time to recovery (Russo & Fouts, 1997).

Dynamic capabilities. Under volatility, firms sense shifts in regulation, technology costs, and stakeholder expectations; seize them via staged pilots, partnerships, and offtake agreements; and reconfigure by retiring carbon-intensive lines, redesigning materials, or re-platforming data governance (Eisenhardt & Martin, 2000; Teece et al., 1997). Advantage scales with learning speed, feedback quality, and redeployment cost. Fast cycle times from signal to capital reallocation convert uncertainty into option value rather than stranded cost.

Industry structure and non-market strategy. ESG can move cost curves through resource productivity and risk reduction, or shift differentiation via reliability, safety, and verified integrity (Porter, 1980). Firms also compete by shaping the rules: coalitions, standards bodies, and disclosure protocols set admissible technologies and verification thresholds (Baron, 1995; Mellahi et al., 2016). Early movers that lock in testing methods or labeling norms raise rivals' compliance costs and reduce demand uncertainty for buyers and lenders.

Institutional and legitimacy theories. Coercive mandates, normative professional standards, and mimetic copying drive diffusion across sectors and geographies (DiMaggio & Powell, 1983; Scott, 2013). Legitimacy depends on congruence between claims and verifiable practice (Suchman, 1995). After incidents, targeted transparency—root-cause disclosure, remediation milestones, and third-party verification—combined with control upgrades restores credibility and lowers regulatory and litigation exposure (Kim & Lyon, 2015).

Creating shared value with discipline. Addressing social problems embedded in the value chain can unlock new demand, cut losses, or secure inputs—e.g., energy-efficient product redesign, inclusive distribution, or supplier safety innovations that reduce downtime (Kramer & Porter, 2011). Discipline is non-negotiable: map mechanisms to cash-flow drivers, apply risk-adjusted hurdle rates, stage investments with stop rules, and link external claims to auditable evidence.

3.5 Finance & Capital-Market Perspectives

Risk pricing. Environmental and social exposures can proxy for systematic risks such as transition policy, liability, and physical climate hazards. If exposures co-move with broad states, ESG characteristics load on priced factors and affect expected returns (Bolton & Kacperczyk, 2021; Fama & French, 1993). If ESG reduces firm-specific operational shocks—fewer incidents, better supplier reliability—it lowers idiosyncratic variance and downside skew, improving Sharpe ratios holding mean returns constant. In incomplete markets, heterogeneous preferences, mandate constraints, and intermediation frictions shift demand curves, altering required returns for screened assets and for high-credibility ESG leaders (Pastor et al., 2022).

Information in prices. Prices reflect ESG only to the extent signals are material, timely, and credible (Fama, 1970). Assured, decision-useful disclosures narrow forecast dispersion and widen analyst coverage; controversy events reprice cash-flow or litigation risk (Krüger, 2015). Carbon and climate disclosures change discount rates when tied to enforceable targets or cap-ex plans; boilerplate does not (Ilhan et al., 2021). Residual anomalies arise from noisy ratings, stale data, and limits to arbitrage that delay correction.

Behavioral channels. Investor values and attention shape flows. Values-aligned portfolios tolerate tracking error to meet sustainability constraints, moving prices via clientele effects (Baker & Wurgler, 2007; Hartzmark & Sussman, 2019). Attention spikes after salient events—accidents, fines, breakthrough targets—causing transient flow-driven mispricing that mean-reverts as fundamentals clarify. Misclassification and greenwashing distort category labels and index eligibility, creating wedge dynamics until assurance, enforcement, or learning realigns perceptions (Marquis & Toffel, 2016).

Cost-of-capital mechanics. Mechanisms are contractual and statistical. On equity, lower downside correlation and incident frequency can compress beta and higher-moment risk. On debt, better process controls and governance raise expected recovery and reduce default intensity, narrowing spreads (El Ghoul et al., 2011; Oikonomou et al., 2014). Lenders and insurers embed ESG into pricing grids: Step-up and step-down pricing, covenant tests based on safety performance or emissions intensity, exclusion lists targeting high-risk activities, and warranty or audit clauses that assign monitoring rights are commonly used contract features to align interests and manage risk (Chava, 2014). Where verification is weak, markets discount claims and the channel attenuates.

Real options under uncertainty. ESG programs are portfolios of staged options. Pilots, offtake contracts, and modular retrofits create growth options if technology costs fall or regulation tightens, and abandonment options if assumptions break (Trigeorgis, 1996). Dynamic capabilities—fast sensing, rapid reconfiguration—lower exercise and switching costs, raising option value relative to irreversible bets (Teece, 2007). Firms maximize value by sequencing learning-rich, reversible investments first, then scaling only when policy credibility and cost curves improve.

3.6 Integrative ESG Strategy Framework

Link inputs, processes, and outputs. Inputs include regulatory context, stakeholder salience, resource endowments, financing constraints, and information quality. Processes cover governance design, capital budgeting with ESG-adjusted hurdle rates, product and process redesign, supplier and workforce contracting, and disclosure with assurance. Outputs are risk metrics, operating cost and yield metrics, innovation revenue, factor loadings, valuation multiples, and legitimacy indicators (Eccles & Krzus, 2018; Khan et al., 2016).

Classify ESG strategic posture by objective and capability. Compliance meets binding rules at minimum cost and stabilizes license to operate. Efficiency targets resource productivity and defect reduction with near-term payback. Innovation pursues new products, markets, and business models aligned with transition demand. Purpose-driven embeds societal problem-solving in core strategy when complementarities with capabilities and market position are strong.

Use a decision matrix. Map the firm's competitive context—regulatory intensity, stakeholder pressure, asset specificity, and demand elasticity—against its resource base—data maturity, operational discipline, supplier control, and balance-sheet capacity. In high-pressure contexts with strong capabilities, pursue innovation or purpose-driven bets with staged financing and option value. In low-pressure contexts with weak capabilities, prioritize compliance and targeted efficiency gains while building data and control systems. Migration across cells should be gated by evidence on unit economics and external validation.

3.7 Conclusion

ESG value creation arises from complementary mechanisms. Economics explains contractual alignment and the governance of externalities; strategy explains capability building and institutional fit; finance translates information and risk into prices and capital access (Barney, 1991; Fama & French, 1993; Williamson, 1985). Integration, not single-theory advocacy, is the result.

Combine plant-level microdata with supply-network maps; study dynamic migration across ESG strategies as regulation and technology evolve; link disclosure quality and assurance to real outcomes using audit-ready measures; quantify real-options value of transition investments; test boundary conditions where ESG destroys value (Berg et al., 2022; Christensen et al., 2021; Pastor et al., 2022).

Treat ESG as capital allocation under uncertainty. Focus on financially material issues, build measurement and control capabilities, price flexibility, and disclose with assurance to convert operational gains into lower financing costs and durable advantage (El Ghoul et al., 2011; Khan et al., 2016; Teece, 2007).

References

Baker, G., Gibbons, R., & Murphy, K. J. (2002). Relational contracts and the theory of the firm. *Quarterly Journal of Economics, 117*(1), 39–84.

Baker, M., & Wurgler, J. (2007). Investor sentiment in the stock market. *Journal of Economic Perspectives, 21*(2), 129–152.

Barney, J. (1991). Firm resources and sustained competitive advantage. *Journal of Management, 17*(1), 99–120.

Baron, D. P. (1995). Integrated strategy. *Advances in Strategic Management, 11*, 47–67.

Berg, F., Kölbel, J. F., & Rigobon, R. (2022). Aggregate confusion: The divergence of ESG ratings. *Review of Finance, 26*(6), 1315–1344.

Bolton, P., & Kacperczyk, M. (2021). Do investors care about carbon risk? *Journal of Financial Economics, 142*(2), 517–549.

Chava, S. (2014). Environmental externalities and cost of capital. *Management Science, 60*(9), 2223–2247.
Christensen, H. B., Hail, L., & Leuz, C. (2021). Mandatory CSR and sustainability reporting: Economic analysis and literature review. *Review of Accounting Studies, 26*(3), 1176–1248.
Coase, R. H. (1960). The problem of social cost. *Journal of Law and Economics, 3*, 1–44.
Dhaliwal, D. S., Li, O. Z., Tsang, A., & Yang, Y. G. (2011). Voluntary nonfinancial disclosure and the cost of equity capital. *The Accounting Review, 86*(1), 59–100.
DiMaggio, P. J., & Powell, W. W. (1983). The iron cage revisited. *American Sociological Review, 48*(2), 147–160.
Eccles, R. G., & Krzus, M. P. (2018). *The Nordic model: An analysis of leading practices in ESG disclosure.* Nordic Council of Ministers.
Eisenhardt, K. M., & Martin, J. A. (2000). Dynamic capabilities: What are they? *Strategic Management Journal, 21*(10–11), 1105–1121.
El Ghoul, S., Guedhami, O., Kwok, C. C. Y., & Mishra, D. R. (2011). Does corporate social responsibility affect the cost of capital? *Journal of Banking & Finance, 35*(9), 2388–2406.
Fama, E. F. (1970). Efficient capital markets: A review of theory and empirical work. *Journal of Finance, 25*(2), 383–417.
Fama, E. F. (1980). Agency problems and the theory of the firm. *Journal of Political Economy, 88*(2), 288–307.
Fama, E. F., & French, K. R. (1993). Common risk factors in the returns on stocks and bonds. *Journal of Financial Economics, 33*(1), 3–56.
Freeman, R. E. (1984). *Strategic management: A stakeholder approach.* Pitman.
Grossman, S. J., & Hart, O. D. (1986). The costs and benefits of ownership. *Journal of Political Economy, 94*(4), 691–719.
Hart, O., & Moore, J. (1990). Property rights and the nature of the firm. *Journal of Political Economy, 98*(6), 1119–1158.
Hart, S. L. (1995). A natural-resource-based view of the firm. *Academy of Management Review, 20*(4), 986–1014.
Hartzmark, S. M., & Sussman, A. B. (2019). Do investors value sustainability? *Journal of Finance, 74*(4), 1913–1968.
Healy, P. M., & Palepu, K. G. (2001). Information asymmetry, corporate disclosure, and the capital markets. *Journal of Accounting and Economics, 31*(1–3), 405–440.
Holmström, B., & Milgrom, P. (1991). Multitask principal–agent analyses. *Journal of Law, Economics, & Organization, 7*(Special Issue), 24–52.
Ilhan, E., Krueger, P., Sautner, Z., & Starks, L. T. (2023). Climate risk disclosure and institutional investors. *The Review of Financial Studies, 36*(7), 2617–2650.
Jensen, M. C., & Meckling, W. H. (1976). Theory of the firm: Managerial behavior, agency costs and ownership structure. *Journal of Financial Economics, 3*(4), 305–360.
Khan, M., Serafeim, G., & Yoon, A. (2016). Corporate sustainability: First evidence on materiality. *Accounting Review, 91*(6), 1697–1724.
Kim, E. H., & Lyon, T. P. (2015). Greenwash vs. brownwash: Exaggeration and undue modesty in corporate sustainability disclosure. *Organization science, 26*(3), 705–723.
Klein, B., Crawford, R. G., & Alchian, A. A. (1978). Vertical integration, appropriable rents, and the competitive contracting process. *Journal of Law and Economics, 21*(2), 297–326.
Kramer, M. R., & Porter, M. (2011). *Creating shared value* (Vol. 17). Boston, MA, USA: FSG.
Krüger, P. (2015). Corporate goodness and shareholder wealth. *Journal of Financial Economics, 115*(2), 304–329.
Lins, K. V., Servaes, H., & Tamayo, A. (2017). Social capital, trust, and firm performance: The value of corporate social responsibility during the financial crisis. *The Journal of Finance, 72*(4), 1785–1824.
Marquis, C., Toffel, M. W., & Zhou, Y. (2016). Scrutiny, norms, and selective disclosure: A global study of greenwashing. *Organization Science, 27*(2), 483–504.
Mellahi, K., Frynas, J. G., Sun, P., & Siegel, D. (2016). A review of the nonmarket strategy literature: Toward a multi-theoretical integration. *Journal of Management, 42*(1), 143–173.

Mitchell, R. K., Agle, B. R., & Wood, D. J. (1997). Toward a theory of stakeholder identification. *Academy of Management Review, 22*(4), 853–886.

Myers, S. C., & Majluf, N. S. (1984). Corporate financing and investment decisions when firms have information that investors do not have. *Journal of Financial Economics, 13*(2), 187–221.

Oikonomou, I., Brooks, C., & Pavelin, S. (2014). The effects of corporate social performance on the cost of corporate debt. *Financial Review, 49*(1), 49–75.

Pastor, Ľ, Stambaugh, R. F., & Taylor, L. A. (2022). Sustainable investing in equilibrium. *Journal of Financial Economics, 145*(2), 287–312.

Porter, M. E. (1980). *Competitive strategy*. Free Press.

Russo, M. V., & Fouts, P. A. (1997). A resource-based perspective on corporate environmental performance and profitability. *Academy of Management Journal, 40*(3), 534–559.

Scott, W. R. (2013). *Institutions and organizations: Ideas, interests, and identities*. Sage publications.

Simnett, R., Vanstraelen, A., & Chua, W. F. (2009). Assurance on sustainability reports: An international comparison. *The Accounting Review, 84*(3), 937–967.

Spence, M. (1973). Job market signaling. *Quarterly Journal of Economics, 87*(3), 355–374.

Suchman, M. C. (1995). Managing legitimacy: Strategic and institutional approaches. *Academy of Management Review, 20*(3), 571–610.

Teece, D. J. (2007). Explicating dynamic capabilities: The nature and microfoundations of (sustainable) enterprise performance. *Strategic Management Journal, 28*(13), 1319–1350.

Teece, D. J., Pisano, G., & Shuen, A. (1997). Dynamic capabilities and strategic management. *Strategic Management Journal, 18*(7), 509–533.

Trigeorgis, L. (1996). *Real options*. MIT Press.

Verrecchia, R. E. (2001). Essays on disclosure. *Journal of Accounting and Economics, 32*(1–3), 97–180.

Williamson, O. E. (1985). *The economic institutions of capitalism*. Free Press.

Social Capital and ESG Engagement 4

4.1 What is Social Capital

Social capital is most often understood as the stock of trust, norms, and networks that enable cooperation and collective action. Unlike financial or physical capital, which reside in tangible resources or monetary claims, social capital is embedded in patterns of relationships and shared understandings. It represents the quality of connections among actors—individuals, organizations, or institutions—and the capacity those connections create for coordinated behavior. At the corporate level, social capital refers to the trust between firms and their stakeholders, the legitimacy conferred by communities, and the credibility that allows organizations to coordinate under uncertainty.

The concept of social capital has evolved across disciplines. In sociology, early scholars emphasized social capital as an individual resource gained through membership in networks that could be converted into economic or cultural advantage. Coleman (1988) extended the concept by framing social capital as a collective good embedded in social structures, facilitating obligations, expectations, and information flows. Later, Robert Putnam popularized the term for broader audiences. His influential book *Bowling Alone* (2000) documented the erosion of civic engagement in the United States—declining participation in associations, clubs, and community activities—and argued that this decline undermined trust and cooperation. The image of Americans "bowling alone" rather than in leagues became a metaphor for the weakening of social connectedness and the negative consequences for collective well-being. While Putnam's work was focused on communities and civic life, it laid a foundation for understanding social capital in organizations and markets by highlighting how networks and trust generate real economic and social benefits.

Economists have also taken up the concept, examining how social capital reduces transaction costs, mitigates principal–agent problems, and supports contract enforcement where legal institutions are weak or incomplete. In political

J. Wang, *ESG Strategies and Financial Markets*, Management for Professionals,
https://doi.org/10.1007/978-981-95-5620-5_4

science, social capital has been used to explain why some regions or nations sustain more effective institutions, higher levels of civic cooperation, and greater resilience to social conflict. In public health, it has been linked to community well-being, stress reduction, and health outcomes. This breadth of applications underscores the interdisciplinary relevance of the concept: wherever collective action is necessary, social capital provides the "glue" that makes coordination possible.

Within business and management, the importance of social capital follows directly from these insights. At the organizational level, trust and cooperative ties reduce frictions in contracting, lower the risk of opportunistic behavior, and increase access to external resources. Firms with strong ties to suppliers and customers are better positioned to manage uncertainty, adapt to shocks, and innovate collaboratively. Employee-level social capital—manifested through networks of cooperation, shared norms, and strong organizational identification—enhances productivity, lowers turnover, and fosters knowledge sharing. Inter-organizational networks provide reputational legitimacy, helping firms attract investors, strategic partners, and favorable regulatory treatment. Social capital also underpins what is often called the "social license to operate," where firms that demonstrate reciprocity and responsibility gain the trust of communities and thereby reduce the risk of protests, litigation, or reputational crises.

The absence of social capital, by contrast, isolates firms from these advantages. Just as Putnam showed that communities with declining networks faced weakened trust and diminished collective capacity, organizations without social capital find themselves exposed to conflict, dependent on costly formal controls, and vulnerable to sudden shocks. In such cases, firms rely heavily on legal contracts, monitoring mechanisms, and external enforcement, all of which raise transaction costs and erode flexibility.

Taken together, the development of social capital as a concept—from its roots in sociology, through its refinement in economics and political science, to its application in business—illustrates its enduring significance. It is not a peripheral construct but a central element in understanding how cooperation, trust, and legitimacy translate into economic performance. For firms, social capital functions as an intangible yet vital resource that sustains resilience, supports strategic initiatives, and ultimately shapes competitive advantage in both product and capital markets.

4.2 Social Capital and ESG

The connection between social capital and ESG engagement is conceptually natural. Both concepts are rooted in relationships, trust, and legitimacy. ESG practices extend beyond compliance to encompass how firms interact with stakeholders: environmental stewardship reflects long-term commitment to society and natural ecosystems; social responsibility involves cultivating trust with workers, protecting customer rights, and supporting communities; governance structures demonstrate accountability and fairness toward shareholders, regulators, and other stakeholders.

In each of these domains, social capital acts as both a foundation and a reinforcing outcome. Firms with strong social capital are more likely to engage credibly in ESG activities, while sustained ESG practices, in turn, build additional trust and reputational legitimacy. This interplay suggests that social capital is both an antecedent to and a consequence of ESG engagement. On the one hand, firms embedded in networks of reciprocity and shared norms face stronger pressures to maintain legitimacy, leading them to adopt ESG practices. On the other hand, ESG engagement strengthens relational value by signaling credibility, responsibility, and fairness, deepening the trust that underpins social capital. The result is a self-reinforcing cycle where social capital and ESG evolve together.

Social capital is typically measured at the regional or community level, reflecting collective trust, civic participation, and cultural norms. Indicators such as voter turnout, community association density, or levels of charitable activity have been widely used in the literature. This regional measurement highlights how local culture and norms shape corporate behavior. Firms located in regions with higher levels of social capital are more likely to adopt ESG practices, as they are subject to stronger community expectations and embedded in cultures that reward cooperation and responsibility. Conversely, in regions with weaker social capital, ESG adoption tends to lag because stakeholder pressures are muted and relational monitoring is weaker.

A growing body of empirical research confirms these mechanisms. Studies find that firms headquartered in regions with higher social capital are more socially responsible, disclose more ESG information, and are less prone to financial misreporting. Social capital is associated with stronger corporate social responsibility (CSR) performance (Guiso et al., 2004; Hasan et al., 2017), greater stakeholder trust (Hilary & Hui, 2009), and lower incidences of unethical behavior. Regional trust has been linked to stronger environmental and community engagement, while community-level norms of reciprocity correlate with improved corporate governance outcomes. This literature demonstrates that the broader social environment in which firms operate strongly influences their ESG decisions, reinforcing the notion that social capital and ESG are interconnected and often inseparable in practice.

Financial markets recognize the deep interconnections between social capital and ESG engagement. Investors routinely confront challenges in assessing whether firms' ESG commitments are credible and capable of generating long-term value. The benefits of ESG initiatives are often uncertain, unfold slowly, and are vulnerable to symbolic or superficial adoption. In this setting, social capital operates as a signal that a firm's ESG practices are genuine and trustworthy.

One channel is the reduction of information asymmetry. Firms embedded in dense social networks face stronger external scrutiny, which enhances the reliability of their disclosures. Investors interpret ESG commitments from such firms as more credible because they are subject to relational monitoring. A second channel is the lowering of monitoring and contracting costs. When a firm enjoys relational credibility with its stakeholders, lenders and investors have less need for restrictive covenants or costly enforcement mechanisms, directly reducing the cost of borrowing. A third channel is the mitigation of non-financial risks. Firms with high social capital are better protected against reputational crises, regulatory sanctions, litigation, or stakeholder boycotts. This insurance-like function strengthens the downside protection that investors value. Finally, social capital facilitates the translation of ESG activities into financial outcomes. Because the payoffs from ESG initiatives are gradual and intangible—emerging through reputation, resilience, and innovation—social capital provides the relational infrastructure for markets to interpret these signals as authentic and meaningful, thereby accelerating their incorporation into firm valuation.

These mechanisms explain why investors consistently reward firms with strong social capital through lower costs of equity and debt, narrower bid–ask spreads, and more favorable analyst coverage. Social capital is not simply a background condition; it is a critical lens through which markets assess the credibility and financial materiality of ESG engagement.

Consequently, firms with high social capital often enjoy lower costs of equity and debt, narrower bid–ask spreads, and more favorable analyst coverage. Bondholders, in particular, value the assurance that social capital provides against default risk. Recent evidence shows that social capital is associated with reduced bond yield spreads, even after controlling for financial fundamentals.

This chapter builds on these foundations to examine in detail how social capital interacts with ESG engagement and how both influence corporate financing outcomes. The empirical centerpiece is the study "The Role of Social Capital in Private Placement: Evidence from Rule 144A Debt Issuances." This paper provides systematic evidence on the role of social capital in debt markets, showing that relational assets mitigate investor concerns over opportunism, information asymmetry, and stakeholder conflicts, thereby reducing the cost of borrowing. Situating this evidence within the broader ESG framework underscores that social capital is not simply a sociological construct, but a critical intangible resource that links ESG engagement to tangible financial benefits.

Through this integration, the chapter highlights a broader implication: in a financial system increasingly attentive to sustainability and stakeholder relations, intangible relational resources like social capital are central to how markets assess risk, allocate capital, and value corporate conduct in the ESG era.

4.3 The Role of Social Capital in Private Placement: Evidence from Rule 144A Debt Issuances

4.3.1 Introduction

The Securities and Exchange Commission has allowed firms to sell securities to qualified institutional buyers (QIBs) under Rule 144A since April 1990. The issuance of Rule144A debt does not require registration, which implies that Rule 144A debt offerings tend to have fewer disclosures, more rapid issuance, and leave less time for investors to conduct due diligence (Fenn, 2000). The Rule 144A debt is mainly adopted by domestic firms who need to quickly issue securities that are eligible to be subsequently registered. Existing studies reveal that most of firms choosing to finance through private placement experience a high degree of information asymmetry and are with low credit quality that below investment grade (Cai et al., 2011; Chandra & Nayar, 2008; Maksimovic & Pichler, 2006). Given the features of the Rule 144A debt issuers and the issuance process, it is difficult for investors to accurately evaluate the qualification of Rule 144A debt issuers. It is noteworthy to explore how to mitigate the information asymmetry and determine the yield spreads of Rule 144A debt.

An emerging line of research explores the informal institutions in economic transactions and financial contracts. For example, Williamson (2009) finds that the presence of informal institutions is a strong determinant of economic development. Estrin and Prevezer (2011) document that informal institutions serve as the corporate governance mechanism and lead to enhanced domestic and foreign investment. Social capital is wildly viewed as a critical component of informal institution that copes with moral hazard and incentive problems (Stiglitz, 2000).

Social capital is defined as a set of norms shared among members in certain groups or communities (Bourdieu, 1986; Fukuyama, 1997; Putnam, 2001). Generally, higher social capital societies display greater trust as well as higher economic payoff (Knack & Keefer, 1997; Putnam, 2000). As an important component of informal institutions, social capital plays a role in decreasing transaction costs of organizing activity and in allowing certain activities (Adhikari & Goldey, 2010; Casson et al., 2010). Recent empirical studies have highlighted the importance of social capital. For example, Jha (2019) finds that firms headquartered in the high social capital region deliver the high quality of the financial report. Lins et al. (2017) document a positive relation between social capital and financial performance during the financial crisis. Hasan et al. (2017), Brockman et al. (2018) and Fogel et al. (2018) find that firms headquartered in counties with higher levels of social capital incur a lower cost of debt.

In this study, we posit that social capital plays an important role in the issuances of Rule 144A debt. We believe that investors incorporate social capital in the pricing scheme of Rule 144A debt offerings for the following three reasons. First, social capital serves as an alternative governance mechanism to deal with agency conflict and moral hazard. Most Rule 144A debt issuers have high information uncertainty and experience agency problems. Agency problems affect firm's financing decisions. Social capital serves as a monitoring mechanism given its information sharing feature and its high level of social punishment towards misbehaviors. Second, social capital facilitates information transmission and mitigates the information asymmetry between Rule 144A debt issuers and investors. The dense social networks in communities with high level of social capital provide more access to information and may speed up the information flow (Gooderham et al., 2011; Lee & Bell, 2013). Consequently, the social capital of the region where Rule 144A debt issuers headquartered provides additional channel to assess issuers' qualification. Third, social capital is always treated as the mutual trust in communities. (Fukuyama, 1997; Putnam, 2001). Empirical studies document that the firms headquartered in the high social capital region are trustworthy for their stakeholders and enjoy more financing access and a lower financing cost (Guiso et al., 2004; Hasan et al., 2017). Social capital in the county where the Rule 144A debt issuers headquartered may affect how much the investors trust the issuers. We extend these streams of literature and empirically examine whether and to what extent social capital affects the cost of Rule 144A debt.

We use data from the Northeast Regional Center for Rural Development (NRCRD) to measure the levels of social capital. We collect data of Rule 144A debt from Thomson Financial SDC Platinum Global New Issues database (SDC) and measure the debt cost using yield spreads relative to the Treasury security of comparable maturity. Using a sample of 1378 debt offerings from 1997 to 2015 in the U.S., we find a significantly negative relation between social capital and Rule 144A debt yield spreads after controlling for the firm, debt and county attributes, and year and industry fixed effects. Our finding is economically meaningful.

The results are robust when we use trust as an alternative social capital measure, and when we adopt a Heckman selection model, an instrumental variable approach and propensity score matching. The effect of social capital on the cost of Rule 144A debt is stronger for weakly monitored firms, such as those with lower institutional ownership. The findings also suggest that the effect of social capital on Rule 144A debt is more prominent after financial crisis.

4.3.2 Related Research

4.3.2.1 Institutional Background for Rule 144A Debt Offerings

Rule 144A debt is mainly adopted by U.S. domestic firms who need to issue securities that are eligible to be subsequently registered quickly (Huang & Ramirez, 2010). When Rule 144A debts are subsequently registered, the debt carries the nature of the public debt, and the investors enjoy the benefit of public-market liquidity (Fenn, 2000). Therefore, Rule144A debt is comparable with public market debt but with distinct differences. Typically, firms issuing Rule144A debt have lower credit quality and more severe information asymmetry issues (Arena, 2011). The issuance of Rule144A debt is lack of registration which implies the fewer disclosures and the faster issuances, and leaves investors less time for due diligence (Fenn, 2000). From investor's perspective, Rule 144A debt carries higher due diligence cost, implies higher information asymmetry, and lack of liquidity. Investors ask for a higher yield to compensate for the uncertain creditworthiness. Prior literature documents that lenders mitigate the potential risks of debt-related investment by adjusting the debt yield spreads (Bharath et al., 2008; Van Binsbergen et al., 2010; Wittenberg-Moerman, 2008). The inadequate disclosure and informational asymmetry are the main drivers of the premium of Rule144 securities (Fenn, 2000; Wittenberg-Moerman, 2008).

4.3.2.2 Related Literature and Hypotheses Development

Informal institutions are socially shared rules that are created, communicated, and enforced outside of the coercive power of the state (Estrin & Prevezer, 2011; Helmke & Levitsky, 2004). Informal institutions play a significant role in economic development and operation of the market by facilitating the access to resources and information, especially when the formal mechanisms are absent. Social capital is an important factor of informal institution that contributes to decreasing transaction costs of organizing activities (Adhikari & Goldey, 2010; Casson et al., 2010; Stiglitz, 2000). Social capital is described as a set of norms shared among members in certain groups or communities (Bourdieu, 1986; Fukuyama, 1997; Putnam, 2001). Portes (1998) adds that social networks generated from social capital are not a free natural given and must be constructed through investment strategies, usable as a reliable source of other benefits. In this process, there must comprise significant trust-based information sharing mechanism and collaboration. Therefore, social capital facilitates access to information and speeds up the information flow within the region (Moran, 2005). Social capital is also an essential determinant of the level of trust (Guiso et al., 2004). As Putnam (2001) and Woolcock (2001) emphasize in their works, although social trust is not part of the definition of the social capital, it is a close consequence and certainly a proxy of social capital. Portes (1998) points out that there are two instrumental values of social capital: enforceable trust and reciprocity exchange. Firms in the regions with high social capital levels earn more social trust. Meanwhile, the high level of social capital indicates a high level of social punishment towards the misbehavior of the society and therefore enhances the altruism level among the participants within the communities (Guiso et al., 2004; Jha, 2019).

A healthy trust-based relationship is beneficial for the long-term contract because it conveys valuable opportunities and information (Chung et al., 2000). A large body of literature investigates the effect of social capital on the strategic decisions and economic outcomes. For example, Jha and Chen (2015) document that the auditors judge the trustworthiness of the clients based on where the firm is headquartered, and that firms pay less if they earn more trust from their auditors. Jha (2019) finds that firms locating in the region with high social capital tend to deliver higher quality of the financial reports and are less likely to commit fraud by misrepresenting financial information. Further, Lins et al. (2017) argue that trust is built through social capital between the firms and that both stakeholders and investors pay off when the markets suffer a negative shock. These empirical studies have highlighted the role of social capital in the firm's operation.

Financial contracts are the ultimate trust-intensive contracts (Guiso et al., 2004). Rule 144A is a great example of the trust-intensive contracts given its low information disclosure requirement and its issuers' financial condition. Such transactions depend not only on the enforceability of contracts but also on the extent to which the investors trust the issuer. Rule 144A bond investors have limited access to public information and lack monitoring mechanisms. Therefore, the trust-based information sharing process is critical in the practice of private placement of Rule

144A debt. Social capital enhances mutual trust of different parties. Firms headquartered in high level of social capital regions are proven to be more trustworthy for stakeholders (Guiso et al., 2004; Jha, 2019). The trust inherited from social capital allows more open and honest information sharing, which gives Rule 144A debt issuers headquartered in high social capital regions more competitive advantages. Investors evaluate the qualification of the issuers and the value of the debt contract before deciding the payoff of their capital. The high social capital region enjoys the information advantage because of the close-knit within the community (Moran, 2005). In this sense, social capital facilitates information transmission and mitigates the information asymmetry between the firms and outsiders. The more information Rule 144A debt investors acquire, the fewer uncertainties they potentially face, and the fewer risks are associated with the deal (Wittenberg-Moerman, 2008). Since there is a causal effect of social capital on the cost of debt, we put forward our first hypothesis as follows:

Hypothesis 1 The cost of Rule 144A debt is lower for issuers headquartered in counties with higher levels of social capital.

Social capital is regarded as an informal community governance mechanism (Boone & White, 2015). Such governance is at the regional level and it mainly depends on participants' self-discipline and interaction with other parties. The governance function of informal institutions is especially strong when the firm-specific governing and monitoring mechanism is absent. Shareholders with large ownership have strong incentives to conduct extensive monitoring of the management (Bhojraj & Sengupta, 2003; Gillan & Starks, 2003; Shleifer & Vishny, 1986). Boone and White (2015) find that firms with high institutional ownership have greater management disclosure and analysts following, resulting in lower information asymmetry. Similarly, Bhojraj and Sengupta (2003) find that firms with larger institutional ownership enjoy higher bond ratings and lower bond yields. These results reinforce that large institutional holding is a firm-specific monitoring mechanism. The high institutional ownership may weaken the informal monitoring role played by social capital in the private placement of Rule 144A debt. We put forward our second hypothesis as follows:

Hypothesis 2 The negative relation between social capital and the cost of Rule144A debt offerings is weaker for issuers with larger institutional ownership.

Religious social norms have been shown as a force to affect the decisions of corporate managers and economic choices and outcomes in a variety of contexts (Chintrakarn et al., 2017; Dyreng et al., 2012). Religiosity is associated with higher ethical norms, and higher ethical norms induce a high punishment towards misconduct. Though religiosity and social capital are all social environment factors, they measure different aspects of cultural norms. Religiosity measures faith in God and induces ethical behavior, while social capital measures the norms for cooperative behavior such as trust and close knit within communities (Dyreng et al., 2012; Jha,

2019). Religiosity and social capital are two important complements for the social environment, and religiosity is also partly incorporated into the wildly used social capital measurement. When these two sources exist simultaneously in the social environment, it would be much better for investors to evaluate the qualification of the firms. We expect that the negative relation between social capital and cost of Rule 144A debt becomes stronger for issuers that are located in more religious counties. We put forward our third hypothesis as follows:

Hypothesis 3 The effect of social capital on cost of Rule144A debt offerings is stronger for issuers located in more religious communities.

4.3.2.3 Data, Sample, and Measures

Data and sample

We construct our sample using several data sources. We use data from the Northeast Regional Center for Rural Development (NRCRD) to measure the levels of social capital. We collect all issues of Rule 144A debt from the Thomas Reuters New Issues Database of the Securities Data Company (SDC). The data of public debt is obtained from the SDC database as well. In our study, we require all the debt data in our sample to be non-convertible, with a fixed coupon rate and with maturity longer than one year. Further, the issuers must be headquartered in the U.S. We retrieve financial information and location of the headquarters of our sample issuers from Standard & Poor's Compustat database. We obtain the demographic data from Bureau of Economic Analysis (BEA). We use state code and county code (fips) of each firm's headquarter location to match Compustat database with NRCRD and BEA. Following the convention, we eliminate financial firms (SIC codes 6000–6900) and utility companies (SIC codes 4900–4999) because these industry segments are highly regulated. We further eliminate the observations with missing information. Our sampling procedure yields a sample of 1378 Rule144A debt offerings from 1997 to 2015.

Measure of cost of Rule 144A debt

We collect data of Rule 144A bond from SDC database. The cost of Rule 144A debt is measured using yield spreads. We calculate yield spread as the difference in basis points between the original yield of Rule 144A bond and that of a U.S. Treasury bond with comparable maturity.

Measures of social capital

We obtain social capital data from the Northeast Regional Center for Rural Development (NRCRD) at Pennsylvania State University. NRCRD provides the U.S. county-level data in the years of 1990, 1997, 2005, 2009 and 2014, respectively. Following Rupasingha et al. (2006), we adopt the principal component analysis to construct the measure of U.S. county-level social capital. Specifically, we use four NRCRD variables as principal factors to capture the strength of the cooperative norms and the density of social capital. Among them, *pvote* is the voter turnover of the county; *respn* reflects the Census Bureau's census response rate of the measured county; *assn* is the aggregate for all social organizations considered in the county divided by population per 1000; *nccs* is the number of non-profit organizations. We first standardize these four variables to have a mean of zero and a standard deviation of one, then we create the social capital score of each county by adopting the principal component analysis using the above four standardized variables. The first principal component is considered as the social capital score of the county in the given data year. The dataset only provides data used for estimating social capital score in 1990, 1997, 2005,2009 and 2014. Existing literature tends to measure social capital over year by filling in the data for the missing years using the social capital score in the preceding year in which data are available. However, this treatment could introduce serial correlation issue. In this study, we adopt the linear interpolation approach to fill the social capital score for the missing year by assuming a constant change from year to year between the two point (Hilary & Hui, 2009; Jha, 2019). For example, the social capital scores have established values for the year of 1997 and 2005. We fill all the missing years' social capital scores between 1997 and 2005 by making them pass through the straight line of two known values evenly.

Other measures
In our study, we include three sets of control variables in the empirical test: the firm-level attributes, debt-level attributes, and county-level attributes. In the first set, firm size is the natural logarithm of the book value of firm assets. We gauge firm performance using Tobin's *Q*, which is the ratio of the market value of the asset to book value of the asset. Market leverage is total debt divided by the market value of equity, which is the product of stock price times the number of shares outstanding. ROA is measured by the ratio of net income to total assets. Tax avoidance is measured using tax expense scaled by pre-tax income (Huseynov & Klamm, 2012). The dividend payout policy is measured using common and preferred dividends scaled by income before extraordinary items (Floyd et al., 2015). Existing literature documents a mixed relation between corporate investment and cost of capital (Frank & Shen, 2016; Gilchrist & Zakrajsek, 2007). We add firm investment in the control set by calculating firm investment as common equity scaled by the invested capital (Grundy & Li, 2010). The second set of the control variables include debt size, debt maturity, and debt rating. In the county-level control set, we include the population size, population growth rate and household income per capita in a county. We take the logarithm of the population and income per capita to normalize the distribution.

Table 4.1 reports the descriptive statistics for all the variables used in baseline regression.

Since the existing literature tends to compare Rule 144A debt with the public issues, in Table 4.1, we also report the descriptive statistics of public debt for comparison. There is a total of 1378 Rule 144A issues and 3707 public issues in the sample period. On average, the Rule 144A issuing size is $567 million and with

392 basis points of Treasury spreads. The average maturity is 9 years. Comparing the Rule 144A debt characteristics with public issues, our sample reveals that Rule 144A original yield and the yield spreads are significantly higher than those of public issues. The issue size of Rule 144A is smaller than that of public issues. In terms of firm attributes, Rule 144A issuers are smaller in size, higher in leverage and with worse operating conditions. Furthermore, Table 4.1 shows that Rule 144A debt issuers are short of cash, pay lower dividend and have fewer investment opportunities. In addition, Rule 144A debt issuers have a typically lower credit rating. When we compare our sample with Arena (2011), we find that the Rule 144A debt and public debt exhibits the similar pattern in terms of firm and issue characteristics like Tobin's *Q*, ROA, credit rating, yield spreads, issue size and maturity.

4.3.3 Empirical Results

In this section, we model Rule 144A debt yield spreads as a function of social capital along with a set of controls. In addition, we include year fixed effects to control for the timely trend and economy-wide shocks. We also add industry fixed effects to control for unobservable time-invariant industry characteristics.[1] Because the same firm can issue debt to different investors, the standard errors in the OLS regression are inefficient when the residuals are correlated for the same issuing firm over time. We, therefore, cluster standard errors by the firm to address this residual dependence across debt for the same firm (Cameron & Miller, 2015). We also perform the bootstrap as an alternative method for estimating the standard errors as the robustness check. Table 4.2 presents the main regression results testing the proposed relation between social capital and Rule144A debt yield spreads. Table 4.2 shows the results of three models. Model 1 controls for the firm attributes only. Model 2 controls for both the firm and debt attributes. Since social capital is measured at county-level, in Model 3, we add county-level controls in the regression. The coefficients on social capital are significantly negative ($p < 0.05$). The coefficients are −0.041, −0.039 and −0.036, respectively. Moreover, the coefficients on the control variables generally are in line with expectations. We find that the yield spreads are negatively related to firm size, investment level and Tobin's *Q*. And the higher a firm's leverage level is, the higher the yield spreads the Rule 144A debt issuers must pay. The relation between the firm's credit rating and Rule 144A debt spreads is significantly negative. The baseline regression output reveals that firms headquartered in the high social capital counties incur lower

[1] The social capital index is constructed at county level. There is limited variation in the social capital within a state. The inclusion of state-fixed effects in the model can take away a large part of social capital's effect on Rule 144A debt cost. Besides, in the panel data analysis, fixed-effect may not work well with data for which within-cluster variation is minimal. Therefore, we didn't control for state-fixed effect in our models.

Table 4.1 Summary statistic

	Rule 144A debt						Public debt						Mean Difference
	N	Mean	S.D.	P25	P50	P75	N	Mean	S.D.	P25	P50	P75	
Social capital	1378	−0.535	0.893	−1.255	−0.428	0.161	3707	−0.347	0.835	−0.920	−0.290	0.223	−0.188***
Yield spreads	1378	392	221	225	360	529	3707	176	137	88	135	211	216.6***
Years to maturity	1378	9.156	4.395	7.108	8.640	10.153	3707	11.828	9.114	5.114	10.144	10.294	−2.672***
Issue size	1378	566.590	922.475	198.764	299.741	540	3707	1370.163	2631.172	298.859	693.494	1500	−803.6***
Debt rating	1378	10.471	3.182	8	10	13	3707	15.545	3.000	14	15	17	−5.074***
Firm size	1378	7.985	1.259	7.137	7.838	8.898	3707	9.715	1.307	8.773	9.768	10.569	−1.730***
Tobin's Q	1378	1.526	0.793	1.105	1.301	1.669	3707	1.926	0.929	1.293	1.627	2.260	−0.400***
ROA	1378	0.024	0.093	0.005	0.029	0.057	3707	0.060	0.056	0.031	0.059	0.090	−0.037***
Market leverage	1378	0.395	0.167	0.287	0.379	0.504	3707	0.284	0.123	0.201	0.268	0.359	0.111***
Investment	1378	0.457	0.208	0.311	0.472	0.601	3707	0.558	0.183	0.446	0.579	0.685	−0.101***
Tax avoidance	1378	0.215	1.706	0.172	0.344	0.382	3707	0.319	0.849	0.248	0.324	0.373	−0.104**
Dividend payment	1378	0.190	2.192	0.000	0.000	0.181	3707	0.288	7.511	0.071	0.278	0.468	−0.098
Cash holding	1378	0.074	0.084	0.016	0.041	0.097	3707	0.084	0.104	0.019	0.046	0.103	−0.010**
Tangibility	1378	0.415	0.126	0.333	0.436	0.512	3707	0.404	0.128	0.316	0.419	0.500	0.012**

(continued)

Table 4.1 (continued)

	Rule 144A debt						Public debt						Mean Difference
	N	Mean	S.D.	P25	P50	P75	*N*	Mean	S.D.	P25	P50	P75	
County population	1378	1,637,875	1,712,076	589,394	952,810	2,246,432	3707	1,592,986	1,727,594	682,071	951,535	1,669,348	44,888.9
County population growth	1378	0.013	0.013	0.004	0.010	0.019	3707	0.009	0.010	0.002	0.007	0.014	0.003***
County personal income	1378	44,980	17,845	33,940	40,596	51,111	3707	54,275	26,577	37,093	46,396	61,193	−0.153***

yield spreads in their Rule144A debt issuances. Our results lend strong support for Hypothesis 1.

We further estimate the economic significance of our finding. Since the dependent variable is in its log-transformed state, and the independent variable is in its original metric in our model, it indicates that for one unit increase in the social capital, the yield spreads will decrease by 3.6%. Moreover, based on the estimate in Model 3 of Table 4.2, a one-standard-deviation increase in social capital in the data leads to a reduction of yield spreads by 12.34 bps.[2] The average issuing size and yield spreads of Rule 144A debt in the sample is $567 million and 392bps, respectively. This implies that a one-standard-deviation increase in social capital reduces issuing cost by 0.027 million ($0.027 = 567 \times 392$ bps $\times$ 12.34 bps). The effect of social capital on cost of Rule 144A debt is economically meaningful.

The major concern for the regression analysis is the endogeneity issue. The endogeneity concern comes from two aspects. On the one hand, there is self-selection endogeneity concern arising from the strategic decision of issuing Rule 144A debt. Rule 144A debt financing is not a random decision but is a deliberate decision to self-select into the preferred choices. Therefore, we need to address this potential issue by incorporating and controlling for the unobservable information that may influence firms' decisions. On the other hand, the estimation can be affected by the endogeneity of social capital because of the omitted variables that are correlated with social capital and debt cost. Arguably firms tend to issue Rule 144A debt might choose to locate in a high social capital region. If this is the case, it might not be that social capital affects Rule144A debt as we argue, but rather that firms with a greater propensity to issue Rule 144A debt choose to locate in the high social capital county. To address these endogeneity issues, following the existing corporate finance application (Chaney et al., 2004; Massa & Žaldokas, 2014), we employ the instrumental variable two-stage least square approach, propensity score matching, and Heckman two-step procedure in our study.

We first use the DealScan database and the SDC database to gather detailed information about different groups of firms seeking external financing, including bank loans (DealScan) and public debts (SDC). According to Heckman (1979), incorporating information from groups of firms using alternative sources of financing allows us to recover the error structure from eliminating bias. Heckman's method needs to perform a Probit model in which firm self-select into one group. In this case, we adopt Probit model to estimate the likelihood of choosing Rule 144A debt versus other financing methods (Denis & Mihov, 2003) where the dependent variable equals one if the firm issues Rule 144A debt in the given year and zero if the firm issues public debt or borrows bank loans. Specifically,

---

[2] In our sample, the average social capital score is −0.535 and the standard deviation is 0.893, and the average Rule144 A debt yield spread in our sample is 392 bps and the standard deviation is 221. Based on the estimate in model 3 of Table 4.3, a 1-standard-devation increase in social capital in the data leads to a reduction in Ln(spread) of −0.032, where $-0.032 = -0.036 * 0.893$. It further suggests a decrease of 12.34 bps based on the average Rule 144A debt spread of 392 bps, where $-12.34 = 392 * \exp(-0.032) - 392$.

Table 4.2 Baseline regressions: the effect of social capital on Rule 144A debt yield spreads

Independent variable	Dependent variable Yield spread (in logs)		
	(1)	(2)	(3)
Social capital	−0.041*** (0.013)	−0.039*** (0.015)	−0.036** (0.019)
Firm size	−0.204*** (0.023)	−0.171*** (0.016)	−0.169*** (0.007)
Tobin's Q	−0.231*** (0.065)	−0.151*** (0.027)	−0.155*** (0.030)
ROA	−0.253 (0.304)	−0.268 (0.288)	−0.288*** (0.080)
Market leverage	0.013 (0.173)	0.075 (0.149)	0.053 (0.136)
Investment	−0.837*** (0.127)	−0.692*** (0.107)	−0.712*** (0.075)
Tax avoidance	0.003 (0.004)	−0.001 (0.010)	−0.001 (0.010)
Dividend payment	0.003 (0.010)	0.004 (0.008)	0.004 (0.004)
Cash holding	0.852*** (0.198)	0.709*** (0.194)	0.780** (0.342)
Tangibility	−0.177 (0.153)	−0.104 (0.121)	−0.142 (0.232)
Years to maturity		0.001 (0.005)	0.000 (0.002)
Issue size		−0.000 (0.000)	−0.000** (0.000)
Debt rating		−0.631*** (0.054)	−0.615*** (0.043)
Ln (POP)			−0.032 (0.021)
Population growth			0.255 (0.201)
Ln (Income)			0.010 (0.028)
Constant	8.470*** (0.282)	8.092*** (0.139)	8.425*** (0.134)
Year FE	Yes	Yes	Yes
Industry FE	Yes	Yes	Yes
Observations	1378	1378	1378
R-squared	0.639	0.673	0.675

Note The sample contains 1378 observations during period of 1997–2015. Model (1) includes controls for firm characteristics. Model (2) adds additional controls for debt characteristics. Model (3) adds additional controls for county demographical factors. Across all models, the dependent variable is Log (Spreadt). It is the natural logarithm of the difference in basis points between the original yield of Rule 144A bond and that of a U.S. Treasury bond with comparable maturity in year t. Section 3.4 define the measures of control variables. Robust standard errors clustered at the firm level in parentheses. Significance at the 10%, 5%, and 1% level is indicated by *, **, and ***, respectively we model the choice of debt financing as a set of variables that have been identified as determinants of financing decisions, which include firm size, leverage, profitability, Altman *Z* score, sales growth rate and credit rating (Akhigbe et al., 2006; Glegg et al., 2012). We drop the observations if the firm issues both of two types of debt in the same year. We calculate the inverse Mills ratio based on the Probit model and include it in all regression models to lead to a consistent estimation (Heckman, 1979). The inverse Mills ratio allows us to control for selection bias when adding it as an additional control variable. Adding of inverse Mills ratio not only controls for selection bias but also signifies the direction of self-selection (Hamilton & Nickerson, 2003).

Next, we adopt an instrumental variable two-stage least square(2SLS) approach. Putnam (2001) points out that the best single predictor of the social capital in the U.S. is the distance to the Canadian border for some historical reasons. Being close to the border means a higher social capital level. However, there is no evidence to expect that distance to the Canadian border to be directly related to the debt cost. The above two factors make the distance to the Canadian border a potential candidate as an instrument of social capital in our study. We accordingly use the latitude of the county in which the firms' headquarters are located as the instrument. Model 1 of Table 4.3 presents results from the first-stage regression. The dependent variable is social capital, and the independent variables is the border distance. We include all control variables as specified in the baseline model as presented in Model 3 of Table 4.2. Coefficient on the instrumental variable is statistically significant. Model 2 of Table 4.3 reports the results from the second-stage regression. The dependent variable is the logarithm of Rule 144A yield spreads, and the independent variable is the fitted value of social capital obtained from the first-stage estimation. The fitted social capital is negative and significant. The results from instrumental variable 2SLS suggest that the endogeneity issue arising from social capital is not a major concern that may bias the estimation of the baseline model. Furthermore, we add the inverse Mills ratio as an additional control in Model 2. The inverse Mills ratio allows us to control for selection bias when adding it as an additional control variable. The coefficient on the inverse Mills ratio is significantly negative, suggesting that within this group, some unobservable reasons make a firm more likely to issue Rule 144A debt. The significance of coefficient on inverse Mills ratio throughout the study indicates the importance of controlling for self-selection.

As an alternative way to address the endogeneity issue arising from financing through Rule 144A debt, propensity score matching (PSM) method is adopted as well. The PSM technique is wildly used in finance literature (Chakraborty & Gantchev, 2013; Faccio et al., 2016) to pair treatment and non-treatment groups on a set of observable characteristics to remove relevant differences. Following the steps of propensity score matching, we divide the sample into two groups based on the median level of social capital. The Rule 144A debt issuing firms with high social capital score are categorized into the treated group, and the firms with low social capital score are grouped into the control group. For each of the observations in the treated and control groups, we calculate the propensity score by performing

Table 4.3 Results from instrumental-variable two-stage regressions

Independent variable	First Stage Social Capital	Second Stage Yield spread (in logs)
Border distance	−0.098*** (0.003)	
Fitted social capital		−0.144*** (0.051)
Firm size	−0.065*** (0.023)	−0.176*** (0.014)
Tobin's *Q*	−0.040* (0.022)	−0.151*** (0.019)
ROA	0.308*** (0.101)	−0.255* (0.135)
Market leverage	0.435** (0.208)	0.064 (0.181)
Investment	0.489** (0.229)	−0.694*** (0.138)
Tax avoidance	−0.011 (0.030)	−0.002 (0.007)
Dividend payment	0.008*** (0.002)	0.005 (0.005)
Cash holding	0.012 (0.258)	0.662*** (0.204)
Tangibility	−0.436 (0.407)	−0.129 (0.150)
Years to maturity	−0.002 (0.003)	0.001 (0.003)
Issue size	−0.000 (0.000)	−0.000 (0.000)
Debt rating	0.017 (0.078)	−0.630*** (0.061)
Ln (POP)	−5.443*** (1.585)	−0.086 (1.076)
Population growth	0.663*** (0.073)	0.035 (0.054)
Ln (Income)	−10.133*** (0.793)	7.756*** (0.611)
Inverse Mills ratio		−0.783* (0.408)
Year FE	Yes	Yes
Industry FE	Yes	Yes

(continued)

Table 4.3 (continued)

Independent variable	First Stage Social Capital	Second Stage Yield spread (in logs)
Observations	1,378	1,378
R-squared	0.616	0.669

Note The sample consists of 1378 observations during the period of 1997–2015. Model 1 presents the estimates of the first-stage regression. The dependent variable is social capital. The independent variable is Log (Border Distance). It is the natural logarithm of the distance between a county and the Canadian border. Model 2 presents the results of the second-stage regression. The dependent variable is Log (Spread), It is the natural logarithm of the difference in basis points between the original yield of Rule 144A bond and that of a U.S. Treasury bond with comparable maturity. We use the same control variables as specified in the Model 3 of Table 4.2. Section 4.3.4 define the measures of control variables. Robust standard errors clustered at the firm level in parentheses. *, **, and *** indicate significance at the 10%, 5%, and 1% levels, respectively

Table 4.4 Propensity score matching: firms in high social capital regions incur lower yield spreads

	Control group ($N = 689$)			Treatment group ($N = 689$)				
	Mean	Median	S.D.	Mean	Median	S.D.	Difference	*t*-statistics
Yield spreads	430.18	390.50	223.88	372.94	345.50	218.05	57.25***	4.376
Market value	5935.92	1607.48	16,587.64	6287.92	2219.19	15,082.27	−352.0	−0.374
MTOB	5.87	2.13	44.40	5.74	1.92	56.69	0.13	0.043
DEBT	0.40	0.39	0.17	0.40	0.37	0.15	0.001	0.176
EBITDA	0.13	0.12	0.08	0.13	0.12	0.07	−0.001	−0.360
CASH	0.09	0.05	0.09	0.08	0.05	0.08	0.01	0.482

The Table 4.4 presents the summary statistics of the treatment, and the matched group. MTOB is the ratio of market value to asset to book value of asset. Debt is the ratio of total debt to total asset. EBITDA is calculated as EBITDA divided by total asset. CASH is calculated as total cash divided by total asset. The t-stats are test the quality of the means for the two groups. *, **, and *** indicate significance at the 10%, 5%, and 1% levels, respectively

the logit model. We carefully select the firm attributes to calculate the propensity scores that include market value, market to book ratio, leverage, EBITDA and cash holding (Jha & Chen, 2015). For each observation in the treated sample, we find the nearest neighbor who has the minimum absolute value of the difference in propensity scores in the control group. We perform a one-to-one match without replacement to construct the matched sample. Next, we test if there is a statistically significant difference in Rule 144A debt yield spreads between firms in the treated group and those in the matched group. The results are reported in Table 4.4.

Table 4.4 compares the summary statistics between the treated group and the matched sample constructed from the control group. The mean yield spreads in the treated group (firms from high social capital region) is substantially lower than the yield spreads in the matched sample (firms from low social capital region). The difference is significant at 1%. The comparison also shows that other firm-level variables are hardly different.

We further test the existence of a statistically significant difference in Rule 144A debt yield spreads between the issuers in the treated group and those in the matched group. The results are reported in Columns 1–3 of Table 4.5. Our results remain the same. The issuing firms headquartered in counties with high social capital level incur a smaller yield spreads than issuer headquartered in the low social capital region.

Our results indicate that social capital has a negative relation with yield spreads of Rule 144A debt issuances. We then explore the boundary conditions of the negative relation. We posit that the effect of social capital on cost of Rule 144A debt may be different for firms with different levels of institutional ownership. A bulk of literature documents that institutional investors perform active monitoring activities, leading to a high quality of financial report, a low financing cost and a high corporate governance level. This direct and strong monitoring mechanism may weaken the effect of informal governance mechanism. Thus, we believe that social capital has a less pronounced impact on the cost of Rule144A for issuers with larger institutional ownership. To test this possibility, we introduce the interaction term in the regression and report results in Table 4.6. We measure firm's institutional ownership by using data from 13f to calculate the percentage of the institutional holding by the top five institutional investors. The first three columns of Table 4.6 show that after adding the interaction term in the regression, the social capital is significantly and negatively associated with yield spreads. The coefficient of the interaction term is positive and significant at 0.01 level. Our results indicate that the effect of social capital on the cost of Rule144A becomes weaker when issuers own a large institutional ownership.

Like social capital, religiosity is another force to create the sense of community and self-esteem and build trust (El Ghoul et al., 2012). Recent studies show that firms headquartered in more religious regions enjoy lower equity financing cost (El Ghoul et al., 2012) and deliver higher quality of financial reports (Dyreng et al., 2012). These studies suggest that religiosity plays a role of governance when the alternative strong monitoring mechanism is lacking. Both the religiosity and social capital represent the important components of informal institutions that help to evaluate the qualification of the firms. If both are available in the process of investment decision-making, it would be much better for investors because of more high-quality information. We interact religiosity with social capital and report the results in Table 4.7. We find that the direction and significance of the coefficient of social capital remain unchanged. Moreover, we find a negative relation between religiosity and Rule 144A yield spreads. The interaction is significantly negative, which indicates that the impact of social capital is more pronounced when the firm is headquartered in a more religious region.

Table 4.5 Results from PSM sample

Independent variable	Dependent variable Yield spread (in logs)		
	(1)	(2)	(3)
Social capital	−0.141*** (0.031)	−0.087*** (0.018)	−0.089*** (0.025)
Firm size	−0.186*** (0.014)	−0.131*** (0.001)	−0.130*** (0.028)
Tobin's *Q*	−0.392*** (0.076)	−0.279*** (0.003)	−0.285*** (0.045)
ROA	−0.439 (0.625)	−0.419 (0.786)	−0.411 (0.401)
Market leverage	0.697*** (0.257)	0.656** (0.305)	0.564*** (0.135)
Investment	−0.187 (0.186)	−0.192 (0.351)	−0.276 (0.188)
Tax avoidance	−0.062** (0.025)	−0.043 (0.066)	−0.049*** (0.014)
Dividend payment	0.003 (0.010)	0.003 (0.005)	0.003 (0.003)
Cash holding	1.336*** (0.247)	1.172*** (0.331)	1.141*** (0.324)
Tangibility	−0.465* (0.238)	−0.183 (0.185)	−0.221 (0.218)
Years to maturity		−0.002 (0.008)	−0.002 (0.004)
Issue size		−0.000*** (0.000)	−0.000* (0.000)
Debt rating		−0.601*** (0.160)	−0.554*** (0.054)
Ln (POP)			−0.081*** (0.031)
Population growth			−0.354 (0.743)
Ln (Income)			0.118* (0.071)

(continued)

Table 4.5 (continued)

Independent variable	Dependent variable Yield spread (in logs)		
Inverse Mills ratio	−0.058 (0.086)	−0.582*** (0.092)	−0.675*** (0.111)
Constant	8.167*** (0.253)	7.511*** (0.184)	7.301*** (0.722)
Year FE	Yes	Yes	Yes
Industry FE	Yes	Yes	Yes
Observations	689	689	689
R-squared	0.587	0.620	0.627

Model (1) includes controls for firm characteristics. Model (2) adds additional controls for debt characteristics. Model (3) adds additional controls for county demographical factors. Across all models, the dependent variable is *Log* $(Spread_t)$. It is the natural logarithm of the difference in basis points between the original yield of Rule 144A bond and that of a U.S. Treasury bond with comparable maturity in year t. Section 3.4 define the measures of control variables. Robust standard errors clustered at the firm level in parentheses. Significance at the 10%, 5%, and 1% level is indicated by *, **, and ***, respectively

The financial crisis highlighted the importance of trust for financial markets and financial stability (Bouslah et al., 2018; Lins et al., 2017). Given that firm's social capital helps build trust and social cooperation (Putnam, 2000), trustworthy should be more valuable and should more likely to be incorporated into market players' pricing scheme. To test whether social capital is valued more after financial crisis, we examine the effect of social capital on the cost of Rule 144A debt by interacting social capital with a dummy variable, which equals to 1 if the issuing date is after year of 2009 and 0 otherwise. The results are presented in Table 4.8. We find that the coefficient on social capital remains significantly negative when controlling for firm characteristics, debt attributes, and county-level demographic factors. Furthermore, the coefficient on the interaction term is significantly negative, suggesting that the effect of social capital on Rule 144A yield spreads is stronger after the financial crisis.

To test the robustness of our result, we use trust as the alternative measure of social capital. The trust data comes from the World Value Survey (WVS), the most comprehensive investigation of political and socio-cultural indicators. We focus on the U.S. data where the county code is 840. The trust-related questions in WVS are V24, V103, V104, V105, and V160B that asking about interviewees' trust level towards their family, neighborhood, and various types of people. We recode the answer variables so that lower values would reflect lower trustworthiness. We get the mean value of each variable by state (V246B) and then perform the principal component analysis to construct the trust score. The results are presented in Table 4.9. We continue to find that the coefficients on social capital's alternative measure, trust, are significantly negative.

Table 4.6 Results of the differential effect of social capital: the role of institutional ownership

Independent variable	Dependent variable Yield spread (in logs)		
	(1)	(2)	(3)
Social capital	−0.130*** (0.034)	−0.163*** (0.035)	−0.229*** (0.042)
Institutional ownership	0.005 (0.046)	0.018 (0.045)	0.033 (0.045)
Social capital × Institutional ownership	0.164*** (0.048)	0.161*** (0.048)	0.160*** (0.048)
Firm size	−0.157*** (0.015)	−0.177*** (0.016)	−0.172*** (0.017)
Tobin's *Q*	−0.197*** (0.036)	−0.156*** (0.033)	−0.156*** (0.033)
ROA	−0.251 (0.282)	−0.285 (0.284)	−0.305 (0.285)
Market leverage	0.145 (0.203)	0.080 (0.202)	0.079 (0.204)
Investment	−0.715*** (0.164)	−0.704*** (0.165)	−0.727*** (0.166)
Tax avoidance	−0.002 (0.004)	−0.004 (0.006)	−0.005 (0.006)
Dividend payment	0.003 (0.003)	0.004 (0.003)	0.004 (0.003)
Cash holding	0.888*** (0.223)	0.744*** (0.217)	0.802*** (0.221)
Tangibility	−0.127 (0.156)	−0.067 (0.153)	−0.104 (0.154)
Years to maturity		0.000 (0.007)	−0.012 (0.009)
Issue size		−0.000 (0.000)	−0.000* (0.000)
Debt rating		−0.702*** (0.221)	−1.086*** (0.284)
Ln (POP)			−0.051*** (0.018)
Population growth			0.293 (1.033)
Ln (Income)			−0.023 (0.063)

(continued)

Table 4.6 (continued)

Independent variable	Dependent variable Yield spread (in logs)		
Inverse Mills ratio	−0.445*** (0.068)	−0.021 (0.212)	−0.448 (0.291)
Constant	8.405*** (0.234)	8.133*** (0.275)	8.787*** (0.637)
Year FE	Yes	Yes	Yes
Industry FE	Yes	Yes	Yes
Observations	1378	1378	1378
R-squared	0.686	0.700	0.703

Note Across all models, the dependent variable is Log (Spreadt). It is the natural logarithm of the difference in basis points between the original yield of Rule 144A bond and that of a U.S. Treasury bond with comparable maturity in year t. Section 3.4 define the measures of control variables. Institutional ownership is the percentage of the holding by firm's top five institutional investors. Robust standard errors clustered at the firm level in parentheses. Significance at the 10%, 5%, and 1% level is indicated by *, **, and ***, respectively

4.3.4 Conclusion and Discussion

In this study, we investigate the effect of social capital on the cost of Rule 144A debt. Rule 144A provides a context to explore how sophisticated investors use informal institution when they have limited information to evaluate the Rule144 debt issuers' creditability. The results of the analysis provide evidence that issuers headquartered in the counties with higher levels of social capital incur significantly lower yield spreads in their Rule 144A debt offerings. The findings are robust to a Heckman selection model, an instrumental variable approach and an alternative measure of social capital. Additionally, the analysis reveals that the effect of social capital is more pronounced for the issuing firms with smaller institutional ownership and located in more religious regions.

Our study makes several contributions. First, our findings provide strong support for the argument that social capital has positive economic payoffs (Guiso et al., 2004). We extend the study of Hasan et al. (2017) and show that the social capital affects the cost of private debt. Since debt is the major source of capital for U.S. firms and the private debt market dominates the public debt market in size, our study suggests that social capital benefits the economic payoffs and the corporations by reducing the cost of debt financing, consequently, benefiting the firm value. Second, our study makes a contribution to the debt contracting literature. Firms that issue 144A private debt are characterized by low credit quality and high information asymmetry. Concerns over creditworthiness, information accuracy and information asymmetry are the main drivers that push Rule 144A yields high. We show that the social capital where the firm is headquartered facilitates information sharing, build enforceable trust and serve as a soft and community-wide monitoring mechanism. Our study sheds further light on how institutional

Table 4.7 Results of the differential effect of social capital: the role of religiosity

Independent variable	Dependent variable Yield spread (in logs)		
	(1)	(2)	(3)
Social capital	−0.068*** (0.020)	−0.067*** (0.020)	−0.061*** (0.022)
Religiosity	−0.008*** (0.003)	−0.008*** (0.002)	−0.008*** (0.002)
Social capital × Religiosity	−0.004*** (0.001)	−0.004*** (0.001)	−0.004*** (0.001)
Firm size	−0.336*** (0.017)	−0.523*** (0.023)	−0.536*** (0.023)
Tobin's *Q*	−0.300*** (0.022)	−0.233*** (0.022)	−0.235*** (0.021)
ROA	−1.629*** (0.445)	−2.224*** (0.490)	−2.337*** (0.479)
Market leverage	0.000*** (0.000)	0.000*** (0.000)	0.000*** (0.000)
Investment	−0.175 (0.118)	0.118 (0.109)	0.109 (0.108)
Tax avoidance	−1.091*** (0.083)	−0.776*** (0.076)	−0.801*** (0.077)
Dividend payment	0.005 (0.005)	0.005 (0.005)	0.004 (0.005)
Cash holding	−0.001 (0.003)	−0.006* (0.003)	−0.006* (0.003)
Tangibility	1.265*** (0.128)	0.597*** (0.130)	0.603*** (0.133)

(continued)

Table 4.7 (continued)

Independent variable	Dependent variable Yield spread (in logs)		
Years to maturity	−0.346*** (0.079)	0.049 (0.078)	0.045 (0.080)
Issue size		−0.008*** (0.001)	−0.009*** (0.001)
Debt rating		0.000*** (0.000)	0.000*** (0.000)
Ln (POP)		−0.629*** (0.027)	−0.627*** (0.028)
Population growth			−0.000*** (0.000)
Ln (Income)			−0.000 (0.000)
Inverse Mills ratio	−0.282*** (0.033)	−0.813*** (0.050)	−0.843*** (0.050)
Constant	9.264*** (0.167)	10.003*** (0.197)	10.189*** (0.194)
Year FE	Yes	Yes	Yes
Industry FE	Yes	Yes	Yes
Observations	1378	1378	1378
R-squared	0.509	0.575	0.578

Across all models, the dependent variable is Log (Spreads). It is the natural logarithm of the difference in basis points between the original yield of Rule 144A bond and that of a U.S. Treasury bond with comparable maturity in year t. Section 3.4 define the measures of control variables. Religiosity is the adherence rate, which is the fraction of a county's population that claims affiliation with an organized religion. Robust standard errors clustered at the firm level in parentheses. Significance at the 10%, 5%, and 1% level is indicated by *, **, and ***, respectively

Table 4.8 Results of the differential effect of social capital: before and after financial crisis

Independent variable	Dependent variable Yield spread (in logs)		
	(1)	(2)	(3)
Social capital	−0.005 (0.029)	−0.021** (0.009)	−0.049** (0.020)
Financial crisis dummy	0.312*** (0.037)	0.178*** (0.037)	0.170*** (0.041)
Social capital × FC_dummy	−0.067*** (0.025)	−0.086** (0.035)	−0.099** (0.041)
Firm size	−0.183*** (0.026)	−0.294*** (0.021)	−0.299*** (0.043)
Tobin's *Q*	−0.244*** (0.044)	−0.203*** (0.051)	−0.208** (0.084)
ROA	−0.514 (0.648)	−0.498 (0.412)	−0.541* (0.295)
Market leverage	0.153 (0.227)	0.285*** (0.102)	0.253 (0.237)
Investment	−0.730*** (0.232)	−0.654*** (0.111)	−0.694*** (0.097)
Tax avoidance	0.000 (0.011)	−0.003 (0.004)	−0.004 (0.015)
Dividend payment	0.004 (0.017)	0.005** (0.002)	0.005*** (0.002)
Cash holding	0.763*** (0.240)	0.596*** (0.138)	0.725** (0.291)

(continued)

Table 4.8 (continued)

Independent variable	Dependent variable Yield spread (in logs)		
Tangibility	−0.038 (0.189)	0.052 (0.082)	−0.015 (0.064)
Years to maturity		−0.011** (0.004)	−0.012** (0.005)
Issue size		−0.000 (0.000)	−0.000 (0.000)
Debt rating		−0.786*** (0.067)	−0.775*** (0.072)
Ln (POP)			−0.049** (0.022)
Population growth			1.120 (1.370)
Ln (Income)			-0.034 (0.040)
Inverse Mills ratio	−0.019 (0.085)	−0.453*** (0.096)	−0.486*** (0.128)
Constant	8.059*** (0.312)	8.681*** (0.182)	9.757*** (0.468)
Industry FE	Yes	Yes	Yes
Observations	1,378	1378	1378
R-squared	0.575	0.616	0.621

Note Across all models, the dependent variable is Log (Spreads). It is the natural logarithm of the difference in basis points between the original yield of Rule 144A bond and that of a U.S. Treasury bond with comparable maturity in year t. Section 4.3.4 define the measures of control variables. FC_Dummy equals to 1 if issuing year is after 2009 and 0 otherwise. Robust standard errors clustered at the firm level in parentheses. Significance at the 10%, 5%, and 1% level is indicated by *, **, and ***, respectively

Table 4.9 Results from alternative measure of social capital

Independent variable	Dependent variable Yield spread (in logs)		
	(1)	(2)	(3)
Trust score	−0.164** (0.076)	−0.167** (0.068)	−0.156** (0.070)
Firm size	−0.094*** (0.029)	−0.205*** (0.045)	−0.219*** (0.042)
Tobin's *Q*	−0.150*** (0.033)	−0.124*** (0.028)	−0.127*** (0.034)
ROA	−0.207 (0.419)	−0.361 (0.479)	−0.394 (0.418)
Market leverage	−0.338* (0.176)	−0.177 (0.176)	−0.191 (0.157)
Investment	−0.892*** (0.136)	−0.805*** (0.135)	−0.818*** (0.137)
Tax avoidance	0.000 (0.010)	−0.001 (0.009)	−0.001 (0.010)
Dividend payment	0.004 (0.007)	0.004 (0.008)	0.004 (0.007)
Cash holding	0.788*** (0.238)	0.595*** (0.204)	0.641*** (0.216)
Tangibility	0.187 (0.117)	0.288** (0.114)	0.260** (0.117)
Years to maturity		0.001 (0.004)	−0.000 (0.005)
Issue size		−0.000 (0.000)	−0.000 (0.000)
Debt rating		−0.704*** (0.092)	−0.722*** (0.088)
Ln (POP)			−0.005 (0.010)
Population growth			1.227 (0.923)
Ln (Income)			−0.038 (0.053)
Inverse Mills ratio	−0.383*** (0.080)	−0.078 (0.151)	−0.127 (0.139)
Constant	7.480*** (0.262)	7.859*** (0.300)	8.409*** (0.650)

(continued)

Table 4.9 (continued)

Independent variable	Dependent variable Yield spread (in logs)		
Year FE	Yes	Yes	Yes
Industry FE	Yes	Yes	Yes
Observations	1,378	1,378	1,378
R-squared	0.583	0.625	0.626

Across all models, the dependent variable is Log (Spreads). It is the natural logarithm of the difference in basis points between the original yield of Rule 144A bond and that of a U.S. Treasury bond. The independent variable is the state-level trust score. We use trust score as alternate measure to capture the effect of social capital. Robust standard errors clustered at the firm level in parentheses. Significance at the 10%, 5%, and 1% level is indicated by *, **, and ***, respectively

investors incorporate the regional social capital in their pricing scheme of private placement of Rule 144A debt.

Acknowledgements This chapter is based on the article previously published as: Jianrong Wang, Haizhi Wang, Desheng Yin, and Yun Zhu. "The role of social capital in private placement: evidence from Rule 144A debt issuances." *Managerial Finance* 48, no. 2 (2022): 181–200.

Reprinted with permission from *Managerial Finance.*

References

Adhikari, K. P., & Goldey, P. (2010). Social capital and its "downside": The impact on sustainability of induced community-based organizations in Nepal. *World Development, 38*(2), 184–194.

Akhigbe, A., Newman, M., & Safieddine, A. (2006). Market expectations and the valuation effects of equity issuance. *Journal of Financial Research, 29*(2), 253–269.

Arena, M. P. (2011). The corporate choice between public debt, bank loans, traditional private debt placements, and 144A debt issues. *Review of Quantitative Finance and Accounting, 36*(3), 391–416.

Bharath, S. T., Sunder, J., & Sunder, S. V. (2008). Accounting quality and debt contracting. *The Accounting Review, 83*(1), 1–28.

Bhojraj, S., & Sengupta, P. (2003). Effect of corporate governance on bond ratings and yields: The role of institutional investors and outside directors. *The Journal of Business, 76*(3), 455–475.

Boone, A. L., & White, J. T. (2015). The effect of institutional ownership on firm transparency and information production. *Journal of Financial Economics, 117*(3), 508–533.

Bourdieu, P. (1986). The forms of capital. In *Handbook of theory and research for the sociology of education* (pp. 241–258). Greenwood Press.

Bouslah, K., Kryzanowski, L., & M'Zali, B. (2018). Social performance and firm risk: Impact of the financial crisis. *Journal of Business Ethics, 149*(3), 643–669.

Brockman, P., El Ghoul, S., Guedhami, O., & Zheng, Y. (2018). Does social trust affect international contracting? Evidence from foreign bond covenants. *Journal of International Business Studies, 53*(6), 1011–1044.

Cai, K. N., Lee, H. W., & Sharma, V. (2011). Underpricing of IPOs that follow private placement. *Journal of Financial Research, 34*(3), 441–459.

Cameron, A. C., & Miller, D. L. (2015). A practitioner's guide to cluster-robust inference. *Journal of Human Resources, 50*(2), 317–372.

Casson, M. C., Della Giusta, M., & Kambhampati, U. S. (2010). Formal and informal institutions and development. *World Development, 38*(2), 137–141.

Chakraborty, I., & Gantchev, N. (2013). Does shareholder coordination matter? Evidence from private placements. *Journal of Financial Economics, 108*(1), 213–230.

Chandra, U., & Nayar, N. N. (2008). The information content of private debt placements. *Journal of Business Finance & Accounting, 35*(9–10), 1164–1195.

Chaney, P. K., Jeter, D. C., & Shivakumar, L. (2004). Self-selection of auditors and audit pricing in private firms. *The Accounting Review, 79*(1), 51–72.

Chintrakarn, P., Jiraporn, P., Tong, S., & Chatjuthamard, P. (2017). Exploring the effect of religious piety on corporate governance: Evidence from anti-takeover defenses and historical religious identification. *Journal of Business Ethics, 141*(3), 469–476.

Chung, S., Singh, H., & Lee, K. (2000). Complementarity, status similarity and social capital as drivers of alliance formation. *Strategic Management Journal, 21*(1), 1–22.

Coleman, J. S. (1988). Social capital in the creation of human capital. *American Journal of Sociology, 94*(Supplement), S95–S120.

Denis, D. J., & Mihov, V. T. (2003). The choice among bank debt, non-bank private debt, and public debt: Evidence from new corporate borrowings. *Journal of Financial Economics, 70*(1), 3–28.

Dyreng, S. D., Mayew, W. J., & Williams, C. D. (2012). Religious social norms and corporate financial reporting. *Journal of Business Finance & Accounting, 39*(7–8), 845–875.

El Ghoul, S., Guedhami, O., Ni, Y., et al. (2012). Does religion matter to equity pricing? *Journal of Business Ethics, 111*(4), 491–518.

Estrin, S., & Prevezer, M. (2011). The role of informal institutions in corporate governance: Brazil, Russia, India, and China compared. *Asia Pacific Journal of Management, 28*(1), 41–67.

Faccio, M., Marchica, M.-T., & Mura, R. (2016). CEO gender, corporate risk-taking, and the efficiency of capital allocation. *Journal of Corporate Finance, 39*, 193–209.

Fenn, G. W. (2000). Speed of issuance and the adequacy of disclosure in the 144A high-yield debt market. *Journal of Financial Economics, 56*(3), 383–405.

Floyd, E., Li, N., & Skinner, D. J. (2015). Payout policy through the financial crisis: The growth of repurchases and the resilience of dividends. *Journal of Financial Economics, 118*(2), 299–316.

Fogel, K., Jandik, T., & McCumber, W. R. (2018). CFO social capital and private debt. *Journal of Corporate Finance, 52*, 28–52.

Frank, M. Z., & Shen, T. (2016). Investment and the weighted average cost of capital. *Journal of Financial Economics, 119*(2), 300–315.

Fukuyama, F. (1997). Social capital and the modern capitalist economy: Creating a high trust workplace. *Stern Business Magazine, 4*(1), 1–16.

Gilchrist, S., & Zakrajsek, E. (2007). *Investment and the cost of capital: New evidence from the corporate bond market*. National Bureau of Economic Research.

Gillan, S., & Starks, L. T. (2003). Corporate governance, corporate ownership, and the role of institutional investors: A global perspective. *Journal of Applied Finance, 13*(2), 4–22.

Glegg, C., Harris, O., Madura, J., et al. (2012). The impact of mispricing and asymmetric information on the price discount of private placements of common stock. *Financial Review, 47*(4), 665–696.

Gooderham, P., Minbaeva, D. B., & Pedersen, T. (2011). Governance mechanisms for the promotion of social capital for knowledge transfer in multinational corporations. *Journal of Management Studies, 48*(1), 123–150.

Grundy, B. D., & Li, H. (2010). Investor sentiment, executive compensation, and corporate investment. *Journal of Banking & Finance, 34*(10), 2439–2449.

Guiso, L., Sapienza, P., & Zingales, L. (2004). The role of social capital in financial development. *American Economic Review, 94*(3), 526–556.

Hamilton, B. H., & Nickerson, J. A. (2003). Correcting for endogeneity in strategic management research. *Strategic Organization, 1*(1), 51–78.

Hasan, I., Hoi, C. K., & Wu, Q. (2017). Social capital and debt contracting: Evidence from bank loans and public bonds. *Journal of Financial and Quantitative Analysis, 52*(3), 1017–1047.

Heckman, J. J. (1979). Sample selection bias as a specification error. *Econometrica, 47*(1), 153–161.

Helmke, G., & Levitsky, S. (2004). Informal institutions and comparative politics: A research agenda. *Perspectives on Politics, 2*(4), 725–740.

Hilary, G., & Hui, K. W. (2009). Does religion matter in corporate decision making in America? *Journal of Financial Economics, 93*(3), 455–473.

Huang, R., & Ramirez, G. G. (2010). Speed of issuance, lender specialization, and the rise of the 144A debt market. *Financial Management, 39*(2), 643–673.

Huseynov, F., & Klamm, B. K. (2012). Tax avoidance, tax management and corporate social responsibility. *Journal of Corporate Finance, 18*(4), 804–827.

Jha, A. (2019). Financial reports and social capital. *Journal of Business Ethics, 155*(2), 567–596.

Jha, A., & Chen, Y. (2015). Audit fees and social capital. *The Accounting Review, 90*(2), 611–639.

Knack, S., & Keefer, P. (1997). Does social capital have an economic payoff? A cross-country investigation. *The Quarterly Journal of Economics, 112*(4), 1251–1288.

Lee, J. Y., & Bell, D. R. (2013). Neighborhood social capital and social learning for experience attributes of products. *Marketing Science, 32*(6), 960–976.

Lins, K. V., Servaes, H., & Tamayo, A. (2017). Social capital, trust, and firm performance: The value of corporate social responsibility during the financial crisis. *The Journal of Finance, 72*(4), 1785–1824.

Maksimovic, V., & Pichler, P. (2006). Structuring the initial offering: Who to sell to and how to do it. *Review of Finance, 10*(3), 353–387.

Massa, M., & Žaldokas, A. (2014). Investor base and corporate borrowing: Evidence from international bonds. *Journal of International Economics, 92*(1), 95–110.

Moran, P. (2005). Structural vs. relational embeddedness: Social capital and managerial performance. *Strategic Management Journal, 26*(12), 1129–1151.

Portes, A. (1998). Social capital: Its origins and applications in modern sociology. *Annual Review of Sociology, 24*(1), 1–24.

Putnam, R. (2000). *Bowling alone: The collapse and revival of American Community.* Simon & Schuster.

Putnam, R. (2001). Social capital: Measurement and consequences. *Canadian Journal of Policy Research, 2*(1), 41–51.

Rupasingha, A., Goetz, S. J., & Freshwater, D. (2006). The production of social capital in US counties. *The Journal of Socio-Economics, 35*(1), 83–101.

Shleifer, A., & Vishny, R. W. (1986). Large shareholders and corporate control. *Journal of Political Economy, 94*(3), 461–488.

Stiglitz, J. E. (2000). Formal and informal institutions. In I. Serageldin & P. Dasgupta (Eds.), *Social capital: A multifaceted perspective* (pp. 59–68). World Bank.

Van Binsbergen, J. H., Graham, J. R., & Yang, J. (2010). The cost of debt. *The Journal of Finance, 65*(6), 2089–2136.

Williamson, C. R. (2009). Informal institutions rule: institutional arrangements and economic performance. *Public Choice, 139*(3), 371–387.

Wittenberg-Moerman, R. (2008). The role of information asymmetry and financial reporting quality in debt trading: Evidence from the secondary loan market. *Journal of Accounting and Economics, 46*(2–3), 240–260.

Woolcock, M. (2001). The place of social capital in understanding social and economic outcomes. *Canadian Journal of Policy Research, 2*(1), 11–17.

Regulatory and Policy Influences on ESG Adoption

5

5.1 From Legal Obligation to Strategic Opportunity: How Regulation and Policy Drive ESG Adoption

Firms do not operate in isolation. Their decisions on whether, when, and how to adopt ESG practices are conditioned by the institutional environment, of which regulation and policy are central components. Regulation defines the hard boundaries of permissible conduct, while policy sets the soft contours of future opportunities and risks. Together, these instruments structure corporate incentives and disincentives, embedding ESG not as a discretionary add-on but as an institutionalized requirement of modern corporate governance.

ESG adoption is a matter of voluntary corporate commitment or managerial moral choice. Yet evidence consistently shows that regulatory and policy shifts are what drive firms to normalize sustainability practices across sectors and geographies. These frameworks reduce coordination problems among firms, level the playing field, and establish credibility with investors and other stakeholders. By providing both sanctions and rewards, regulators and policymakers transform ESG from a reputational narrative into a measurable dimension of firm strategy and performance.

The most immediate influence of regulation is to establish a compliance floor—a non-negotiable baseline of behavior that all firms must meet. This function has been especially visible in the ESG domain.

In Europe, the Corporate Sustainability Reporting Directive (CSRD) marks a turning point. Over 50,000 companies are now required to disclose sustainability information in standardized formats, subject to third-party audit and digital tagging. The scope covers climate, biodiversity, human rights, and governance practices, thereby broadening sustainability disclosure beyond voluntary, selective communication. Parallel measures like the Sustainable Finance Disclosure Regulation (SFDR) impose obligations on financial intermediaries, ensuring that sustainability claims about funds and investment products are verifiable rather than

J. Wang, *ESG Strategies and Financial Markets*, Management for Professionals,
https://doi.org/10.1007/978-981-95-5620-5_5

marketing devices. Together, these measures institutionalize transparency as the minimum expectation.

In the United States, although contested, regulatory change is reshaping practice. The SEC's proposed climate disclosure rule would compel firms to report greenhouse gas emissions (Scopes 1 and 2, and in some cases Scope 3), climate risk governance, and scenario planning in their 10-K filings. Even before implementation, anticipation of this rule has triggered internal investments in ESG data systems, reporting processes, and cross-functional risk management committees. This demonstrates how regulation exerts influence even in draft form by raising expectations of investors and auditors.

In China, the baseline is linked to national strategic goals. The carbon peaking (2030) and neutrality (2060) pledges cascade into sectoral mandates, green bond eligibility criteria, and disclosure obligations for listed companies. Energy-intensive sectors face quota systems and technology benchmarks that compel efficiency upgrades and renewable transitions. State-owned enterprises are especially under pressure to align their operations with the government's carbon strategy, but private firms increasingly face the same floor through supply-chain and financing channels.

Thus, across jurisdictions, regulation compels ESG adoption by setting a hard floor below which firms cannot fall. What differs is the breadth, enforceability, and political consensus underlying these baselines.

While regulation defines the minimum, policy often pushes firms toward the frontier of ESG adoption by offering incentives and signaling long-term strategic direction. These interventions are less about penalties and more about opportunities.

In Europe, the EU Taxonomy provides a classification system for environmentally sustainable activities. This functions as a guide for both firms and investors, channeling capital flows toward compliant activities and away from those deemed environmentally harmful. The EU Green Bond Standard and sustainability-linked finance instruments further create financial incentives: lower interest rates and broader investor demand for firms that align projects with ESG objectives. These policies reward innovation and accelerate sectoral transitions.

In the United States, the Inflation Reduction Act (IRA) represents the most substantial policy push to date. Through tax credits, subsidies, and grants, the IRA lowers the cost of investing in renewable energy, electric vehicles, carbon capture, and clean manufacturing. Even without federal mandatory ESG disclosure, firms now view ESG alignment as a strategic necessity to access policy-driven capital and market growth. At the state level, programs like California's Cap-and-Trade system and Renewable Portfolio Standards set de facto national benchmarks, as large firms harmonize practices across their operations.

In China, policy acts as both carrot and stick. The Green Credit Guidelines direct banks to incorporate ESG into lending criteria, rewarding firms that meet sustainability benchmarks with cheaper financing. At the same time, firms with weak ESG records find access to capital increasingly constrained. Pilot programs in green supply chains, circular economy development, and renewable deployment embed ESG considerations into industrial upgrading, making sustainability inseparable from competitiveness in the long run.

These examples show how policy initiatives operate as catalysts, pushing firms to reframe ESG not as cost compliance but as strategic advantage. They also illustrate that the most forward-looking firms treat policy signals as reliable indicators of future regulation, positioning themselves early for competitive gains. Beyond compliance and incentives, regulation has a less tangible but equally powerful effect: it sets norms. Legal mandates codify societal expectations, and once institutionalized, these expectations diffuse into corporate practice.

Anti-discrimination laws changed not only hiring practices but also workplace cultures. Occupational safety regulations reduced workplace accidents but also fostered cultures of prevention and care. Environmental protection laws reduced emissions but also created a shared understanding that pollution is a corporate responsibility, not an externality to be ignored. ESG regulation functions in the same way. By requiring firms to disclose and manage climate risk, regulators implicitly define sustainability as a legitimate and integral part of business performance.

Firms adjust their ESG and CSR activities in direct response to regulatory and policy shifts, and these adjustments often unfold in stages that move from compliance to deeper organizational change and ultimately to strategic repositioning. At the most basic level, new regulations compel firms to align with mandatory standards by upgrading reporting systems, adopting recognized disclosure frameworks, and embedding compliance into governance structures. This alignment ensures that firms can meet legal obligations on issues such as emissions reporting, diversity metrics, or supply-chain due diligence. Beyond this compliance floor, regulatory pressure also triggers organizational adaptation. Companies begin to integrate ESG into everyday routines by revising investment appraisal processes with internal carbon pricing, linking executive compensation to sustainability key performance indicators, and restructuring supply chains to reflect extended responsibility obligations. The most forward-looking firms go further by treating policy shifts as indicators of future competitive landscapes and strategically repositioning themselves to capture new opportunities. They innovate in products and services, expand access to sustainable finance through green or sustainability-linked bonds, and adjust geographic footprints to take advantage of regions offering strong regulatory incentives. Examples are visible across jurisdictions: European utilities accelerating renewable transitions under EU finance and disclosure rules, U.S. automakers expanding electric-vehicle investment to benefit from Inflation Reduction Act subsidies, and Chinese state-owned enterprises installing carbon-capture technologies to align with national carbon neutrality pledges and secure preferential lending under the Green Credit Guidelines. Anticipating regulation itself becomes a strategic advantage, as firms that prepare early can avoid costly retrofits, strengthen stakeholder trust, and capture first-mover benefits from policy-driven incentives. In this way, regulation and policy not only set the minimum standards for ESG adoption but also operate as catalysts for organizational learning and as signals that guide long-term strategic direction.

Norm-setting matters because it shapes stakeholder expectations. Investors begin to price ESG risk into capital allocation. Employees evaluate employers not only on pay but also on sustainability commitments. Consumers reward or punish firms based on alignment with social and environmental norms. Regulation thus influences ESG adoption not only through direct cost–benefit shifts but by redefining the very meaning of legitimacy in business.

The economic logic of ESG regulation is mirrored in broader social legislation. Our study of marriage equality legislation, published in the Journal of Business Research, demonstrates this. Between 2003 and 2015, thirty-six U.S. states legalized same-sex marriage. At first glance, this appears to be a moral or social issue detached from corporate performance. Yet, by exploiting the staggered implementation of marriage equality laws across states, we showed that firms headquartered in states that legalized same-sex marriage experienced significant improvements in financial performance compared with peers.

The mechanisms provide critical insight. Legal recognition of same-sex marriage reduced heterosexist stigma, improved organizational climates, and enhanced psychological well-being among LGBTQ employees. These gains diffused to heterosexual employees as well, through more inclusive, fair, and cohesive workplaces. The passage of legislation therefore reshaped social norms at the societal level, organizational climates at the firm level, and performance at the economic level. In short, law altered institutions, and institutions shaped firm outcomes.

This case parallels ESG regulation. Just as marriage equality laws created a more inclusive social and workplace environment that translated into firm performance gains, ESG regulation embeds sustainability and governance into the institutional fabric of business, producing measurable benefits. Both demonstrate that regulation is not merely restrictive—it is constitutive, shaping the conditions under which firms can thrive.

Our marriage equality paper applied the framework of institutional racism to heterosexism, showing how social norms at different levels conditioned the impact of legislation. The same logic applies to ESG regulation. At the highest level, regulation reflects and reinforces societal norms. Just as marriage equality laws signaled that inclusivity is a social value, ESG regulation signals that sustainability and accountability are non-negotiable societal commitments. Public concern about climate change, biodiversity loss, and inequality provides the legitimacy for governments to legislate ESG adoption. In Europe, this is visible in the principle of double materiality, which explicitly requires firms to account for both financial and societal impacts. Different industries internalize regulation differently. In our marriage equality study, industries with masculine dominance showed slower acceptance of LGBTQ inclusion. In ESG, carbon-intensive industries face stricter rules, such as emissions caps in aviation or steel. Service sectors may feel the impact through disclosure obligations or reputational exposure. Sectoral policy design—whether energy efficiency standards for manufacturing or circular economy rules for packaging—conditions how ESG is adopted across industries.

Within industries, organizational climate determines how regulation translates into outcomes. In the marriage equality context, firms with pro-LGBTQ climates captured greater performance benefits from legal change. In ESG, firms with strong sustainability governance, board oversight, and integrated risk management are able to convert regulatory compliance into strategic advantage. Firms lacking these structures reduce ESG to "box-ticking," missing opportunities for innovation and value creation.

This three-level mapping underscores that regulation exerts influence through nested layers. Law sets the societal signal, industries adapt through sectoral standards, and firms internalize change through organizational climates. The result is a chain of institutional adaptation that produces both social progress and firm-level value.

Regulation and policy influence ESG adoption by operating simultaneously as compliance floors, strategic catalysts, and norm setters. They compel, reward, and legitimate sustainability practices. The case of marriage equality demonstrates the broader point that laws aimed at social progress can yield firm-level economic benefits by reshaping institutional contexts. ESG regulation follows the same trajectory: it embeds sustainability into the rules of business, enabling both societal advancement and corporate performance.

For scholars, this underscores the need to situate ESG within institutional and regulatory frameworks rather than treating it as voluntary choice. For policymakers, it highlights the potential of well-designed regulation to accelerate ESG adoption and generate dual benefits for society and firms. For companies, it signals that regulatory anticipation and proactive adaptation are not merely defensive strategies but pathways to resilience and competitive advantage.

In the remainder of this chapter, we present empirical evidence that illustrates how social legislation—though not explicitly framed as ESG regulation—can reshape firm behavior and performance through institutional channels. The case in point is the legalization of same-sex marriage across U.S. states, a landmark social reform with unanticipated but measurable corporate effects. By analyzing how firms responded to this legal shift, we show how regulation—especially when it carries moral and cultural significance—can alter organizational climates, reduce workplace stigma, and generate economic value.

This case is directly relevant for ESG scholarship. It demonstrates that laws reflecting broader societal values—such as inclusion, fairness, and human dignity—can produce firm-level benefits, particularly when internalized through aligned cultures, policies, and managerial systems. The institutional logic that underpins successful ESG adoption—legal signal, normative shift, organizational response—is already visible in how firms reacted to marriage equality legislation.

We now turn to the full text of our study, "Marriage Equality for Everyone? The Business Case for Same Sex Marriage Legislation," originally published in the *Journal of Business Research*. The article provides both theoretical framing and causal evidence on how social regulation affects corporate outcomes, and offers a transferable model for understanding how ESG-related laws may influence firms in similar multi-level ways.

5.2 Marriage Equality for Everyone? The Business Case for Same Sex Marriage Legislation

Abstract

The impact of legislation in shaping social norms has captured both scholarly and practitioner attention in the past decades. However, limited understanding exists on how social legislation can create economic value for firms and thereby strengthen the business case for such legislation. We attempt to theorize and test this phenomenon in the context of marriage equality. We first attempt to understand the role of state-wise same-sex marriage social legislation on financial performance of firms headquartered in states where the legislation is passed. Adapting the model of institutional racism to the context of heterosexism, we then develop a framework to examine the role of societal-cultural, institutional, and individual factors in shaping the effect of state-wise same-sex marriage legislation on firm performance. In a sample of publicly traded U.S. firms, we conduct a difference-in-difference analysis to test and find support for our arguments.

5.2.1 Introduction

Equality is indeed a core need of all human beings; however, this need is often denied to minority groups in the institutions of society. Marriage equality is one such right that was long refused to sexual and gender minorities (LGBTQ). In 2003, Massachusetts became the first state in the U.S. to provide this right, thirty-five other states slowly followed suit, and finally in a landmark ruling on June 26, 2015, the U.S. Supreme Court legalized same-sex marriage in all 50 states and the D.C. This ruling prohibited the 14 remaining states of the U.S. from enforcing their state-wide laws limiting the right to marry based on gender. The ruling granted "equal dignity in the eyes of the law" to same-sex couples (Savage & Phelps, 2015). However, this ruling was not universally welcomed. The governor of Texas said the justices "have imposed on the entire country their personal views on an issue that the Constitution and the Court's previous decisions reserve to the people of the states" (Blake, 2015). A year later, a same-sex couple seeking marriage license was verbally abused and harassed by officials in the Gilmer, W. Virginia county clerk's office (Wootson Jr. & Somashekhar, 2017). Having a federal law that must be complied with is only the first step towards the equality being sought by LGBTQ individuals. In a diverse society like the U.S., it's no mean feat to get everyone to fully support non heteronormative or gender-blind marriage; however, it's only when everyone comes on board that the LGBTQ individuals will feel fully accepted and included.

We believe legal compliance without full acceptance will keep creating hurdles for same-sex couples, unless researchers try to mitigate this situation by explicating the benefits of gender-blind marriage to the entire society. While the U.S.

Supreme Court extended Civil Rights Act of 1964 to provide protection to individuals from employment discrimination based on their sexual orientation, there are still seventy seven countries where individuals can be discriminated in the workplace based on their sexual orientation (Catalyst, 2018). Further, the U.S. Supreme Court also ruled recently that federal employment discrimination laws do not protect employees from discrimination by their employer based on religious liberty (Human Rights Watch, 2018; Liptak, 2020). Though many organizations are adopting inclusive workplace policies, LGBTQ employees continue to report incidents of discrimination and harassment in the workplace which impact their psychological well-being and performance (King et al., 2017; Van Laer, 2018). Workplace bullying and lack of perceived support in the workplace also adversely impact their work attitudes and strain (Webster et al., 2018). We believe these challenges may be mitigated if it becomes clear how everyone, not just the LGBTQ employees, benefits by protecting the rights of LGBTQ employees. We argue that though LGBTQ individuals constitute only about 7 percent of the U.S. population (Jones, 2022) and thus a small minority in the workplace, ensuring their rights can still create value for everyone by creating a progressive and inclusive workplace where every employee receives fair treatment. We therefore attempt to shed light on the value engendered to firms and thus for the surrounding society when states provide marriage equality to all denizens.

Firms are influenced by their external context such as regulatory structures and legislations (Anand et al., 2018; Duncan, 1972). Research in this realm has largely focused on the effect of business-related state laws such as non-compete covenants on financial outcomes (Anand et al., 2018), and paid scant attention to how legislation directed towards societal residents impacts firm outcomes, including performance. We argue that social legislations affect most activities and outcomes of firms in which societal residents are employed. For instance, the enactment of Employment Non-Discrimination Acts that prohibit discrimination based on sexual orientation and gender identity by a firm's headquarter state has been shown to enhance corporate innovation (Gao & Zhang, 2017). The effects of social legislation on firm outcomes are increasingly of interest to scholars, practitioners, and policy makers (Flammer & Kacperczyk, 2016; Gao & Zhang, 2017). We add to this emerging literature by examining how firms benefit in terms of increased performance when their home state passes pro-LGBTQ legislation. We draw on stigma theory (Goffman, 1963) to propose that passage of state-wise same-sex marriage (SSM) legislation in a firm's home state improves its performance, because LGBTQ employees are less likely to be discriminated and harassed in the workplace when governmental support is clearly communicated through inclusive legislation. This improves their psychological well-being and job satisfaction, which leads to greater productivity in the workplace (Ragins, 2008; Wang & Schwarz, 2010). Further, heterosexual employees may be engaged to a greater degree if their LGBTQ coworkers receive equal treatment (Dahling et al., 2016).

Further, we contend that the effect of SSM on firm performance is not uniform across all firms. Legislation providing equal rights to a state's minority citizens should lead to a win–win situation for society and firms alike; however, there may be several macro and micro factors existing at the societal-cultural, institutional, and individual firm levels that determine the positive impact of legislation on critical firm outcomes. We therefore applied the framework of institutional racism (Jones, 1972) in the context of heterosexism (Smith & Ingram, 2004; Willis, 2012) to develop a multi-level model to investigate the contingency factors shaping the effects of social legislations on firm outcomes. The framework of institutional racism (Jones, 1972) is relevant to our study since stigma based on sexual orientation or gender identity is like that of racism, where individuals with a higher social status enjoy the privileges that come with their status and denounce individuals with a lower social status. We therefore posit that heterosexism exists at three hierarchical levels. At the highest macro level, societal-cultural norms such as values and beliefs embedded in close-knit and loose-knit cultures determine acceptance of LGBTQ individuals (Erez & Gati, 2004). At the next macro-level, norms embedded in an industry or occupation in which the firm operates shape attitudes towards LGBTQ individuals (Plug et al., 2014). Lastly, at the micro level, firm climate shaped through different organizational policies is likely to determine the effects of social legislation (Li & Nagar, 2012; Wang & Schwarz, 2010). We therefore theorize three such factors that manifest as a form of heterosexism in societal institutions—community connectedness (the extent to which members of a community interact with each other) (Gelfand et al., 2011) at the highest societal-cultural level, industry masculinity (male dominance and likely lower acceptance of LGBTQ individuals) (Anderson, 2009; Miller et al., 2003) at the middle level, and organizational pro-LGBTQ climate (Shan et al., 2017) at the individual firm level. By applying Jones' (1972) framework of institutional racism to investigate how social norms, industry type and organizational climate influence the SSM-firm performance relationship we contextualize this research and make an important contribution to social legislation literature.

Finally, we answer diversity scholars' call for research that quantifies the value of diversity friendly laws and policies (Everly & Schwarz, 2015; Huffman et al., 2008; Nishii, 2013). We advance research on workplace performance of employees with stigmatized identities based on their sexual orientation or gender identity (Ragins & Cornwell, 2001; Ragins, 2004, 2008). By analyzing the causal link between diversity-friendly legislation and firm performance we attempt to build a business case for diversity management (Ely & Thomas, 2001). While, LGBTQ individuals are still subject to widespread prejudice, discrimination, harassment, and hostility in heteronormative workplaces (Fu, 2017; Webster et al., 2018), government and organizations will be more likely to adopt further initiatives to create a psychologically safe space for them in the society and workplace, given strong research evidence for the value generated by marriage equality. This may also have positive implications for other employees, as individuals are more likely to more productive when their coworkers feel included and engage themselves fully in the workplace (Westman et al., 2009).

We note that the concern of reverse causality exists in the relationship between SSM passage and firm performance. For instance, a state with better economy (i.e., better firm performances) maybe more likely to have progressive laws such as SSM. Therefore, establishing the causal direction is critical to understanding the effect of social legislation on firm outcomes. We therefore utilize a natural experiment provided by the staggered passage of same sex marriage law in 36 states from 2003 to 2015 to investigate the causal relationship between the legislation and firm outcomes. We use a difference-in-difference approach to explore the exogenous variation provided by staggered SSM passage and its effect on firm performance. We focus on the "treatment" group composed of firms headquartered in states that passed SSM and utilize the "control" group of firms headquartered in states not passing SSM in the same years, even if those states have already passed SSM or will pass SSM later in our sample. This approach fully controls for unobserved firm differences and aggregate shocks through the inclusion of firm fixed effects and year fixed effects and draws causal inferences about the effects of variation in the legislation on firm performance. To further ensure robustness of our findings, we employ a propensity score matching (PSM) method to pair the "treated" firms with "non-treated" firms and run the analyses in a propensity-scored-matched sample. In addition, we track historic state locations of headquarters for our sample firms and identify any firms that shifted their headquarters state in the study period to explore the effects of time-series change of state SSM legislation on firm performance.

5.2.2 Literature Review and Hypotheses Development

5.2.2.1 State-Wise Same-Sex Marriage Legislation and Firm Performance

Stigmas refer to individual attributes that are perceived as flaws in a social context (Goffman, 1963). Stigmatized individuals often become victims of harassment and discrimination in the workplace because of their perceived repulsive or undesirable characteristics (Crocker & Major, 1989; Dovidio et al., 2000). These negative experiences also occur in the workplace through social interactions (Pescosolido & Martin, 2015). Employees may be stigmatized in the workplace for many reasons, such as health-related issues (e.g., mental illness, HPV/HIV), financial status, relationship status (e.g., same sex couple), family status (e.g., infertility), association with past crimes, and living in certain neighborhoods (Pescosolido & Martin, 2015; Summers et al., 2018). Stigmatized identities are not necessarily always visible in a social setting (Ragins, 2008). One such kind of invisible stigma arises from an individual's sexual orientation or gender identity (Summers et al., 2018), and leads to workplace discrimination for LGBTQ employees (Catalyst, 2021). While U.S. Supreme Court recently extended the Civil Rights Act of 1964 to protect LGBTQ individuals from employment discrimination, employers may still be granted religious exemptions to discriminate against LGBTQ individuals (Liptak, 2020). Moreover, many organizations are yet to implement family-friendly policies covering same-sex partner or spousal benefits (Catalyst, 2018).

Discrimination exacts a considerable cost from our society in many implicit ways. Extant research shows that discrimination based on an individual's sexual orientation or gender identity adversely impacts their personal well-being (Martinez & Hebl, 2010) and the performance of the firm in which these individuals are employed (Johnston & Malina, 2008; Wang & Schwarz, 2010). The absence of civil marriage rights for LGBTQ individuals excludes them from the protections that law assigns to heterosexual marriages (Duhigg et al., 2010). Absence of civil marriage rights for LGBTQ employees further devalues their identity in social and workplace settings (Crocker et al., 1998). After all, an employee's work and family domain are intertwined, rather than two independent entities with no observable influences on one another (Jennings & McDougald, 2007). As a result, LGBTQ employees end up concealing their identity in the workplace to avoid discrimination and prejudiced reactions (Ragins, 2008). This identity concealment takes a heavy toll on their mental and physical health leading to emotional stress, psychological strain, and stress-related illnesses (Ragins, 2008). Altogether, these employees are not able to fully engage themselves in work because of the constant struggles they experience to validate their identity in both work and non-work domain (Clair et al., 2005). This has a negative effect on their psychological well-being impacting their workplace productivity. Productivity loss may also occur due to a mood or affect spillover in the form of negative affect (van Hooff et al., 2006), cognitive spillover in the form of ruminating thoughts (Maertz & Boyar, 2011), and physiological spillover in the form of reduced energy due to elevated cortisol levels (Repetti et al., 2009).

Firm performance may also decrease through spillover effects to heterosexual employees. Heterosexual employees may feel a psychological connection with their LGBTQ coworkers, and be morally outraged and less productive if the latter do not receive fair treatment (Dahling et al., 2016). LGBTQ employees constitute a small percentage of the workforce; however, ensuring their rights can create sizable economic effects at the firm level because the resulting progressive and inclusive environment enhances productivity of many others in the workforce (Conti et al., 2018). This is because employees are more likely to be productive in workplaces where all individual feels free to express their authentic selves (Roussin et al., 2016). Team effectiveness is higher (Tasheva & Hillman, 2019) when members from different diverse backgrounds can fully engage themselves and contribute to sharing their perspectives (Nishii, 2013). Firm performance may thus rise due to enhanced collaboration between diverse individuals facilitated by social liberalization laws (Vakili & Zhang, 2018).

Lastly, extant research on emotion crossover suggests that one employee's stress may lead to strain in other team members (Westman, 2001; Westman et al., 2009; Zagenczyk et al., 2020). LGBTQ employees may experience a greater degree of burnout due to a decrease in psychological well-being because of their stigmatized identity (Riggle et al., 2017). However, the burnout may also crossover to their heterosexual coworkers decreasing their productivity and the overall team engagement levels (Bakker et al., 2006). This impacts a firm's competitive advantage and long term performance as it prevents a firm from achieving returns on investments that it has incurred in acquiring and developing its human capital (Anand et al., 2018). Thus, firms are more likely to have higher performance if they are headquartered in states where same-sex marriage is legalized.

Hypothesis 1 Same-sex marriage legislation in a firm's home state boosts firm performance.

5.2.2.2 State-Wise Same-Sex Marriage Legislation and Firm Performance: Boundary Effects of Institutional Racism

The impact of social legislation on firm financial performance may be contingent on several contextual factors. We adapt Jones's (1972) model of institutional racism in the context of heterosexism to provide a better understanding of the effect of SSM legislation on firm performance. Herek et al. (1992) defined heterosexism as "an ideological system that denies, denigrates, and stigmatizes any non-heterosexual form of behavior, identity, relationship or community" (p. 89). Jones's model of institutional racism examines racism in societal institutions through the lens of a multi-level framework, which can be applied to get new insights into heterosexism in the LGBTQ employee's community and the workplace. Jones (1972) summarized and bridged the existing definitions of racism into a single idea which posits that "one group enjoys privilege and retains the powerful position needed to maintain it, define it as natural, and reject others who deviate from the standards that has set up to reflect its way of life" (p. 373). This notion of racism can be applied in the context of heterosexism since heterosexual individuals claim a higher social status and reject LGBTQ individuals labeling them as unnatural because of their deviant sexual orientation or gender identity (Kertzner et al., 2009). Further, Jones (1972) conceptualized that racism exists at three hierarchical levels—societal-cultural (at the top level), institutional (at the middle level), and individual (at the bottom level). At the highest macro-level, societal-cultural racism outlines the cultural values and beliefs of the community in which an individual resides. At the second macro-level, institutional racism depicts the cultural artifacts of the industry or occupation in which an individual works. Finally, at the micro-level, individual racism delineates the workplace climate in an individual organization. To apply Jones' model to understand how heterosexism shapes the effects of SSM legislation on firm performance we investigate 3 factors relevant to organizations: community connectedness at the highest societal-cultural level, industry masculinity at the middle level, and organizational pro-LGBTQ climate at the individual level.

Jones (1972) conceptualized societal-cultural racism as "superiority of one race's cultural heritage over that of another race" (p. 6). Though sexual orientation and gender identity are distinct from race, the widespread societal beliefs regarding the inferiority of LGBTQ individuals can be explained through Jones's definition. Our assertion is in line with diversity literature, which suggests that negative attitudes towards LGBTQ individuals are widely prevalent (Ragins, 2008). We maintain that LGBTQ individuals experience societal-cultural racism in the form of discrimination. We further argue that societal-cultural racism towards LGBTQ employees may vary across communities and this variation may determine the impact of SSM legislation on these employees' morale and subsequent workplace performance.

Within any social group or community culture shapes behavioral norms and expectations, and defines the core values for the group members. Culture manifests itself in a top-down process of socialization where individuals internalize the shared beliefs and meaning system of their community that shape their behaviors. Further, the degree of internalization depends upon the strength of a culture (Erez & Gati, 2004). Close-knit cultures are characterized by clear consistent expectations, rigid community norms, and little tolerance of socially deviant behaviors, whereas loose-knit cultures are characterized by vague expectations, feeble community norms, and high tolerance of socially deviant behaviors (Gelfand et al., 2011; Schein, 1992). It's therefore likely that LGBTQ individuals, who defy the prevalent norms, are more stigmatized in a close-knit community. LGBTQ individuals in a highly connected or tight community are thus less likely to disclose their sexual orientation to other members.

In a loose-knit community on the other hand, where the members are not governed by strict social norms and socially deviant behavior is not punished (Erez & Gati, 2004; Ragins & Cornwell, 2001), LGBTQ individuals are less likely to be stigmatized and treated differently than their majority counterparts who are heterosexual and cisgender. Diversity scholars maintain that discrimination is more likely to be experienced in communities marked by an absence of legislation providing LGBTQ rights equal to those of the majority members of the community (Ragins & Cornwell, 2001). However, we argue that the absence of LGBTQ-friendly legislation may not increase the challenges of these individuals to that degree in less connected loose-knit communities as they do in close-knit ones where norms are more rigid and do not tolerate any type of deviation. We therefore expect the impact of LGBTQ-friendly legislation to be stronger in highly connected communities, as it helps reduce societal-cultural racism and change strong social norms intolerant of stigmatized individuals. LGBTQ individuals in highly connected communities are also more likely to benefit in terms of increased societal acceptance and belongingness when SSM legislation is passed. This increased sense of positive affect and well-being may spill over to their workplace and enhance their productivity.

Hypothesis 2 The positive effect of state-wise same-sex marriage legislation on firm performance is moderated by community connectedness, such that the positive effect is stronger in more rather than less connected communities.

After community, the next lower macro level of analysis is an industry for which we turn to Jones's definition of institutional racism. Jones (1972) defines institutional racism as "those established laws, customs, and practices which systematically reflect and produce racial inequities" (p. 131). This conceptualization brings a lesser macro perspective to heterosexism and allows an examination of prejudice and biases prevalent in certain industries or occupations. We argue that the impact of SSM legislation on LGBTQ employees' morale and workplace productivity is contingent upon institutional practices that may be systematically creating disadvantages for them. Our argument draws on diversity research, which suggests that industries that tend to be more masculine are fraught with disadvantages for LGBTQ individuals. Heteronormative discourse adversely impacts the labor market job prospects of LGBTQ individuals (Drydakis, 2015), and occupational segregation based on one's sexual orientation is not uncommon (Bérubé, 2011). LGBTQ individuals are more likely to be found in gender-segregated industries, which they find less prejudiced and more tolerant (Plug et al., 2014). For example, gay men gravitate more towards feminine occupations or industries such as nursing, front-desk hospitality, and commercial airline steward jobs (Tilcsik et al., 2015).

This is because masculine industries (such as automotive, construction, oil and gas) are characterized by masculine, heterosexual work styles and create tremendous pressure for LGBTQ individuals to be muscular and display masculine emotions in order to fit in (Sánchez et al., 2009). Further, such industries characterized by isolation and discrimination carry a strong stigma against sexual or gender minorities making it difficult for them to form close trusting relationships with their coworkers (Collins, 2013). The only way to thwart the bigoted and prejudiced institutional practices (Jones, 1972) dominant in masculine industries is to introduce law, policy, or legislation, which are supportive of LGBTQ individuals. LGBTQ-inclusive laws are more likely to challenge the heteronormativity existing in masculine industries and reduce implicit biases and practices existing in the workplace.

Hypothesis 3 The positive effect of state-wise same-sex marriage legislation on firm performance is moderated by industry masculinity, such that the positive effect is stronger in more rather than less masculine industries.

Individual racism as introduced by Jones (1972) and applied to organizational settings is believed to stem from the racial climate in the workplace (Ragins & Cornwell, 2001). The heterosexist climate in an organization in this case is manifested in the form of employee shared perceptions (Schneider & Reichers, 1983) about the degree of heteronormative cisgender policies, practices, and procedures that an organization expects, supports, and rewards. LGBTQ individuals are more likely to be stigmatized in organizations where the policies and practices do not provide equal benefits to all employees regardless of their sexual orientation or gender identity.

This is because organizational policies discriminating sexual or gender minorities further delegitimize their identities leading to increased prejudice and biases against them in heterosexual cisgender employees (Chuang et al., 2018). LGBTQ individuals are further motivated to conceal their stigmatized identities in such non-supportive work environment due to fear of backlash from their supervisors and coworkers (Ragins, 2008). On the other hand, organizations that provide fair treatment to all employees are more likely to influence heterosexual cisgender employees to take the role of an ally and demonstrate supportive behaviors towards their LGBTQ coworkers (Martinez & Hebl, 2010). These organizations are less likely to benefit from pro-LGBTQ legislation as they already have pro-LGBTQ policies in place to improve the morale and thereby productivity of LGBTQ employees. Further, firms with more progressive LGBTQ non-discrimination policies such as adoption of same-sex domestic partnership benefit (SSDPB) policies are already found to outperform otherwise equivalent firms (Li & Nagar, 2012; Wang & Schwarz, 2010). Thus, pro-LGBTQ legislation is more likely to have a positive effect on LGBTQ employees' morale when there is lack of supportive organizational policies, as it will allow them to be their authentic selves in the workplace without fear of discrimination.

Hypothesis 4 The positive effect of state-wise same-sex marriage legislation on firm performance is moderated by organizational pro-LGBTQ climate, such that the positive effect is stronger for firms with lower degree of pro-LGBTQ climate.

5.2.3 Method

5.2.3.1 Sample

The primary goal of this research is to explore the staggered timing of SSM legislation across different states as exogenous shock and its effect on firm performance. We therefore focus on the 18 states where same-sex marriage was legalized between year 2003 and year 2013 (Kail et al., 2015). To supplement our dataset, we also checked court records for each state to verify the ruling date and effective date. The time-period of this study begins in year 2003 when Massachusetts became the first state to legalize same-sex marriage. Table 5.1 provides a list of legal ruling dates for these 18 states. We note that California had a long and winding path toward the legislation of same-sex marriage. We only consider the ruling date in 2013 in our empirical study because it provides a clear time point to implement the difference-in-difference approach. On May 15, 2008, California Supreme Court ruled that same-sex couples' access to marriage is a fundamental right under Article 1, Section 7 of the California Constitution; however, this ruling was overturned in November when Prop 8 was approved by 52 percent of California voters and marriage for same-sex couples was excluded from California state constitution. It was not until April 26, 2013 that Federal court found Prop 8 unconstitutional and same-sex marriage again became legal in California.

Using information on the staggered timing of SSM legislation across the 50 U.S. states and the District of Columbia, we identified all publicly traded U.S. firms whose headquarters were located in one of the aforementioned 18 states. Our sample included firms that had financial information in Compustat database for at least two years before and after the state legislation passage (i.e., ruling

Table 5.1 State-wise same-sex marriage legislation dates

State	State code	Ruling year	Effective year
Alaska	AK	2014	2014
Arizona	AZ	2014	2014
California	CA	2013	2013
Colorado	CO	2014	2014
Connecticut	CT	2008	2008
Delaware	DE	2013	2013
District of Columbia	DC	2009	2010
Florida	FL	2014	2015
Hawaii	HI	2013	2013
Idaho	ID	2014	2014
Illinois	IL	2013	2014
Indiana	IN	2014	2014
Iowa	IA	2009	2009
Maine	ME	2012	2012
Maryland	MD	2012	2013
Massachusetts	MA	2003	2004
Minnesota	MN	2013	2013
Montana	MT	2014	2014
Nevada	NV	2014	2014
New Hampshire	NH	2009	2010
New Jersey	NJ	2013	2013
New Mexico	NM	2013	2013
New York	NY	2011	2011
North Carolina	NC	2014	2014
Oklahoma	OK	2014	2014
Oregon	OR	2014	2014
Pennsylvania	PA	2014	2014
Rhode Island	RI	2013	2013
South Carolina	SC	2014	2014
Utah	UT	2014	2014
Vermont	VT	2009	2009
Virginia	VA	2014	2014
Washington	WA	2012	2012
West Virginia	WV	2014	2014
Wisconsin	WI	2014	2014
Wyoming	WY	2014	2014

date) to ensure the comparability of our sample firms experiencing the regulation changes. We excluded firms in financial industry (SIC code 6000–6999) and utility industry (SIC code 4900–4999), because both are highly regulated. Our final sample included 105,767 firm-year observations for 9,450 unique firms. For testing Hypothesis 4, our sample size was 5,492 because data regarding the effect of organizational pro-LGBTQ climate were not available for all firm-year observations. For supplementary analyses, the sample size was 53,726 because data regarding headquarters change were not available for all firm-year observations.

5.2.3.2 Measures

Return on assets (ROA). We used ROA as a financial indicator offirm performance because this measure captures the efficiency of utilizing firm assets to generate returns. We calculated ROA as the ratio of income before extraordinary items and firm total book assets (Grullon & Michaely, 2002).

Profitability per 100 employees. Instead of using firm book assets as the scaling factor, we divided the firm income before extraordinary items in million dollars by number of employees in hundreds to calculate profitability per 100 employees. We chose this operationalization because it captures the impact of a firm's human capital, its employees (Girma et al., 2004; Guest et al., 2003).

State-wise same-sex marriage legislation (SSM). Following extant literature (Bertrand & Mullainathan, 2003; Jayaratne & Strahan, 1996), we treated the passages of SSM legislation in a state as exogenous shocks. To explore the staggered timing of SSM legalization across different states as exogenous shock, we defined a dummy variable that equals 1 from year t onward for a particular firm if the state, in which the same firm is headquartered, passed the SSM protection in year t, and 0 otherwise. Table 5.1 has details of SSM passage dates.

Community connectedness. We measured community connectedness by adopting the view that an individual is linked to other individuals in a particular community through their participation in various organizations such as civic groups, religious organizations, sports clubs, fitness centers, professional organizations, labor unions, political and business groups (Rupasingha et al., 2006). Social interactions between individuals belonging to the same groups tend to build mutual trust and facilitate cooperation. Therefore, the number of organizations and their members can serve as a proxy for the extent to which members of a community interact and are connected to each other. We note that for the entire U.S. county-level data on community connectedness has been computed by Rupasingha et al. (2006). Because larger counties are likely to have more clubs and organizations, Rupasingha and colleagues calculated the number of organizations per 10,000 people at the county level to standardize the measure. We conceptualized community connectedness at the level of the society/culture in which a firm is embedded. Therefore, following extant research (Hasan et al., 2017; Jha & Chen, 2015) we focused on the county where a particular firm is headquartered, and used this measure for all analyses.[1]

Industry masculinity. We used industry-wise employee demographic data[2] provided by the Bureau of Labor Statistics (BLS) to calculate industry masculinity, that is the extent to which an industry is dominated by men and likely less accepting of LGBTQ individuals (Anderson, 2009; Miller et al., 2003). First, we mapped the industry description in the BLS data against the 1987 SIC code list provided by the Census Bureau.[3] Following extant research, we defined masculine industries as those in which women constituted 25% or less of the total employed (Catalyst, 2018; Linstead & Marechal, 2015; United States Department of Labor Women's Bureau, 2014). For instance, in 2018, construction was a masculine industry with women making 9.1% of the total employed (BLS, 2018). Accordingly, we assigned a dummy variable that equals to 1 for industries with SIC codes 1510 (general building contractors) and 1530 (operative builders). In a similar fashion, we identified a list of SIC codes and classified those as masculine industries.

Organizational pro-LGBTQ climate. To measure organizational pro-LGBTQ climate, we used a firm's Corporate Equality Index (CEI) score given by the Human Rights Campaign (HRC). Since 2002, HRC sends an annual survey to the managing partner or CEO as well as to the head of human resources of all Fortune 1000 organizations. HRC's mission is to capture the degree to which these organizations have adopted pro-LGBTQ workplace policies (Kaplan & Berkley, 2021). The CEI scores are not just calculated based on the organization's self-reported information but also HRC research data which include LGBTQ discrimination incidents reported about the organization in the media, organization's SEC filings, primary reports from the organization's LGBTQ employees, and reports prepared by HRC Foundation Workplace Project (Human Rights Campaign Foundation, 2015).

HRC assigns scores in the range of 0 to 100. We divided the original scores by 100 to scale those in the range of 0 to 1, which was consistent with all other study variables.

Control variables. A firm's performance is likely affected by the extent to which its home state offers legal protection from discrimination based on employee gender identity and sexual orientation. We assessed "state LGBTQ regulation" as the strength of LGBTQ employment discrimination law at the ruling date of same sex marriage law. This indicator ranges from 0 to 4, such that 0 = no protection, 1 = protection from sexual orientation-based discrimination for state employees, 2 = protection from sexual orientation and gender identity-based discrimination for state employees, 3 = protection from sexual orientation-based discrimination for all employees, and 4 = protection from sexual orientation and gender identity-based discrimination for all employees (Kanuer, 2010). Finally, it is plausible that a particular firm's performance depends on the economic development in its home

[1] https://aese.psu.edu/nercrd/community/social-capital-resources.
[2] https://www.bls.gov/cps/cpsaat18.htm.
[3] https://www.census.gov/prod/techdoc/cbp/cbp96/sic-code.pdf.

state. Therefore, using data from Bureau of Economic Analysis, we used state GDP growth rate as an additional control, which is calculated as the percentage change of state GDP from year $t - 1$ to year t.

In addition to state-level variables, we also controlled for several firm-level variables capturing various aspects of an individual firm relevant to its performance. Past research (Huynh & Petrunia, 2010) indicates that firm size and leverage affect performance, therefore we controlled for both variables. We measured "Firm size" as the natural logarithm of firm book assets, and "Book leverage" as book value of long-term debt plus short-term debt divided by book value of firm assets. We also controlled for firm research and development (R&D) and capital investments in physical assets—two key sources of performance improvement (Amir et al., 2007). We measured "R&D intensity" by scaling firm R&D expenditures by net sales, and "Capital expenditure" as the ratio of capital expenditures to firm book assets. Finally, we also controlled for two indicators of a firm's financial health -payout ratio and asset tangibility. Payout ratio of a firm reflects whether it has free cash flow after satisfying all investment demands and is computed as the ratio of the sum of dividend payment and stock repurchase to firm book assets (Fenn & Liang, 2001). We measured asset tangibility as the ratio of tangible assets (i.e., net property, plant & equipment net of depreciation plus inventories) to total assets.

5.2.3.3 Analytical Strategy

The staggered timing of state regulation regarding the same-sex marriage provides an ideal setting to explore empirically whether and to what extent these regulatory changes affect firm performance. In this study, we adopt a difference-in-difference (DID) approach to perform our analysis, which has been used in numerous studies to explore the effects of policy changes (e.g., Black & Strahan, 2002; Stan & Puranam, 2017; Wang et al., 2016). This econometric approach (see Eq. 5.1) can be easily understood with an example. To estimate the effects of SSM legislation on firm performance in Connecticut in 2008, we can compare labor productivity before and after 2008 for firms headquartered in Connecticut. However, the change in performance could be primarily driven by shocks that are common to the entire economy (e.g., the 2008 financial crisis). Therefore, we choose a second state Texas and focus on firms headquartered in Texas as our control group. As the firms headquartered in Texas are subject to the same economic condition in year 2008 but same-sex-marriage was not legalized there at that time, the difference in performance for Texas firms before and after 2008 can serve as an estimate of the extent that the 2008 financial crisis affected firms' performance in year 2008. By comparing the difference in firm performance pre- and post-2008 in Connecticut with the difference in firm performance pre- and post-2008 in Texas (i.e., difference in difference), we are able to estimate the effect of SSM legislation on performance for individual firms headquartered in Connecticut. As shown in Eq. 5.1, *treatment* is a location dummy for which Connecticut firms have a value of 1 and Texas firms have a value of zero. Accordingly, *post* is a time dummy for which years of 2008 and onward have a value of 1 and zero otherwise. Our focus is the coefficient β_3 of the interaction term of *treatment* and *post*, which captures the effect of the regulation change on performance of individual firms headquartered in Connecticut.

$$Y_{i,t} = \beta_0 + \beta_1 \text{ treatment} + \beta_2 \text{ post} + \beta_3 \text{ post} \times \text{treatment} + \beta X_{i,t} + \varepsilon_{i,t} \quad (5.1)$$

Because different states gradually removed the restriction on the same-sex marriage at different time points, we thereby used a generalized difference-in-difference approach proposed by Bertrand and Mullainathan (2003) to explore the impact of the legalization of same sex marriage on firm performance. Specifically, at the individual firm's level, the regression model is as follows with dependent variable being ROA and profit per 100 employees, respectively.

$$Y_{i,k,t} = \gamma D_{k,t} + \beta X_{i,k,t} + \gamma_i + \lambda_t + \varepsilon_{i,k,t} \quad (5.2)$$

where, i indexes firms, k indexes the state in which the firm is headquartered, t indexes time, $Y_{i,\,k,\,t}$ is the dependent variable, $X_{i,\,k,\,t}$ is a vector of control variables, γ_i are firm fixed effects, λ_t are year fixed effects, and $\varepsilon_{i,\,k,\,t}$ is a random error term. $D_{k,\,t}$ is a dummy variable that equals 1, if same sex marriage has been legalized in year t (and onward) and in state k, and 0 otherwise. Our estimate of the effect of SSM is γ.

In summary, DID method accounts for any time-invariant factors by including firm fixed effects in the regression models. The inclusion of firm fixed effects in the regression models allows us to fully control for any time-invariant factors for a particular firm such as firm locations. We also include year fixed effects to control for economy-wide shocks and time trends. Consequently, the indicator (i.e., $D_{k,\,t}$) in Eq. 5.2 replaces the term post × treatment in Eq. 5.1 and allows us to capture the true effect of SSM on firm performance. In other words, we treat staggered regulatory changes as exogenous shocks, and the generalized difference-in-difference approach enables us to test the causal direction of input-outcome relationships. Moreover, the DID approach implicitly uses firms in states that did not legislate same-sex marriage as the control group even if those states eventually allow for same-sex marriage later on. We note that the inclusion of firm fixed effects in our models addresses concerns about any confounds with state-level attributes, both observed and unobserved. For instance, Alaska has a unique culture that likely influences employee attitudes and performance of firms in Alaska; however, we do not need to include this state fixed effect in our models because for any given firm these do not change from year to year, and thus are accounted for in firm fixed effects. Nonetheless, it is plausible that the economic condition in a particular state, which is time varying, may affect firm performance in addition to the effect induced by the regulatory changes we focused on. We thereby include the state GDP growth rate as an additional control in our model specifications. Finally, we clustered the standard errors at state level to account for interdependence of error terms over time for firms located in the same state so that the statistical significance is not inflated (Bertrand et al., 2004).

5.2.4 Results

Table 5.2 presents the mean, median and correlation coefficients for all of the study variables. Prior to running our analyses, we performed a 5 percent winsorization (Brownen-Trinh, 2019) to mitigate the influences of extreme values. Specifically, we transform all values below the 2.5th percentile to the 2.5th percentile. Similarly, we perform data transformation for values above the 97.5th percentile. Winsorization allows us to improve statistical efficiency and increase the robustness of statistical inferences. Moreover, winsorization introduces less bias than deletion of these extreme data points.

Hypothesis 1 suggests that the passage of SSM legislation in a firm's headquarter state causes a boost in the firm's performance. We created Model 1 and 2 to test the effect of SSM on ROA, and profit per 100 employees (i.e., profit/employee) respectively. Table 5.3 provides the results of difference-in-difference analysis for testing Hypothesis 1. As detailed in the method section, we focused on the indicator of passage of SSM legislation in a particular state to capture its true effect on firm performance, using all other firms in states that do not experience the legislative change as the control group. As shown in Table 5.3, for both the performance measures the effect is positive and significant (ROA: $b = 0.009$, $p < 0.01$; profit/employee: $b = 0.058$, $p < 0.01$). We thus found support for Hypothesis 1. Further, as shown in column 1, the coefficient of 0.01 indicates that the passage of SSM is associated with a 0.9% increase in ROA. The coefficient of 0.058 reported in column 2 suggests a $60,000 increase in income before extraordinary items per 100 employees due to the passage of SSM. These values attest to the economic significance of our results.

Hypothesis 2 suggests that the positive effect of SSM legislation on firm performance is stronger in more connected communities. As shown in Table 5.4, for both performance measures, the interaction effect is positive and significant (ROA: $b = 0.012$, $p < 0.01$; profit/employee: $b = 0.008$, $p < 0.05$). We thus found support for Hypothesis 2. In addition, result in column 1 of Table 5.4 indicates that, with a one-standard deviation increase in community connectedness, the marginal effect of passage of SSM is associated with a 0.5% increase in ROA. We plotted Fig. 5.1 to visualize the moderating effect of community connectedness on the SSM-Firm performance link (Wang et al., 2016). We note that Fig. 5.1 is different from the typical two-way effect interaction graphs because of the difference-in-difference approach that we adopted to conduct our analysis. Specifically, the horizontal axis in Fig. 5.1 depicts the moderating variable and the vertical axis indicates the effect of the passage of SSM law on firm performance, which is given by the sum of the coefficients of SSM and interaction term conditional on the moderator. Figure 5.1 also shows the 95% confidence interval calculated from the estimated coefficient and standard error. The vertical axis in Fig. 5.1a shows that the effect of SSM regulation change on ROA is positive. From the slope of the curve, we can infer that the effect of passage of SSM law on ROA increases as community connectedness increases. Figure 5.1b offers similar insights for profit per 100 employees.

Table 5.2 Summary statistics and pairwise correlation matrix for the study variables

	Variables	Mean	STD	1	2	3	4	5	6	7	8	9	10	11	12	13	14
1	ROA	0.01	0.13	1.00													
2	Profit/employee	2.21	1.25	**0.44**	1.00												
3	SSM	0.21	0.41	**0.01**	**0.08**	1.00											
4	State LGBTQ regulation	1.78	1.56	**0.04**	**0.02**	**0.36**	1.00										
5	State GDP growth rate	0.02	0.02	**0.02**	0.01	**−0.04**	**0.01**	1.00									
6	Firm size	18.25	2.86	**0.13**	**0.26**	**−0.01**	**−0.04**	**−0.06**	1.00								
7	Book leverage	1.87	52.11	**0.06**	**−0.01**	**0.01**	0.00	**−0.01**	**−0.12**	1.00							
8	Capital expenditure	0.05	1.18	**0.03**	**0.04**	−0.01	**−0.01**	**0.07**	**−0.02**	**0.01**	1.00						
9	Payout ratio	0.06	3.04	**0.06**	**0.02**	**0.00**	−0.01	0.00	**−0.04**	**0.03**	0.00	1.00					
10	R&D intensity	0.11	0.31	**−0.28**	**−0.21**	**0.07**	**0.13**	**0.04**	**−0.26**	**0.01**	−0.03	0.00	1.00				
11	Asset tangibility	0.44	0.20	**−0.04**	**−0.04**	**0.04**	**0.10**	**0.06**	**−0.27**	**0.04**	**0.01**	**0.03**	**0.34**	1.00			
12	Industry Masculinity	−0.15	0.58	**0.02**	**0.03**	**−0.06**	**0.03**	**−0.06**	**0.06**	**0.02**	**0.00**	0.00	**−0.05**	**−0.03**	1.00		
13	Community Connectedness	0.29	0.45	**0.02**	**0.05**	**−0.04**	**−0.05**	**0.08**	**0.08**	0.00	0.00	0.00	**−0.05**	**−0.02**	0.00	1.00	
14	Organizational Pro-LGBTQ Climate	0.66	0.32	0.03	0.00	**0.05**	**0.25**	**0.03**	**0.31**	**−0.11**	**−0.19**	**0.04**	**0.21**	**−0.09**	**0.04**	**−0.13**	1.00

Note $N = 105{,}767$. Bold indicates significance *** $p < 0.01$

Table 5.3 Difference-in-difference analysis results for testing hypothesis 1 regarding the effect of SSM on firm performance

Independent variables	Dependent variables			
	OLS	PSM		
	Return on assets	Profit/employee	Return on assets	Profit/employee
	(1)	(2)	(3)	(4)
Intercept	−1.777*** (−88.181)	−3.894*** (−7.914)	−3.990*** (−12.586)	−0.544*** (−24.681) (0.022)
State LGBTQ regulation	0.003*** (3.352)	0.002 (0.121)	0.018* (1.881)	0.001 (0.001)
State GDP growth rate	0.061* (1.790)	0.086 (0.335)	0.047 (0.906)	0.063 (1.121)
Firm size	0.094*** (88.833)	0.213*** (8.047)	0.185*** (11.195)	0.131*** (6.952)
Book leverage	−0.221*** (−52.707)	−0.743*** (−4.280)	−0.114** (2.074)	−0.119*** (−6.156)
Capital expenditure	−0.042*** (−3.024)	0.221 (0.775)	−0.095** (−2.318)	0.014 (0.942)
Payout ratio	0.004 (0.202)	0.848* (1.899)	0.093 (0.723)	0.047*** (2.603)
R&D intensity	−0.426*** (−83.858)	−2.523*** (−16.394)	−1.041*** (13.023)	−0.279*** (−5.292)
Asset tangibility	0.092*** (18.106)	0.186* (1.868)	0.684*** (8.814)	0.004 (0.749)
SSM	0.009*** (3.465)	0.058*** (3.208)	0.027** (2.131)	0.008*** (3.114)
Year fixed effects	Yes	Yes	Yes	Yes
Firm fixed effects	Yes	Yes	Yes	Yes
Clustered standard errors	State	State	State	State
Observations	105,767	105,767	51,236	51,236
F-statistic	1062***	92.53***	26.28***	284.33***
Adjusted R-squared	0.711	0.582	0.716	0.561

Hypothesis 3 suggests that the positive effect of SSM legislation on firm performance is stronger in more masculine industries. We created Model 1 and 2 to test this moderating effect of industry masculinity on the link between SSM and ROA and SSM and profit per 100 employees. We note that, unlike the traditional models for testing interaction effects, Model 1 & 2 do not include main or first order effects for industry masculinity. This is because the masculinity of an industry is similar to culture in that it is change-resistant and takes a long time to vary (Schein, 1990). Industry masculinity should thus be treated as a time-invariant factor. Further, we recall that any time-invariant factors for a particular firm are accounted for

Table 5.4 Difference-in-difference analysis results for testing hypothesis 2 regarding the moderating effect of community connectedness

Independent variables	Dependent variables	
	Return on assets	Profit/employee
	(2)	(1)
Intercept	−1.730*** (−85.44)	−4.094*** (−26.644)
State LGBTQ regulation	0.003*** (3.491)	0.001 (0.190)
State GDP growth rate	0.060* (1.828)	0.101 (0.530)
Firm size	0.094*** (88.627)	0.210*** (29.218)
Book leverage	−0.220*** (−52.561)	−0.740*** (−25.948)
Capital expenditure	−0.043*** (−3.082)	−0.213** (−2.268)
Payout ratio	0.003 (0.197)	0.852* (1.811)
R&D intensity	−0.426*** (−83.736)	−2.516*** (−72.763)
Asset tangibility	0.092*** (18.134)	0.184*** (5.328)
SSM	0.008*** (3.055)	0.046*** (2.655)
Community connectedness	0.008*** (6.928)	0.097*** (11.905)
SSM × Community connectedness	0.012*** (3.668)	0.008** (2.380)
Year fixed effects	Yes	Yes
Firm fixed effects	Yes	Yes
Clustered standard errors	State	State
Observations	105,767	105,767
F-statistic	963.91***	401.20***
Adjusted *R*-squared	0.711	0.583

Note *t* statistics are in parentheses. * $p < 0.10$, ** $p < 0.05$, *** $p < 0.01$. $N = 105{,}767$

by including "firm fixed effects" in the difference-in-difference analytical models. Thus, we only included SSM and its interaction term with the indicator of industry masculinity in our Models 1 & 2. We thereby relied on the variation in the interaction term to estimate its coefficients and make statistical inferences. As shown in Table 5.5, for both the performance measures the interaction effect is positive and significant (ROA: $b = 0.008$, $p < 0.10$; profit/employee: $b = 0.219$, $p <$

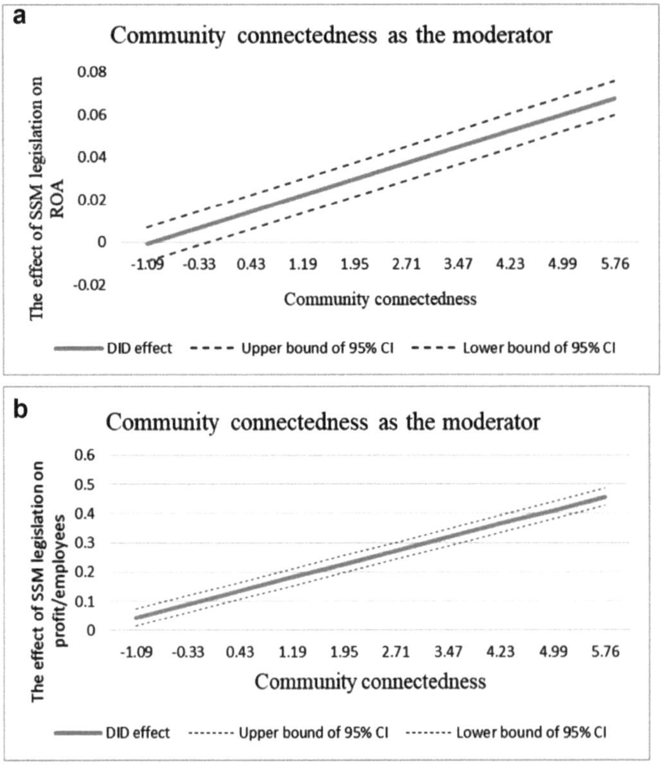

Fig. 5.1 A and B: Community connectedness as moderator

0.05). We thus found support for Hypothesis 3. In addition, result in column 1 of Table 5.5 indicates that, for industry masculinity, the marginal effect of passage of SSM is associated with a 0.8% increase in ROA. Figure 5.2 illustrates the moderating effect of industry masculinity on the SSM-Firm performance link. Given that our measure of industry masculinity is a binary indicator, we drew bar charts in Fig. 5.2a and 5.2b, which show that the effect of SSM on firm performance is stronger in more masculine industries.

Table 5.6 provides the results of difference-in-difference analysis for testing Hypothesis 4. Model 1 and 2 respectively tested the moderating effect of organizational pro-LGBTQ climate on the link between SSM and ROA and SSM and profit per 100 employees. Hypothesis 4 suggests that the positive effect of SSM legislation on firm performance is stronger for organizations with a weaker pro-LGBTQ climate. As shown in Table 5.6, for ROA the interaction effect is negative and significant ($b = -0.026$, $p < 0.01$), and non-significant (– 0.140, ns) for profit per 100 employees. We thus found partial support for Hypothesis 4. In addition, the result in column 1 of Table 5.6 indicates that, with a one-standard deviation decrease in organizational pro-LGBTQ climate, the marginal effect of passage of

Table 5.5 Difference-in-difference analysis results for testing hypothesis 3 regarding the moderating effect of industry masculinity

Independent variables	Dependent variables	
	Return on assets	Profit/employee
	(2)	(1)
Intercept	−1.777*** (−88.163)	−3.876*** (−7.956)
State LGBTQ regulation	0.003*** (3.353)	0.001 (0.100)
State GDP growth rate	0.061** (2.189)	0.082 (0.322)
Firm size	0.094*** (88.821)	0.213*** (8.089)
Book leverage	−0.221*** (−52.697)	−0.746*** (−4.302)
Capital expenditure	−0.042*** (−3.021)	0.207 (0.718)
Payout ratio	0.004 (0.203)	0.847* (1.895)
R&D intensity	−0.426*** (−83.848)	−2.526*** (−16.517)
Asset tangibility	0.092*** (18.106)	0.184* (1.849)
SSM	0.009*** (3.072)	0.042** (2.158)
Industry Masculinity	Absorbed	absorbed
SSM × Industry Masculinity	0.008*	0.219**
	(1.912)	(2.227)
Year fixed effects	Yes	Yes
Firm fixed effects	Yes	Yes
Clustered standard errors	State	State
Observations	105,767	105,767
F-statistic	1009.14***	91.22***
Adjusted *R*-squared	0.711	0.625

Note *t* statistics are in parentheses. Industry masculinity (IM) is absorbed in firm fixed effects, because for the same firm IM does not change over time. It takes a very long period for IM to change. * $p < 0.10$, ** $p < 0.05$, *** $p < 0.01$; $N = 105{,}767$

SSM is associated with a 0.8% increase in ROA. Figure 5.3 shows the moderating effect of organizational pro-LGBTQ climate on the relationship between SSM and ROA. Figure 5.3 indicates that the effect of SSM legislation on ROA is positive and decreases with increases in the level of organizational pro-LGBTQ climate.

Fig. 5.2 A and B: Industry masculinity as moderator

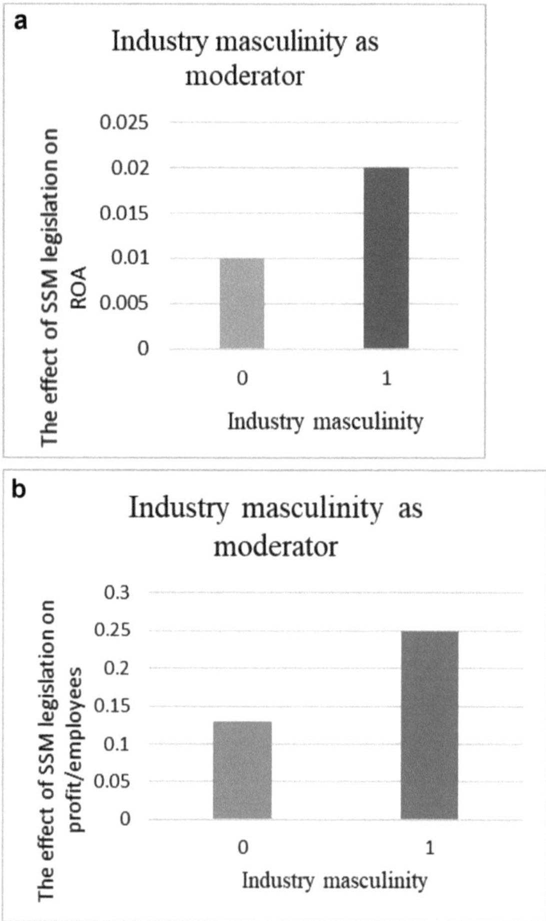

Although difference-in-difference approach allows us to treat the staggered passage of SSM legislation in states as exogenous shocks and draw causal inference, it is based on the assumption that all firms in our sample follow a parallel trend in the absence of the treatment (i.e., the passage of SSM legislation in the firm's headquarters state). Therefore, to further ensure the robustness of our findings, we adopted propensity score matching (PSM) method to form a sample of treated firms and untreated firms. The PSM method (Dehejia & Wahba, 2002) has been widely adopted to pair treatment and nontreatment groups on a set of observable characteristics and obtain consistent estimates of the treatment effect (e.g., Bharath et al., 2011). We implemented PSM method in a two-step procedure. In the first step, we employed a probit model to perform a 1-to-5 match for all firms in the treatment group with firms in the control group. We included all variables in models 1 and 2 (i.e., columns 1 and 2 in Table 5.3) for the first-step probit model, which yielded a log-likelihood of –7,967.56 and a McFadden's pseudo R-squared

Table 5.6 Difference-in-difference analysis results for testing hypothesis 4 regarding the moderating effect of organizational pro-lgbtq climate.

Independent variables	Dependent variables	
	Return on assets	Profit/employees
	(1)	(2)
Intercept	−0.088** (2.194)	−0.941 (1.719)
State LGBTQ regulation	0.005*** (3.482)	0.021 −0.972
State GDP growth rate	0.036 (0.670)	0.337 −0.461
Firm size	0.001 (0.683)	0.007 (0.316)
Book leverage	−0.201*** (−7.953)	−1.012*** (−6.622)
Capital expenditure	−0.075 (−1.387)	−1.286* (−1.744)
Payout ratio	0.410*** (5.998)	2.812*** (2.996)
R&D intensity	−0.769*** (−11.135)	−6.095*** (−6.489)
Asset tangibility	0.042 (0.803)	0.050*** (2.633)
SSM	0.012*** (3.453)	0.009* (1.837)
Org. pro-LGBTQ climate	0.032** (2.294)	0.235** (2.132)
SSM × Org. pro-LGBTQ climate	−0.026*** (−2.100)	−0.140 (−1.319)
Year fixed effects	Yes	Yes
Firm fixed effects	Yes	Yes
Clustered standard errors	State	State
Observations	5,492	5,492
F-statistic	30.36***	12.94***
Adjusted *R*-squared	0.514	0.377

Note t statistics are in parentheses. * $p < 0.10$, ** $p < 0.05$, *** $p < 0.01$. $N = 5492$

of 0.22. The firms in the treatment group is 21 percent of all sample firms. Following Veall and Zimmermann (1996), we compared the prediction accuracy of our model (0.84) with a blind guess (0.79) by calculating $\lambda' = (0.84 - 0.79)/(1 - 0.79) = 0.24$, which reveals a significant 24 percent improvement (Hoetker, 2007). These statistics indicate appropriateness of the choice of independent variables and the overall fit of the probit model. In the second step, we re-ran our DID regression

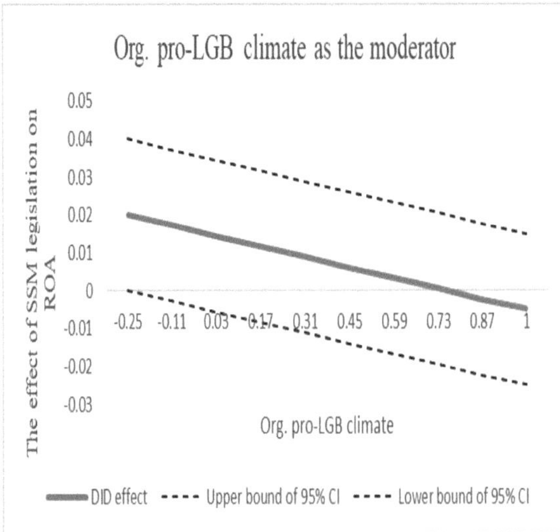

Fig. 5.3 Organizational pro-lgb climate as moderator

using the propensity-score-matched sample. The results reported in columns 3 and 4 of Table 5.3 are consistent with the previous DID results reported in columns 1 and 2 for testing Hypothesis 1. In addition, we conducted 1-to-1 match and 1-to-10 match as robustness checks and found qualitatively similar results. In summary, results reported in Table 5.3 lend strong support for Hypothesis 1.

We also note that during the study period a firm may have moved from one state that has legalized same sex marriage to one that hasn't, or vice versa. We therefore ran additional tests relating firm performance to time-series change of state SSM legislation to make sure our findings accounted for any changes in firm headquarter locations in the study sample. We utilized historic data on headquarters states of our sample firms to identify any firms that had shifted their headquarters during the study period. Following Garmaise (2011), we created a variable named SSM increase that can take 3 values: −1 (headquarters relocated from a state that has adopted SSM legislation to one that hasn't), 0 (no change in headquarters state or the SSM legislation remains the same before and after the change in headquarters state), and +1 (headquarters relocated from a state that hasn't adopted SSM legislation to one that has). We used this variable to capture the time-series change of state SSM legislation as a result of relocation of a firm's headquarters. We modeled firm performance as a function of SSM increase along with a set of control variables. We excluded firm fixed effects from this model because the states of firm headquarters are relatively stable, and inclusion of firm fixed effects in our regression specification would have created near-perfect multicollinearity problem. The results in Table 5.7 indicate that shifting to a state with adoption of SSM legislation is positively associated with firm performance, which is consistent with our main findings.

Table 5.7 Does relocation of firm headquarters matter?

Independent variables	Dependent variables	
	Return on assets	Profit/employees
	(1)	(2)
Intercept	−5.587** (−2.135)	−0.366*** (−31.891)
State LGBTQ regulation	0.008 (0.712)	0.001 (1.074)
State GDP growth rate	0.254 (0.965)	0.566 (1.232)
Firm size	0.261** (2.206)	0.020*** (38.915)
Book leverage	−0.245* (−1.857)	−0.095*** (−16.432)
Capital expenditure	−0.156* (−1.787)	−0.096*** (−2.718)
Payout ratio	0.493** (2.126)	0.279*** (6.419)
R&D intensity	−0.195* (1.781)	−0.200*** (−5.057)
Asset tangibility	0.601 (0.763)	0.032*** (3.878)
SSM Increase	0.013* (1.872)	0.013*** (2.733)
Year fixed effects	Yes	Yes
Firm fixed effects	No	No
Clustered standard errors	State	State
Observations	53,726	53,726
F-statistic	30.795***	316.65***
Adjusted R-squared	0.141	0.221

Note t statistics are in parentheses
$^{*}p < 0.10$, $^{**}p < 0.05$, $^{***}p < 0.01$

5.2.5 Discussion

Findings of this study establish that legalization of SSM leads to enhancements in performance of firms headquartered in that state. SSM legislation likely makes employees feel included, accepted, and appreciated, which shows up in the improved firm performance. However, these effects are not universal. We adapted Jones' (1972) framework in the context of heterosexism to investigate 2 contingency factors from the external environment of the firm: connectedness of the communities from which the firm draws its human capital, and masculinity of the industry in which the firm competes, and one contingency factor from the internal environment of the firm: the firm's pro-LGBTQ climate. We chose these 3 factors because they manifest as a form of heterosexism in societal institutions—community connectedness at the highest societal-cultural level, industry masculinity at the middle institutional level, and organizational pro-LGBTQ climate at the individual level. We found that the effects of SSM legislation were stronger in more connected communities and more masculine industries. In firms with high pro-LGBTQ climate the law's effects were not strong. In other words, when the external environment is not supportive of same sex marriage, the legal change goes a long way in improving employee productivity and firm performance. In tightly connected communities or in masculine industries where the norms are against same sex marriage, SSM legislation increases tolerance and acceptance. On the other hand, in loosely connected communities or less masculine industries the norms are not clear or strong for or against SSM, so the effects of SSM law are not that visible. Similarly, in a firm with low pro-LGBTQ climate the effects of law are more obvious because employees likely feel the need for protection provided by the law.

These findings contribute to literatures on employee stigmas (Goffman, 1963; Ragins, 2008) and diversity management (Cha & Roberts, 2019; Konrad et al., 2016; Roh & Kim, 2016). The impact of legislation on organizational behavior has been catching scholarly interest in last few years (Chuang et al., 2018). Legislation may impact firm activities in multiple ways by causing a switch in employment structures, wage structures, employee relations, and employee working conditions (Walmsley et al., 2019). Scholars argue that government laws are a critical component of a firm's external environment; however, it's not clear how a law not directly related to a firm's line of business can have an impact on its outcomes. We establish this link by investigating increases in firm performance upon passage of SSM law in its home state. Moreover, we theorized and showed that legislation favoring stigmatized individuals is not a blessing for all LGBTQ individuals alike. The effects of law are dependent on several other factors arising from social norms, industry type, and organizational climate. We advance research on stigmas (Dovidio et al., 2000; Goffman, 1963). Employees can be stigmatized based on their sexual and gender minority status (Fu, 2017; Ragins, 2004). We show that social legislation directed towards such stigmatized individuals may also have an impact on their workplace productivity contingent upon a number of factors at the societal-cultural, institutional, and individual firm level. We hope our study will advance research on the business case of marriage equality and further highlight the role of such stigmatized employees as an important source of a firm's human capital.

5.2.5.1 Strengths, Limitations, and Future Research

Our research design incorporated longitudinal data on performance from a large number of firms. Moreover, the 50 states of the U.S. and D.C. passed the SSM law at different times, and the variability afforded us a natural experiment to investigate the causal relationship between the legislation and firm outcomes. We used a generalized difference-in-difference (DID) approach (Ashenfelter & Card, 1984) to explore the impact of the legalization of same sex marriage on firm performance. DID is the correct approach to study the association between policy or law changes and subsequent outcomes, because simply looking at the outcomes before and after the change is subject to time trend problem, for the observed outcome differences could be due to the uniqueness of the sample period, such as business cycles. By adding a control group that experiences the same time trends as the treatment group but isn't exposed to the policy/law change being studied, one can capture the time trend effects by calculating the outcome differences before and after the policy change for the control group. The policy effect then is the difference between the respective outcome difference before and after the policy change between a treatment and a control group. Another strength of the study is our extensive use of theory-backed control variables. Finally, our use of both social and financial indicators of firm performance in the form of labor productivity and return on equity, and additional analyses to check robustness of study findings boost confidence in our results.

Despite these strengths the study is not without limitations. We argued that SSM law makes employees feel more accepted and included; however, our research design did not include primary data collection from employees to assess these perceptions of inclusion. Future scholars may design studies with both primary and secondary data collections to explore various mediational mechanisms underlying the link between SSM laws and firm performance. In addition, by implementing DID approach, we are only able to test the mean effect of SSM legislation on firm performance. It is equally important to explore the variation of such effect so that we can better understand the contingencies as to when and why the regulatory change may have a stronger effect for some firms. Further, we tested our theoretical arguments using a sample of U.S. firms alone. This limits the generalizability of our claims. With different countries passing marriage equality legislation, future research can test the applicability of our model across different country samples. Scholars can also examine the cultural and social norms existing in these countries where marriage equality legislation is passed. For example, western countries with an individualistic culture may have a different response to passage of marriage equality legislation compared to countries which are high on collectivism.

5.2.5.2 Managerial Implications

Our findings have implications for managers and policy makers. Findings of the study attest to long-term effects of SSM legislation and discourage any questions on legitimacy of the law itself. If ever there is any talk of overturning this law, or if one of the 50 states of the U.S. decide to do away with this law, findings of the study will serve as a reminder that the law does not have just intangible benefits such as employee happiness, but also tangible benefits in the form of firm performance.

Policy makers and managers also need to recognize that passage of law is only the first step; community, industry, and firm level factors set boundaries to the positive effects of the law. Policy makers need to take this in account and design programs of training and monitoring so the positive effects of SSM legislation can be reaped by all firms.

5.2.6 Conclusion

Although, past research has examined the impact of legislation and regulatory structures on important organizational outcomes, limited understanding exists of the impact of social legislation on business outcomes along with the factors that might influence this relationship. We build the business case for social legislation and test it in the context of marriage equality. We also outline and examine the contingency factors impacting the effect of marriage equality legislation on firm performance. We hope our findings will advance future discussion on the influence of cultural, occupational, and organizational norms and beliefs and the role they play in shaping the impact of social legislation on organizational outcomes.

Acknowledgements This chapter is based on the article previously published as: Wang, Jianrong, Smriti Anand, Hui Li, and Wei Du. "Marriage equality for everyone? The business case for same sex marriage legislation." *Journal of Business Research* 148 (2022): 190–202. https://doi.org/10.1016/j.jbusres.2022.04.021

Reprinted with permission from *Journal of Business Research.*

References

Amir, E., Guan, Y., & Livne, G. (2007). The association of R&D and capital expenditures with subsequent earnings variability. *Journal of Business Finance & Accounting, 34*(1–2), 222–246.

Anand, S., Hasan, I., Sharma, P., & Wang, H. (2018). State enforceability of noncompete agreements: Regulations that stifle productivity! *Human Resource Management, 57*(1), 341–354.

Anderson, E. D. (2009). The maintenance of masculinity among the stakeholders of sport. *Sport Management Review, 12*(1), 3–14.

Ashenfelter, O., & Card, D. (1984). *Using the longitudinal structure of earnings to estimate the effect of training programs* (National Bureau of Economic Research).

Bakker, A. B., van Emmerik, H., & Euwema, M. C. (2006). Crossover of burnout and engagement in work teams. *Work and Occupations, 33*(4), 464–489.

Bertrand, M., Duflo, E., & Mullainathan, S. (2004). How much should we trust differences-in-differences estimates? *The Quarterly Journal of Economics, 119*(1), 249–275.

Bertrand, M., & Mullainathan, S. (2003). Enjoying the quiet life? Corporate governance and managerial preferences. *Journal of Political Economics, 111*(5), 1043–1075.

Bérubé, A. (2011). 'Queer work' and labor history. In J. D'Emilio & E. B. Freedman (Eds.), *My desire for history: Essays in gay, community, and labor history* (pp. 259–269). University of North Carolina Press.

Bharath, S. T., Dahiya, S., Saunders, A., & Srinivasan, A. (2011). Lending relationships and loan contract terms. *Review of Financial Studies, 24*(4), 1141–1203.

Black, S. E., & Strahan, P. E. (2002). Entrepreneurship and bank credit availability. *The Journal of Finance, 57*(6), 2807–2833.

Blake, P. (2015). *US Supreme Court rules gay marriage is legal nationwide.* https://www.bbc.com/news/world-us-canada-33290341

BLS. (2015). *Labor force statistics from the current population survey*. https://www.bls.gov/cps/cpsaat18.htm

Brownen-Trinh, R. (2019). Effects of winsorization: The cases of forecasting non-GAAP and GAAP earnings. *Journal of Business Finance & Accounting, 46*(1–2), 105–135.

Catalyst. (2018). *Lesbian, gay, bisexual, and transgender workplace issues*. https://www.catalyst.org/knowledge/lesbian-gay-bisexual-transgender-workplace-issues

Cha, S. E., & Roberts, L. M. (2019). Leveraging minority identities at work: An individual-level framework of the identity mobilization process. *Organization Science, 30*(4), 735–760.

Chuang, Y.-T., Church, R., & Hu, C. (2018). Effects of movements and opportunities on the adoption of same-sex partner health benefits by corporations. *Journal of Management, 44*(7), 2766–2800.

Clair, J. A., Beatty, J. E., & Maclean, T. L. (2005). Out of sight but not out of mind: Managing invisible social identities in the workplace. *Academy of Management Review, 30*(1), 78–95.

Collins, J. C. (2013). Stress and safety for gay men at work within masculinized industries. *Journal of Gay & Lesbian Social Services, 25*(3), 245–268.

Crocker, J., & Major, B. (1989). Social stigma and self-esteem: The self-protective properties of stigma. *Psychological Review, 96*(4), 608–630.

Crocker, J., Major, B., & Steele, C. (1998). Social stigma. *Handbook of Social Psychology* (Vols 1–2 4th ed., pp. 504–553). McGraw-Hill.

Conti, R., Kacperczyk, A. J., & Valentini, G. (2018). Discrimination and entrepreneurship: Evidence from LGBT rights laws. *Academy of Management Proceedings* 2018.

Dahling, J. J., Wiley, S., Fishman, Z. A, et al. (2016). A stake in the fight: When do heterosexual employees resist organizational policies that deny marriage equality to LGB peers? *Organizational Behavior and Human Decision Processes, 132*.

Dehejia, R. H., & Wahba, S. (2002). Propensity score-matching methods for nonexperimental causal studies. *The Review of Economics and Statistics, 84*(1), 151–161.

Dovidio, J. F., Major, B., & Crocker, J. (2000). Stigma: Introduction and overview. *The Social Psychology of Stigma* (pp. 1–28). Guilford Press.

Drydakis, N. (2015). Sexual orientation discrimination in the United Kingdom's labour market: A field experiment. *Human Relations, 68*(11), 1769–1796.

Duhigg, J. M., Rostosky, S. S., Gray, B. E., et al. (2010). Development of heterosexuals into sexual-minority allies: A qualitative exploration. *Sexuality Research and Social Policy, 7*(1), 2–14. https://doi.org/10.1007/s13178-010-0005-2

Duncan, R. B. (1972). Characteristics of organizational environments and perceived environmental uncertainty. *Administrative Science Quarterly, 17*(3), 313–327.

Ely, R. J., & Thomas, D. A. (2001). Cultural diversity at work: The effects of diversity perspectives on work group processes and outcomes. *Administrative Science Quarterly, 46*(2), 229–273.

Erez, M., & Gati, E. (2004). A dynamic, multi-level model of culture: From the micro level of the individual to the macro level of a global culture. *Applied Psychology, 53*(4), 583–598.

Everly, B. A., & Schwarz, J. L. (2015). Predictors of the adoption of LGBT-friendly HR policies. *Human Resource Management, 54*(2), 367–384.

Fenn, G. W., & Liang, N. (2001). Corporate payout policy and managerial stock incentives. *Journal of financial economics, 60*(1), 45–72.

Flammer, C., & Kacperczyk, A. (2016). The impact of stakeholder orientation on innovation: Evidence from a natural experiment. *Management Science, 62*(7), 1982–2001.

Fu, L. (2017, June 25). *LGBTQ workers still face legal discrimination*. http://fortune.com/2017/06/25/lgbtq-employment-discrimination/

Garmaise, M. J. (2011). Ties that truly bind: Non-competition agreements, executive compensation and firm investment. *Journal of Law, Economics and Organization, 27*(2), 376–425.

Gao, H., & Zhang, W. (2017). Employment nondiscrimination acts and corporate innovation. *Management Science, 63*(9), 2982–2999.

Gelfand, M. J., Raver, J. L., Nishii, L., et al. (2011). Differences between tight and loose cultures: A 33-nation study. *Science, 332*(6033), 1100–1104.

Girma, S., Görg, H., & Strobl, E. (2004). Exports, international investment, and plant performance: Evidence from a non-parametric test. *Economics Letters, 83*(3), 317–324.
Goffman, E. (1963). *Stigma: Notes on the management of spoiled identity*. Simon and Schuster.
Grullon, G., & Michaely, R. (2002). Dividends, share repurchases, and the substitution hypothesis. *Journal of Finance, 57*(4), 1649–1684.
Guest, D. E., Michie, J., Conway, N., et al. (2003). Human resource management and corporate performance in the UK. *British Journal of Industrial Relations, 41*(2), 291–314.
Hasan, I., Hoi, C. K., Wu, Q., et al. (2017). Social capital and debt contracting: Evidence from bank loans and public bonds. *Journal of Financial and Quantitative Analysis, 52*(3), 1017–1047.
Herek, G. M., Berrill, K. T., & Berrill, K. (1992). *Hate crimes: Confronting violence against lesbians and gay men*. SAGE.
Huffman, A. H., Watrous-Rodriguez, K. M., & King, E. B. (2008). Supporting a diverse workforce: What type of support is most meaningful for lesbian and gay employees? *Human Resource Management, 47*(2), 237–253.
Human Rights Campaign Foundation. (2015). *Corporate equality index: On gay, lesbian, bisexual and transgender social responsibility*. Retrieved November 7, 2015 from http://hrc-assets.s3-website-us-east-1.amazonaws.com/files/documents/CEI-2015rev.pdf
Human Rights Watch. (2018, February 18). *United States: State laws threaten LGBT equality 'License to discriminate' bills imperil access to services.*
Huynh, K. P., & Petrunia, R. J. (2010). Age effects, leverage and firm growth. *Journal of Economic Dynamics and Control, 34*(5), 1003–1013.
Jayaratne, J., & Strahan, P. E. (1996). The finance-growth nexus: Evidence from bank branch deregulation. *Quarterly Journal of Economics, 111*(3), 639–670.
Jennings, J. E., & McDougald, M. S. (2007). Work-family interface experiences and coping strategies: Implications for entrepreneurship research and practice. *Academy of Management Review, 32*(3), 747–760.
Jha, A., & Chen, Y. (2015). Audit fees and social capital. *The Accounting Review, 90*(2), 611–639.
Johnston, D., & Malina, M. A. (2008). Managing sexual orientation diversity: The impact on firm value. *Group & Organization Management, 33*(5), 602–625.
Jones, J. M. (1972). *Prejudice and racism*. Addison-Wesley.
Kail, B. L., Acosta, K. L., & Wright, E. R. (2015). State-Level marriage equality and the health of same-sex couples. *American Journal of Public Health, 105*(6), 1101–1105.
Kaplan, D. M., & Berkley, R. A. (2021). Promoting LGBT inclusion and scholarship: using the human rights campaigns corporate equality index. *Handbook on Diversity and Inclusion Indices,* 202–218.
Kertzner, R. M., Meyer, I. H., Frost, D. M., et al. (2009). Social and psychological well-being in lesbians, gay men, and bisexuals: The effects of race, gender, age, and sexual identity. *American Journal of Orthopsychiatry, 79*(4), 500–510.
King, E. B., Mohr, J. J., Peddie, C. I., et al. (2017). Predictors of identity management: An exploratory experience-sampling study of lesbian, gay, and bisexual workers. *Journal of Management, 43*(2), 476–502.
Kanuer, N. (2010). *Gay and lesbian elders: History, law and identity politics in the United States* (1st ed.). Routledge.
Konrad, A. M., Yang, Y., & Maurer, C. C. (2016). Antecedents and outcomes of diversity and equality management systems. *Human Resource Management, 55*(1), 83–107.
Li, F., & Nagar, V. (2012). Diversity and performance. *Management Science, 59*(3), 529–544.
Linstead, S. A., & Maréchal, G. (2015). Re-reading masculine organization: Phallic, testicular and seminal metaphors. *Human Relations, 68*(9), 1461–1489.
Liptak, A. (2020, July 8). Job bias laws do not protect teachers in catholic schools, supreme Court rules. *New York Times*. https://www.nytimes.com/2020/07/08/us/job-bias-catholic-schools-supreme-court.html
Maertz, C. P., & Boyar, S. L. (2011). Work-family conflict, enrichment, and balance under "levels" and "episodes" approaches. *Journal of Management, 37*(1), 68–98.

Martinez, L. R., & Hebl, M. R. (2010). Additional agents of change in promoting lesbian, gay, bisexual, and transgendered inclusiveness in organizations. *Industrial and Organizational Psychology-Perspectives on Science and Practice, 3*(1), 82–85.

Miller, S. L., Forest, K. B., & Jurik, N. C. (2003). Diversity in blue: Lesbian and gay police officers in a masculine occupation. *Men and Masculinities, 5*(4), 355–385.

Nishii, L. H. (2013). The benefits of climate for inclusion for gender-diverse groups. *Academy of Management Journal, 56*(6), 1754–1774.

Pescosolido, B. A., & Martin, J. K. (2015). The stigma complex. *Annual Review of Sociology, 41*(1), 87–116.

Plug, E., Webbink, D., & Martin, N. (2014). Sexual orientation, prejudice, and segregation. *Journal of Labor Economics, 32*(1), 123–159.

Ragins, B. R. (2004). Sexual orientation in the workplace: The unique work and career experiences of gay, lesbian and bisexual workers. In *Research in personnel and human resources management* (pp. 35–120). 23. Emerald Group Publishing Limited.

Ragins, B. R. (2008). Disclosure disconnects: Antecedents and consequences of disclosing invisible stigmas across life domains. *Academy of Management Review, 33*(1), 194–215.

Ragins, B. R., & Cornwell, J. M. (2001). Pink triangles: Antecedents and consequences of perceived workplace discrimination against gay and lesbian employees. *Journal of Applied Psychology, 86*(6), 1244–1261.

Repetti, R., Wang, S., & Saxbe, D. (2009). Bringing it all back home: How outside stressors shape families' everyday lives. *Current Directions in Psychological Science, 18*(2), 106–111.

Riggle, E. D. B., Rostosky, S. S., Black, W. W., et al. (2017). Outness, concealment, and authenticity: Associations with LGB individuals' psychological distress and well-being. *Psychology of Sexual Orientation and Gender Diversity, 4*(1), 54–62.

Roh, H., & Kim, E. (2016). The business case for gender diversity: Examining the role of human resource management investments. *Human Resource Management, 55*(3), 519–534.

Roussin, C. J., MacLean, T. L., & Rudolph, J. W. (2016). The safety in unsafe teams: A multilevel approach to team psychological safety. *Journal of Management, 42*(6), 1409–1433.

Rupasingha, A., Goetz, S. J., & Freshwater, D. (2006). The production of social capital in US counties. *The Journal of Socio-Economics, 35*(1), 83–101.

Sánchez, F. J., Greenberg, S. T., Liu, W. M., et al. (2009). Reported effects of masculine ideals on gay men. *Psychology of Men & Masculinity, 10*(1), 73–87.

Savage, D. G., & Phelps, T. M. (2015, June 26). Supreme court ruling: 'Equal dignity in the eyes of the law.' *The Seattle Times*. https://www.seattletimes.com/nation-world/supreme-court-extends-same-sex-marriage-nationwide/

Schein, E. H. (1990). *Organizational culture* (Vol. 45, No. 2, p. 109). American Psychological Association.

Schein, E. H. (1992). *Organizational culture and leadership*. Jossey-Bass.

Schneider, B., & Reichers, A. E. (1983). On the etiology of climates. *Personnel Psychology, 36*(1), 19–39.

Shan, L., Fu, S., & Zheng, L. (2017). Corporate sexual equality and firm performance. *Strategic Management Journal, 38*(9), 1812–1826.

Smith, N. G., & Ingram, K. M. (2004). Workplace heterosexism and adjustment among lesbian, gay, and bisexual individuals: The role of unsupportive social interactions. *Journal of Counseling Psychology, 51*(1), 57–67.

Stan, M., & Puranam, P. (2017). Organizational adaptation to interdependence shifts: The role of integrator structures. *Strategic Management Journal, 38*(5), 1041–1061.

Summers, J. K., Howe, M., McElroy, J. C., Buckley, M. R., Pahng, P., & Cortes-Mejia, S. (2018). A typology of stigma within organizations: Access and treatment effects. *Journal of Organizational Behavior, 39*(7), 853–868.

Tasheva, S., & Hillman, A. J. (2019). Integrating diversity at different levels: Multilevel human capital, social capital, and demographic diversity and their implications for team effectiveness. *Academy of Management Review, 44*(4), 746–765.

Tilcsik, A., Anteby, M., & Knight, C. R. (2015). Concealable stigma and occupational segregation: Toward a theory of gay and lesbian occupations. *Administrative Science Quarterly, 60*(3), 446–481.

United States Department of Labor Women's Bureau. (2014). *Nontraditional (Male-Dominated) Occupations, 2014 Annual Averages.*

Vakili, K., & Zhang, L. (2018). High on creativity: The impact of social liberalization policies on innovation. *Strategic Management Journal, 39*(7), 1860–1886.

van Hooff, M. L. M., Geurts, S. A. E., Kompier, M. A. J., et al. (2006). Work–home interference: How does it manifest itself from day to day? *Work & Stress, 20*(2), 145–162.

Van Laer, K. (2018). The role of co-workers in the production of (homo)sexuality at work: A Foucauldian approach to the sexual identity processes of gay and lesbian employees. *Human Relations, 71*(2), 229–255.

Veall, M. R., & Zimmermann, K. F. (1996). Pseudo-R2 measures for some common limited dependent variable models. *Journal of Economic Surveys, 10*(3), 241–259.

Walmsley, A., Partington, S., Armstrong, R., et al. (2019). Reactions to the national living wage in hospitality. *Employee Relations, 41*(1), 253–268.

Wang, H., Zhao, S., & He, J. (2016). Increase in takeover protection and firm knowledge accumulation strategy. *Strategic Management Journal, 37*(12), 2393–2412.

Wang, P., & Schwarz, J. L. (2010). Stock price reactions to GLBT nondiscrimination policies. *Human Resource Management, 49*(2), 195–216.

Webster, J. R., Adams, G. A., Maranto, C. L., et al. (2018). Workplace contextual supports for LGBT employees: A review, meta-analysis, and agenda for future research. *Human Resource Management, 57*(1), 193–210. https://doi.org/10.1002/hrm.21873

Westman, M. (2001). Stress and strain crossover. *Human Relations, 54*(6), 717–751.

Westman, M., Brough, P., & Kalliath, T. (2009). Expert commentary on work–life balance and crossover of emotions and experiences: Theoretical and practice advancements. *Journal of Organizational Behavior, 30*(5), 587–595.

Willis, P. (2012). Witnesses on the periphery: Young lesbian, gay, bisexual and queer employees witnessing homophobic exchanges in Australian workplaces. *Human Relations, 65*(12), 1589–1610.

Wootson Jr. C. R., & Somashekhar, S. (2017, April 19). A lesbian couple got their marriage license—After a county clerk called them an 'abomination.' *The Washington Post.*

Zagenczyk, T. J., Powell, E. E., & Scott, K. L. (2020). How exhausting!? Emotion crossover in organizational social networks. *Journal of Management Studies, 57*(8), 1589–1609.

Part II

ESG and Financial Markets: Real Effects

ESG Adoption and Corporate Risk-Taking

6

6.1 Introduction: ESG and the Dynamic Risk

In recent years, the relationship between corporate social responsibility (ESG) and firm risk-taking has gained considerable scholarly attention. As ESG frameworks continue to influence corporate strategy and investor expectations, an important question arises: how do firms' environmental, social, and governance actions shape their overall risk profile and affect managerial risk-taking behavior? While ESG is often associated with reputational capital and long-term value preservation, its influence on financial and operational risk exposure remains multifaceted and nuanced.

Classical theories of corporate risk-taking emphasize agency costs, risk aversion, managerial incentives, and capital constraints. In this tradition, risk-taking is both an opportunity and a liability: firms must pursue value-enhancing investments that carry uncertainty while simultaneously managing downside exposure. ESG adds a new layer to this decision-making calculus. By investing in socially responsible practices, firms may be seen as reducing exposure to idiosyncratic and systemic risks, such as regulatory sanctions, environmental disasters, supply chain disruption, labor unrest, and governance failures. At the same time, ESG engagement may constrain managerial discretion, influence firm culture, or alter risk preferences—either amplifying or moderating risk-taking tendencies depending on institutional context and firm characteristics.

Empirical research has begun to map out these complex relationships. On one hand, several studies suggest that ESG reduces firm-specific risk. For example, Albuquerque et al. (2014) show that firms with high ESG performance experience lower stock return volatility. Similarly, Lins et al. (2017) find that social capital built through ESG served as a buffer during the 2008–2009 financial crisis. ESG actions may thus serve as a form of risk insurance by building stakeholder trust and mitigating the severity of adverse events.

J. Wang, *ESG Strategies and Financial Markets*, Management for Professionals,
https://doi.org/10.1007/978-981-95-5620-5_6

On the other hand, ESG is not inherently risk-reducing. While its adoption can generate reputational benefits and stakeholder goodwill, it may also create overconfidence in managerial decision-making or encourage inefficient capital allocation—particularly when ESG efforts are symbolic rather than substantive. Some studies indicate that ESG-oriented firms may engage in more exploratory innovation and undertake riskier R&D investments, suggesting that sustainability commitments do not uniformly translate into risk aversion (Bae et al., 2021). Furthermore, the effects of ESG adoption are not homogenous across all categories of risk. For example, ESG actions may reduce market risk by lowering firms' exposure to tail events and enhancing investor perceptions, thereby decreasing overall market beta. In the context of liquidity risk, firms with strong ESG engagement may benefit from improved stakeholder relationships and better access to capital, which helps alleviate refinancing constraints and stabilize cash flows. Operational risk may also be mitigated through robust environmental and labor practices that enhance supply chain resilience and reduce the frequency of disruptions. When it comes to legal and regulatory risk, effective governance and proactive compliance with regulations can reduce the probability of litigation, regulatory fines, and enforcement actions. Lastly, reputational risk is often attenuated when firms engage in transparent ESG disclosures and demonstrate meaningful engagement with social issues, thereby lowering the impact of negative publicity and stakeholder backlash.

Taken together, the evolving literature suggests that the relationship between ESG and firm risk is not unidirectional but contingent on the type of risk under consideration, the firm's industry and institutional context, and the authenticity of ESG practices. Thus, understanding ESG's role in risk-taking behavior requires careful empirical investigation grounded in specific risk dimensions.

In general, there are consensuses over the negative association between CSR activities and firm risk.

Luo and Bhattacharya (2009) develop a theoretical framework that predicts the corporate social performance helps reduce firm idiosyncratic risk. In particular, from the risk management perspective, they argue that CSR initiatives generate the moral capital such as brand faith and credibility among customers and the other stakeholder groups, which serve as an insurance-like protection for firms. Firms with more moral capital may absorb more internal and external shocks, which in turn lower firm idiosyncratic risk by creating a reservoir of goodwill and mitigating negative stakeholder assessments. In this way, better CSP helps the firm build a bulwark against future loss of economic value, likely reducing the risk and vulnerability of future cash flows (Luo & Bhattacharya, 2009), therefore lower the idiosyncratic risk. In their empirical study, they measure idiosyncratic risk using daily stock return data and measure CSP with fortune's MAC source. The result indicates that CSP has a strong negative effect on idiosyncratic risk.

Based on the panel data ranging from 1991 to 2011, Cheung (2016a, 2016b) finds that CSR investment is negatively related to firm systematic risk and idiosyncratic risk, which is consistent with the finding in Luo and Bhattacharya (2009) and Albuquerque, Durnev, and Koskinen (2014). In particular, they measure CSR using the relative aggregation method extracted from KLD database and measure systematic risk and idiosyncratic risk using market model. They adopt the Maximum Likelihood (ML) method for the empirical model. Their findings are robust when accounting for the endogeneity and the alternative definition of CSR and firm risk.

Harjoto and Jo (2015) employ the sample of U.S. public firms during 1993 to 2009 and find that the CSR intensities may reduce the volatility of stock return, the cost of capital and increase firm value. In their study, they contrast the CSR actions that are required by law (legal CSR) and voluntary CSR (normative CSR). Based on the KLD database, they measure the overall CSR and classify the legal CSR and normative CSR. They find that CSR activities reduce the firm measured by stock return volatility. In addition, their findings indicate that the normative CSR has a lag effect on firm risk reduction compared with legal CSR given that the market analysts and the other participants will not be informed immediately if firms conduct the CSR activities not required by law.

Similarly, Cai et al. (2016) find the empirical evidence based on the U.S. public firms during 1991 to 2012 that corporate environmental responsibility(CER) engagement inversely affects firm risk after controlling for various firm characteristics. In their study, they only focus on one CSR category-the environment in KLD to measure the CER. They measure risk adopting CAMP model and Fama–French four factors model, as well as stock volatility. Results from the regression analysis indicate that CER engagement reduces firm risk.

Hsu and Chen (2015) examine the effect of CSR performance on firm financial risk based on a panel dataset of U.S. public firm from 1991 to 2012. They measure firm default risk following Merton Model and measure credit risk using firm's credit rating. They use the net score of CSR rating from KLD to measure firm CSR activities. Consistent with their hypotheses, they find evidence that good CSP help to reduce the credit risk and bankruptcy risk.

Kim et al. (2014) examine if the CSR can mitigate the stock price crash risk, which is the conditional skewness of return distribution. Engaging more CSR activities makes firms have a high standard of transparency and engage in less bad news hoarding, therefore lower the crash risk. In their study, they rely on MSCI ESG to measure CSR and employ two measures of firm-specific crash risk: the negative conditional skewness of firm-specific weekly returns over the fiscal year and the down-to-up volatility measure of the crash likelihood. After controlling factors that may affect future stock price crash risk, results show that CSR is negatively associated with crash risk. Their study indicates that firm with higher CSR score tends to have a lower future stock price crash risk.

Chang et al. (2014) aggregate different dimensions of CSR activities following the stakeholder framework and get the conclusion consistent with prior study that CSR has a unique impact on firm risk reduction. Especially, they differentiate CSR activities as institutional CSR and technical CSR and construct the longitudinal analysis based on S&P 500 firms over the period of 1995–2009. They find a negative link between institutional CSR and firm risk and such link is more salient in volatile markets and for firms with no social impact and high intangible assets (Chang et al., 2014).

Based on a sample of U.S. firms during 1998–2011, Harjoto and Laksmana (2016) measure CSR using the data from MSCI ESG (KLD) and adopt five measures to proxy corporate risk taking. They find that CSR performance is negatively associated with the deviations from optimal risk taking level. Their findings provide evidence that CSR can reduce excessive risk taking and risk avoidance.

This chapter contributes to this line of inquiry by examining the link between ESG and one critical yet understudied dimension of corporate risk: liquidity risk. In particular, we present the study titled "Environmental, Social, and Governance (ESG) and Firm Liquidity Risk: U.S. Evidence," which investigates how firms' ESG practices are associated with their ability to manage liquidity-related challenges. Liquidity risk—the risk that a firm may not be able to meet its short-term obligations or access external financing under stress—has become increasingly relevant in volatile financial environments.

Drawing on U.S. firm-level data, the featured study examines whether stronger ESG performance correlates with lower liquidity risk. It explores mechanisms through which ESG may enhance firm resilience: improved stakeholder trust, stronger relationships with creditors, and better access to capital markets. The study also tests whether the effect varies across ESG dimensions (environmental, social, and governance) and whether investor responses differ under constrained vs. unconstrained liquidity environments.

By analyzing how ESG commitments influence firms' exposure to liquidity shocks and refinancing pressure, this chapter advances our understanding of the risk-management value of sustainability practices. To provide a concrete empirical grounding for these theoretical insights, the remainder of this chapter presents the study titled "Corporate Social Responsibility and Firm Liquidity Risk: U.S. Evidence." This paper investigates whether ESG performance is associated with firms' exposure to liquidity risk, particularly in the context of short-term financing constraints and cash flow volatility. Drawing on U.S. firm-level data, the study explores the channels through which ESG can influence liquidity management, creditor perception, and investor response under varying financial conditions. Through this lens, the paper offers evidence on how sustainability practices extend beyond ethical signaling to materially affect firms' financial resilience in times of liquidity stress. It situates ESG within the broader discourse on corporate resilience, offering both theoretical insight and empirical evidence on how responsible business conduct may mitigate one of the most pressing financial risks firms face today.

6.2 Corporate Social Responsibility and Firm Liquidity Risk: U.S. Evidence

6.2.1 Introduction

Corporate social responsibility (CSR) has become an increasingly important component of the business practice of most US firms' operation over the last decade (Jo & Harjoto, 2011). Although scholars across different business disciplines have extensively examined the effects of CSR on firm financial performance, the results are largely inconclusive (Friede et al., 2015; Liu, 2006). An emerging line of research turns to look at the relationship between CSR and firm risk because firm risk can be an important mechanism through which CSR affects firm value. There is a large body of literature that documents a negative relationship between CSR and firm risk. The rationale behind these empirical observations is as follows: On the one hand, CSR can function as a tool for firms to engage in risk management and thus to mitigate the consequences of negative outcomes or unforeseen events. This effect is also known as "insurance-like" protection, which can be used to preserve firms' financial performance by generating moral capital or goodwill (Godfrey, 2005). For example, firms experiencing big challenges, lawsuits, or fines may face increased risk. The moral capital created by CSR can serve as a cushion to alleviate the adverse influence of such events on firms' cash flow (Sharfman & Fernando, 2008). On the other hand, CSR represents a transparent resource management that leads to the expected results including economic, political, social, and environmental. Therefore, the firms that engage into intensive CSR may not maximize their profit in the short term but are likely to become sustainable firms in the long term because of the "sustainable hand" which, within a market, seeks the social optimum (Datar et al., 1998; Mishra & Modi, 2013). In this case, CSR firms not only focus on profit maximization but also consider objectives and responsibilities in the social, environmental, ethical, and, of course, economic fields. The "sustainable hand" reallocates the resources to these firms optimally with the objective of seeking social optimum. Specifically, when there is a resources misallocation in the market, this "sustainable hand" will reallocate the scarce resources to those firms with intensive CSR engagements as these firms will lead to social optimum in the long run. This reallocation generated by the "sustainable hand" will help these CSR firms operate, develop, and hedge risk in the long run.

Liquidity risk measures how firm's stock returns will be affected by the shocks in market-wide aggregated liquidity, and it has been shown to be an independent source of systematic risk in empirical asset pricing literature (Acharya & Pedersen, 2005; Pástor & Stambaugh, 2003). The shortage of market liquidity may have a detrimental effect on the whole economic system and that is when "insurance" is expected to pay off. For example, the recent financial crisis is a liquidity crisis. The dry-out of liquidity and fear of recession cause large drops in the equity market globally. If CSR can provide "insurance-like" protection, it is natural to ask: Can CSR engagements protect firms from liquidity risk? If so, to what extent and through what channel does the moral capital created by CSR affect firm's liquidity risk? In this study, we focus on the relation between CSR and firm liquidity risk to add new evidence and shed further light on this line of research.

To test the relationship between firm's CSR and the liquidity risk, we define firm's liquidity risk as "liquidity betas". Mathematically, "liquidity betas" are the covariance between a firm's stock returns and market-wide liquidity shocks, and it has been shown that stocks with higher liquidity risk, represented by "liquidity betas", exhibit higher expected returns. Unlike the other risk metrics that have a consensus in their measurements, liquidity risk is a broad concept and one single measure cannot capture all aspects of liquidity risk. In this study, we employ two widely used market-wide liquidity (illiquidity) measures: Amihud's illiquidity measure (Amihud, 2002) and Pástor and Stambaugh's liquidity measure (Pástor & Stambaugh, 2003). These two measures are different in terms of their liquidity dimension: The former treats liquidity as asset's price pressure while the latter captures asset's price reversal. Our study finds evidence of a mitigating effect of CSR on firms' liquidity risk. Using a large sample of U.S. public firms from 1993 to 2018, we document a significantly negative relationship between CSR and the liquidity risk, indicating that socially responsible firms have lower liquidity risk. Our results are robust after controlling for firm-level characteristics including firm size, book-to-market ratio, financial leverage, ROA, capital expenditure, R&D, sales growth, and corporate governance. We also control for the liquidity level that may correlate with both of the CSR and the liquidity risk. We employ two-stage least square regression and dynamic Generalized Moment of Method (GMM) to control for the endogeneity issue. In addition, we examine an economic channel through which CSR could affect firm's liquidity risk. Firms with better CSR performance pay special attention to stakeholder's well-being, including banks and investors, who serve as important part of stakeholders. In addition, firms with better CSR performance represent higher financial and operation transparency, reinforcing bankers' and investors' trust during liquidity shortage periods. Both of these factors facilitate firms' access to capital from banks and investors, and thus these firms can maintain healthy cash flow for operation. As a consequence, stock returns of these firms will less likely to be affected negatively when market-wide liquidity experiences negative shocks. We find that the negative relationship between CSR and the liquidity risk to be more prominent for firms heavily relying on external capital finance.

6.2.2 Related Literature

Our research builds on to two strands of existing literature. First, our work relates to a growing literature that examines the effect of corporate socially responsibility (CSR) on risk. For example, Husted (2005) concludes that CSR is negatively associated with the firm's ex ante downside business risk; Harjoto and Jo (2015) find that CSR intensities reduce the volatility of stock return and the cost of capital and increase firm value; Kim et al. (2014) document a negative relationship between CSR and stock price crash risk owing to high-CSR firms committing to a high standard of financial and operation transparency and engaging in less bad-news hoarding; Hsu and Chen (2015) examine the effect of CSR performance on firm default risk, and they find evidence that good CSR helps to reduce the credit risk and bankruptcy risk; Cai et al. (2016) conclude that CSR engagement negatively affects firm risk proxied by several risk measures including CAPM beta, Fama–French market beta, standard deviation of daily stock returns, and downside risk; Lins et al. (2017) find that firms with high CSR intensity have higher stock returns during financial crisis as social capital pays off when market suffers a negative shock; Mishra and Modi (2013) contend that CSR has a significant effect on the idiosyncratic risk of firms, with positive CSR reducing risk and negative CSR increasing it; Harjoto and Laksmana (2018) find that CSR performance is negatively associated with the deviations from optimal risk-taking level; Albuquerque et al. (2019) provide a theoretical model predicting that CSR decreases systematic risk and the effects are prominent for firms with high product differentiation; El Ghoul et al. (2011) add new insight to this strand of literature by studying the relation between CSR and cost of equity. They point out that high-CSR firms have lower cost of equity than low-CSR firms as low-CSR firms have a reduced investor base and higher perceived risk; later, they extend their study by documenting a negative relationship between CSR and the cost of equity on a global basis (El Ghoul et al., 2018).

Liquidity has shown to be a priced state variable, and this risk-based view of liquidity has attracted much attention in past two decades, which has led to several studies confirming the pricing role of liquidity risk (Acharya & Pedersen, 2005; Pástor & Stambaugh, 2003). Scholars also propose an illiquidity measure and confirm the pricing role of the liquidity risk by showing that market-wide shocks in this illiquidity measure negatively affect contemporaneous realized returns (Amihud, 2002; Amihud & Noh, 2021). Watanabe and Watanabe (2008) examine how the pricing relationship varies across different economic states. Some studies investigate liquidity risk outside the U.S. market. For example, scholars employ the portion of the zero daily returns over a month as a liquidity measure and confirm the liquidity being a priced factor in 18 emerging markets (Bekaert et al., 2007). Lee (2011) points out that the pricing role of the liquidity risk varies across countries because of different geo-graphic, economic, and political environments. Liang and Wei (2012) build on Lee's (2011) research and confirm that the liquidity risk is a pricing factor on both local and global bases. In addition, existing studies also employ liquidity risk to explain documented classical anomalies (Liu, 2006; Sadka, 2006). Building upon these strands of existing literature, we put forward the hypothesis as follows:

H1 Corporate social performance is negatively related to firm's liquidity risk.

The unexpected shortage of market liquidity has a detrimental effect on firm's operation when market-wide liquidity experiences a negative shock. Financial constraint has an adverse effect on firms, exhausting the internal capital and deteriorating their operating performance, both of which may pull down the stock price. CSR investments aim to improve stakeholders' well-being and therefore can enhance stakeholders' willingness to provide critical resources or effort to support firms' operation. Banks and investors are important stakeholders. During a liquidity crisis, banks and investors are more likely to supply capital to socially responsible firms as such firms have allocated resources to fulfill stakeholders' demands. We argue that the negative relationship between CSR and the liquidity risk will be more pronounced for firms with higher external capital reliance. We put forward the hypothesis as follows:

H2 The negative relationship between CSR and firm's liquidity risk is more pronounced for firms with higher external capital reliance.

External environment has been shown as a force to influence the magnitude of the effect of business strategy on economic outcomes. In this study, we further focus on the regional trust level to present a contextual background and investigate the differential effect of CSR on liquidity risk at regions with different trust levels. Firms located at trustworthy regions enjoy advantages in accessing to finance, obtaining capital at lower price and withstanding risk. When the trustworthy appearance of a region lacks, the moral capital accumulated by the individual firms should be valued more by outsiders. CSR activities can build trust with stakeholders directly and this trust building will eventually transfer into the access to capital. When firms operate in low-trust areas, where it is hard to build trust, those firms with intensive CSR engagements will be viewed as more trustworthy by capital providers and thus these capital providers are more willing to supply capital to these firms. Therefore, we propose the hypothesis as follows:

H3 The negative relationship between CSR and firm's liquidity risk is more pronounced when the regional trust level is low.

6.2.3 Data, Sample and Measures

6.2.3.1 Data

To investigate the relationship between firms' CSR and the liquidity risk, we rely on three data sources to construct our sample. We obtain corporate social ratings data from the MSCI ESG database, which is also known as KLD database. Firms are rated on variety of strengths and concerns on the following seven attributes: community, diversity, employee relations, environment, product, human rights, and governance.

We first recover the missing CUSIP from 1991 to 1995 by stock ticker and company name and then merge KLD data with the Compustat for the financial information using CUSIPs as firm identifiers. Before we merge this combined dataset with Center for Research in Security Prices (CRSP) database, we employ several screenings on CRSP data to construct our liquidity risk measures, which will be discussed in details shortly. After matching cross all three databases and accounting for lags in variables, we end up with a final sample of 30,753 firm-year observations from 1993 to 2018.

6.2.3.2 Corporate Social Responsibility Measure

We rely on KLD to construct CSR measures. KLD assigns a binary rating to a set of concerns and strengths with each of following seven areas: community, diversity, employee relations, environment, human rights, product, and corporate governance. For each firm-year, we calculate a net score for each of attributes equal to the number of strengths minus the number of concerns. We then sum up all strengths and concerns respectively across all attributes to obtain overall CSR_str and CSR_con. Our main interested variable, CSR_net, is obtained by subtracting CSR_con from CSR_str. We exclude corporate governance when constructing CSR_str, CSR_con and CSR_net following the literature (D'Adamo et al. 2021).

6.2.3.3 Measure of Firm Liquidity Risk

Liquidity is a broad and elusive concept and is not directly observed. There are many empirical measures as liquidity has numerous aspects that cannot be captured into one single measure. Generally, it denotes the ability to trade large quantities quickly at low cost with little price impact. Along the empirical asset pricing literature, it has been widely shown that liquidity affects cross-sectional differences of asset returns through two different channels, either a characteristic (level of liquidity) or a risk factor. For example, numerous studies investigate whether expected returns are related to level of liquidity, including (Brennan et al., 1998; Brockman & Chung, 2003; Chiyachantana et al., 2004; Datar et al., 1998; Eleswarapu & Venkataraman, 2006; Lesmond, 2005). On the contrary, some scholars have paid more attention to the systematic liquidity risk as opposed to the level of liquidity per se (Acharya & Pedersen, 2005; Lee, 2011; Liang & Wei, 2012; McAlister et al., 2007; Pástor & Stambaugh, 2003; Sadka, 2006; Sharfman & Fernando, 2008).

In this study, we do not consider other levels of liquidity measures that capture the bid-ask spread, transaction cost, or market depth. Instead, we focus on two types of liquidity risk betas of firms, which are our main dependent variables. The liquidity risk beta is defined as the sensitivity of stock returns to the market-wide liquidity risk. In order to estimate betas, we employ two widely used market-wide liquidity (illiquidity) measures: Amihud's illiquidity measure (Amihud, 2002) and Pástor and Stambaugh's liquidity measure (Pástor & Stambaugh, 2003). The former describes liquidity as asset's price pressure while the latter captures asset's price reversal.

Pástor and Stambaugh's Liquidity Risk Measure

We start off with the Pástor and Stambaugh's liquidity measure (Pástor & Stambaugh, 2003): They define liquidity as being associated with temporary price fluctuations induced by order flows. The market-wide liquidity level is calculated as the equally weighted average of the liquidity measures of individual stocks using CRSP daily data within the month. We closely follow Pástor and Stambaugh's (2003) procedure to exclude stocks on NASDAQ because volume data on NASDAQ include interdealer trades, and this results in an artificially higher volume on NASDAQ. Therefore, we only retain common shares (CRSP share codes 10 and 11) on NYSE and AMEX (CRSP exchange codes 1 and 2). The liquidity is the coefficient "γ" "i,t" presented in the following OLS regression:

$$r^{e}_{i,d+1,t} = \alpha_{i,t} + \beta_{i,t} r_{i,d,t} + \gamma_{i,t} \times sign\left(r^{e}_{i,d,t}\right) \times \nu_{i,d,t} + \varepsilon_{i,d+1,t}\ d = 1, \ldots, D, \tag{6.1}$$

where "r" _"i,d,t" is the stock i's return on day in month t. "r" _"i,d,t" ^"e" is the return of stock i over and above the market return and mathematically "r" _ "i,d,t" ^"e" " = " "r" _"i,d,t" "-" "r" _"m,d,t" where "r" _"m,d,t" is the return on CRSP value-weighed return on day d in month t. "v" _"i,d,t" represents the trading volume measured in ten million dollars. We apply the similar screening procedure suggested by Pástor and Stambaugh (2003): We retain stocks with share price between USD 5 and USD 1000 at the end of the previous month; we only retain stocks that have return and volume data for more than 15 observations with which to estimate the above regression; we also exclude a stock for the first and last partial month that it appears on the CRSP tape. One special attention is deserved for Pástor and Stambaugh (2019), who point out that we should also impose the screen "v" "i,d,t" > 0, thereby excluding days with zero trading volume. This condition was inadvertently neglected to mention in the original paper (Pástor & Stambaugh, 2003).

Once we obtain liquidity measure "γ" _"i,t", innovation in liquidity is constructed as follows:

$$\Delta\gamma_t = \left(\frac{m_t}{m_1}\right) \times \frac{1}{N}\sum_{i=1}^{N_t}\left(\gamma_{i,t} - \gamma_{i,t-1}\right), \quad i = 1, \ldots, N_t \tag{6.2}$$

where m stands for market value of market and scaling factor "m" _"t" /"m" _"1" is meant to adjust inflation. We then regress market liquidity innovation "Δ" "γ" _ "t" in an AR (1) model as follows:

$$\Delta\gamma_t = \alpha + \beta\Delta\gamma_{t-1} + c\left(\frac{m_t}{m_1}\right) \times \gamma_{t-1} + \varepsilon_t \tag{6.3}$$

We extract the fitted residual term "ε" _"t" from above regression and then define Pástor & Stambaugh's market-wide liquidity risk "L" _"t" ^"PS" as follows:

$$L^{PS}_t = \varepsilon_t/100 \tag{6.4}$$

Amihud's Liquidity Measure

Amihud (2002) applies a different philosophy and defines illiquidity measure as average across stocks of the daily ratio of absolute stock returns to dollar volume. It serves as a rough measure of price impact because it can be interpreted as the daily price response associated with one dollar of trading volume. He finds market-wide shocks in illiquidity negatively affect stock's contemporaneous realized returns. In calculating Amihud's illiquidity measure (Amihud, 2002; Amihud & Noh, 2016), we follow the convention by including common shares (CRSP share codes 10 and 11) only listed on NYSE and AMEX (CRSP exchange code 1 and 2). Following Amihud and Amihud and Noh (Amihud, 2002; Amihud & Noh, 2016), we first construct this illiquidity measure as follows:

For each stock i:

$$\mathrm{illiq}_{i,d,t} = \left|r_{i,d,t}\right|/\mathrm{dvol}_{i,d,t} \tag{6.5}$$

where "r" _"i,d,t" and ⟦"dvol" ⟧ _"i,d,t" are return and dollar volume of stock i on day d in month t. A stock is included if, during a 12-month period, its price is between $5 and $1000 and it has more than 200 days of valid return and volume data. We then estimate monthly illiquidity ⟦"ILLIQ" ⟧ _"i,t", calculated for each stock i from daily return and volume data over a 12-month periods that ends in month t, as the average of daily value of ⟦"illiq" ⟧ _"i,d,t". We exclude stocks whose ⟦"ILLIQ" ⟧ _"i,t" are at the highest or lowest 1% tails of the distribution to eliminate outliers. Once we have individual monthly ⟦"ILLIQ" ⟧ _"i,t", we will aggregate them to obtain market-wide monthly illiquidity ⟦"ILLIQ" ⟧ _"t". Specifically, it is calculated as month-t cross-stock value-weighted and the weights are the market capitalizations at the end of the preceding month.

We transform the resulting market-wide monthly series into logarithm and denote it as ⟦"Log_ILLIQ" ⟧ _"t". This series is analogous to "γ" _"i,t" obtained from Pástor & Stambaugh's procedure. The next task is to estimate market-wide liquidity risk, which is the unexpected components in market-wide liquidity. It is calculated by running an AR (2) model over a rolling window of 6

$$\mathrm{Log\_ILLIQ}_t = \alpha_0 + \alpha_1 {*} \mathrm{Log\_ILLIQ}_{t-1} + \alpha_2 {*} \mathrm{Log\_ILLIQ}_{t-2} + \alpha_3 {*} T_t + \varepsilon_t \tag{6.6}$$

where "T" _"t" is the serial number of observations in order to account for a time trend. The shock in month n + 1 denoted ⟦"d_Log_ILLIQ" ⟧ _"n + 1" is the difference between the actual value of and its corresponding fitted value using the slope coefficients estimated over the previous 60 months. Our final unexpected liquidity components, which represents market-wide liquidity risk, is rescaling by negative one as we can thus make it comparable with "L" _"t" ^"PS" we obtained before.

$$L_t^A = -1 \times d\_Log\_ILLIQ_t \tag{6.7}$$

We find that the pooled correlation between "L" _"t" ^"PS" and "L" _"t" ^"A" is only 0.006 suggesting that these two measures capture different aspects of liquidity and making them supplementary to each other.

Liquidity Risk Betas Estimations

We've constructed two market-wide liquidity risk measures, "L" _"t" ^"PS" and "L" _"t" ^"A", and we employ the following OLS regression using the past 60 months of data to estimate two types of liquidity risk betas for each stock:

$$r_{i,t} = \beta_0 + \beta_i^L L_t + \beta_i^M MKT_t + \beta_i^S SMB_t + \beta_i^H HML_t + \varepsilon_t \quad (6.5)$$

where "r" _"i,t" denotes stock's return, "L" _"t" is the market-wide liquidity risk, MKT, SMB and HML are the three factors of Fama and French (1993). By feeding "L" _"t" ^"PS" and "L" _"t" ^"A" into above regressions respectively, we will end up with two sets of stock's liquidity risk betas, Beta_PS and Beta_A, serving as our two main dependent variables. We are aware that Pástor and Stambaugh (2003) put a larger emphasis on predicted liquidity risk beta estimation compared with historical liquidity risk beta estimations. The reason we shift attention to the latter is because they find that historical betas do a better job than predicted betas when extending the timeline in a later study (Pástor & Stambaugh, 2019).

6.2.3.4 Control Variables

We control for variables that have been shown to affect the CSR–risk relationship in prior studies. We first control for the betting against beta measure (BAB) (Frazzini & Pedersen, 2014) as it most likely affects liquidity risk. It is also well documented in many studies that firm size has predictive power (Harvey & Siddique, 2000; Jo & Harjoto, 2011), hence we control for firm size, calculated as the log value of total assets. We further control for other variables known to be associated with firm systematic risk: market-to-book ratio (MB), calculated as market value of equity divided by book value of equity; financial leverage (LEV), calculated as total long-term debts divided by total assets; and profitability, measured by return on assets (ROA). In addition, McAlister et al. (2007) show that R&D expenditures have an impact on systematic risk, and we thus control for R&D, calculated as research and development expenses divided by total sales. Following prior literature, we also control for sales growth (SALEG) (Servaes & Tamayo, 2013). Finally, we control for investment opportunities by capital expenditure expense divided by total assets (CAPEX), and we control for the effect of corporate governance using the net score of KLD ratings in the governance area (GOV). All independent variables are lagged by one year except for GOV. All of our regressions include industry and year fixed effects. Our industry classification is based on the first two digits of the SIC code.

6.2.4 Empirical Results

Table 6.1 reports the summary statistics of variables used in our regression analyses. The sample firms have an average CSR net score of 0.458, CSR strengths score of 1.738, and a CSR concerns score of 1.281. One thing we should notice is that our main independent variable CSR net score ranges from − 9 to 18 and it has a high standard deviation, both of which indicate our sample consists of a wide cross section of firms across the CSR spectrum. Moving on to control variables, the average firm in our sample has a firm-specific BAB of 1.426, a firm size of 7.689, a market-to-book ratio of 2.781, a financial leverage of 0.235, a return on assets of 0.031, a capital investment of 0.045, a sales growth of 0.085, and an R&D ratio of 0.065. The average governance score is – 0.212, indicating that, on average, the firms have more KLD concerns than strengths in this field.

In addition to the variables used in our baseline regression analysis, we also use the following variables in our supplementary analysis: On average, the sample firms have a quoted spread of 0.032, an effective spread of 0.009, a price impact of 0.012, measured by Amihud's (2002) price response, and a share turnover of 9.360, measured by volume divided by total shares outstanding. Inspired by Moshirian et al. (2021) on external equity finance dependence, we construct CapitalDep, calculated as the sum of net equity issuance and net debt issuance divided by capital expenditures. It has a negative average of – 0.001, indicating our sample firms

Table 6.1 This table reports the summary statistics of liquidity risk measures, CSR measures, firm various characteristics, liquidity level, and external capital reliance

Statistic	Min	Pctl(25)	Mean	Pctl(75)	Max	Median	SD
Beta_PS	– 3.275	– 0.169	– 0.01	0.148	2.856	– 0.012	0.295
Beta_A	– 1.813	0.682	1.1	1.417	9.061	1.025	0.621
CSR_net	– 9	– 1	0.458	1	18	0	2.529
CSR_str	0	0	1.738	2	21	1	2.445
CSR_con	0	0	1.281	2	15	1	1.641
BAB	0.037	0.712	1.426	1.898	5.142	1.216	1.003
Size	4.183	6.516	7.689	8.73	11.926	7.586	1.606
MB	– 10.106	1.222	2.781	3.305	22.853	1.949	3.652
LEV	0	0.068	0.235	0.349	0.918	0.211	0.198
ROA	– 0.548	0.009	0.031	0.078	0.251	0.039	0.107
CAPEXP	0	0.013	0.045	0.061	0.263	0.031	0.048
SALEG	– 0.511	– 0.013	0.085	0.15	1.191	0.062	0.225
RNDR	0	0	0.065	0.033	1.917	0	0.229
GOV	– 4	– 1	– 0.21	0	3	0	0.671
CapitalDep	– 1.646	– 0.003	– 0	0.025	1.158	0.004	0.266
Quoted_ spread	0.006	0.021	0.032	0.038	0.155	0.028	0.016
Effective_ spread	0.002	0.006	0.009	0.011	0.05	0.008	0.005
Price_impact	3E–05	0.0003	0.012	0.005	3.927	0.001	0.075
Share_ turnover	0.638	4.368	9.36	11.661	117.42	7.174	8.165
CapitalDep	– 1.646	– 0.003	– 0	0.025	1.158	0.004	0.266

Table 6.2 This table presents mean (Panel A) and median (Panel B) comparison tests for the liquidity risk estimations across subsamples of high (above median) and low (below median) CSR net score (CSR_net). Beta_A and Beta_PS are two liquidity risk measures based on Amihud and Pástor and Stambaugh

		N	Beta_A	Beta_PS
Panel A: Means				
CSR_net ≥ median	(1)	19,015	1.087	– 0.0205
CSR_net < median	(2)	11,738	1.1208	– 0.0016
Difference	(1)–(2)		– 0.0338***	– 0.0189***
t_Stat			[−49.55]	[−44.67]
Panel B:Medians				
CSR_net ≥ median	(1)	19,015	1.0185	– 0.0229
CSR_net < median	(2)	11,738	1.0466	0.0038
Difference	(1)–(2)		– 0.0281***	– 0.0267***
t_Stat			[−47.10]	[−70.75]

do not rely heavily on external capital financing on average. However, it ranges from – 1.646 to 1.158, generating a large dispersion for our further analysis.

Table 6.2 reports the mean (Table 6.2, Panel A) and median (Panel B) liquidity risk betas of firms with low and high CSR net scores, respectively. The mean (median) liquidity risk, measured by Beta_A, of firms with a high CSR net score is 1.0870 (1.0185), while it is 1.1208 (1.0466) for firms with a low CSR net score. The results suggest that the mean (median) Beta_A of firms with a high CSR net score is 0.0338 (0.0281) lower than that of firms with a low CSR net score. These differences are significant at the 1% level. A similar pattern is observed for Beta_PS. These preliminary findings suggest firms with better CSR ratings have significantly lower liquidity risk.

$$\begin{aligned}\beta_t^L &= \alpha_0+\alpha_1 \mathrm{CSR}_{\mathrm{net}\ t-1}+\alpha_2 \mathrm{BAB}_{t-1}+\alpha_3 \mathrm{Size}_{t-1}+\alpha_4 \mathrm{MB}_{t-1}+\alpha_5 \mathrm{LEV}_{t-1}\\ &+ \alpha_6 \mathrm{ROA}_{t-1}+\alpha_7 \mathrm{CAPEX}_{t-1}+\alpha_8 \mathrm{SALEG}_{t-1}+\alpha_9 \mathrm{RD}_{t-1}+\alpha_{110} \mathrm{GOV}_t\\ &+\alpha_m(\mathrm{DIndustry})+\alpha_n(\mathrm{DYear})+\varepsilon_t \end{aligned} \tag{6.9}$$

We report the results from our baseline regressions in Table 6.3. We conduct univariate regressions in Models 1– 2 by regressing liquidity risk betas on the lagged CSR net score, as well as the industry and time dummy variables. A significant negative relationship is observed for both Beta_A and Beta_PS, indicating that corporations with better socially responsible performance tend to have lower liquidity risk. To mitigate the systematic differences existing in a list of firm characteristics between low- and high-liquidity-risk firms, we conduct multivariate regressions in Models 3 to 6. In models 3–4, we investigate this relationship by controlling for a set of variables. We find that the coefficients on the CSR net score remain significantly negative for both of Beta_A and Beta_PS, while the coefficients on firm features are quite different. This is not beyond our expectation as we have shown Beta_A and Beta_PS contain very different information (a correlation of 0.006). Generally, larger and less profitable firms experience higher liquidity risk. The negative relationship between CSR and liquidity risk is also significant economically. On average, an increase of one standard deviation in CSR net score in year t− 1 is associated with a decrease of 1.80% in Beta_A and 3.24% in Beta_PS in year t. Thus, the effect of CSR on liquidity risk is both statistically and economically significant. In Models 5–6, we investigate if strength and concern capture different dimensions and thus have different effect on future liquidity risk. We decompose the CSR net score into the CSR strength score and concern score, and we find that the coefficients on the CSR strength score are significantly negative while the coefficients on the CSR concern score are significantly positive. This means both the individual components are the driving force of the observed negative relationship in Models 3 and 4.

6.2.4.1 Components Analysis

In this section, we examine the effect of individual categories of CSR on liquidity risk. In each of the categories, namely, community, diversity, employee relations, environment, human rights, and product, we compute the corresponding net score as the sum of strengths minus the sum of concerns. We rerun our baseline regression for each of the individual categories' net scores. We find the most of categories show a negative effect on liquidity risk in Table 6.4. For Beta_A, all coefficients are significantly negative except for human right and product. A similar pattern is observed for Beta_PS, however, the coefficient is significantly positive for product category, indicating that a higher product net score is associated with higher liquidity risk represented by Beta_PS. In addition, it shows that community category has largest negative effect on Beta_A while the environment category has the largest negative effect on Beta_PS. Overall, these results indicate that the observed negative relationships in Models 3–4 are not driven solely by any individual component but by a combined effect.

6.2.4.2 Addressing the Endogeneity Concern

As suggested in related literature (Cheng et al., 2014; Jo & Harjoto, 2011), we are aware that our results can be biased by the endogeneity issue, and we thus conduct tests to address endogeneity concerns due to simultaneity, reverse causality, and omitted variables. We first include liquidity level as it can be correlated with both CSR and liquidity risk. We also employ two additional conventional methods, the instrumental variables method and the dynamic GMM method, to estimate the model. We now discuss these analyses in detail.

Although we control for several important factors affecting the liquidity risk, our results on the importance of CSR to liquidity risk may be driven by omitted variables that are correlated with both CSR and the liquidity risk. In this study, we add the liquidity level to our model given that it can potentially affect both the CSR and the liquidity risk (Egginton & McBrayer, 2019; Johnson, 2008). To

Table 6.3 The dependent variables in model 1 to model 8 are two liquidity risk betas, Beta_A and Beta_PS: In model (1) and model (2), we estimate univariate regressions

	Dependent Variable:							
	Beta_A	Beta_PS	Beta_A	Beta_PS	Beta_A	Beta_PS	Beta_A	Beta_PS
	(1)	(2)	(3)	(4)	(5)	(6)	(7)	(8)
Intercept	1.278** [−0.054]	0.092*** [−0.027]	0.023 [−0.135]	0.08 [−0.088]	0.026 [−0.135]	0.08 [−0.088]	0.055 [−0.135]	0.107 [−0.088]
CSR_net (t − 1)	− 0.004*** [−0.001]	− 0.003*** [−0.001]	− 0.004*** [−0.001]	− 0.004*** [−0.001]				
CSR_str (t − 1)					− 0.003** [−0.001]	− 0.003*** [−0.001]		
CSR_con (t − 1)							0.006*** [−0.002]	0.004*** [−0.001]
BAB (t − 1)			0.381*** [−0.003]	− 0.006*** [−0.002]	0.381*** [−0.003]	− 0.006*** [−0.002]	0.381*** [−0.003]	− 0.006*** [−0.002]
AT (t − 1)			0.042*** [−0.002]	0.005*** [−0.001]	0.042*** [−0.002]	0.006*** [−0.002]	0.037*** [−0.002]	0.001 [−0.001]
MB (t − 1)			− 0.001 [−0.001]	− 0.001* [−0.001]	− 0.001 [−0.001]	− 0.001* [−0.001]	− 0.001* [−0.001]	− 0.001** [−0.001]
LEV (t − 1)			0.160*** [−0.016]	− 0.0003 [−0.011]	0.160*** [−0.016]	− 0.0004 [−0.011]	0.164*** [−0.016]	0.003 [−0.01]
ROA (t − 1)			− 0.117**** [−0.033]	− 0.077*** [−0.022]	− 0.120*** [−0.033]	− 0.080*** [−0.022]	− 0.119*** [−0.033]	− 0.079*** [−0.022]
CAPEX (t − 1)			− 0.03 [−0.073]	0.066 [−0.048]	− 0.033 [−0.073]	0.064 [−0.048]	− 0.037 [−0.073]	0.06 [−0.048]

(continued)

Table 6.3 (continued)

	Dependent Variable:							
	Beta_A	Beta_PS	Beta_A	Beta_PS	Beta_A	Beta_PS	Beta_A	Beta_PS
	(1)	(2)	(3)	(4)	(5)	(6)	(7)	(8)
SALEG (t − 1)			0.001 [−0.012]	− 0.024*** [−0.008]	0.0005 [−0.012]	− 0.024*** [−0.008]	0.003 [−0.012]	− 0.022*** [−0.008]
RD (t − 1)			0.135*** [−0.016]	− 0.075*** [−0.01]	0.134*** [−0.016]	− 0.076*** [−0.01]	0.132*** [−0.016]	− 0.078*** [−0.01]
GOV			− 0.015*** [−0.004]	− 0.005* [−0.003]	− 0.016*** [−0.004]	− 0.006** [−0.003]	− 0.016*** [−0.004]	− 0.007** [−0.003]
Industry FE	Yes	Yes	Yes	Yes	Yes	Yes	Yes	Yes
Year FE	Yes	Yes	Yes	Yes	Yes	Yes	Yes	Yes
Observations	30,753	30,753	27,096	27,096	27,096	27,096	27,096	27,096
R^2	0.154	0.047	0.5	0.058	0.499	0.058	0.499	0.058
Adjusted R^2	0.151	0.044	0.498	0.055	0.497	0.054	0.498	0.054

In model (3) and model (4), we control for various firm-level characteristics. In model (5) to model (8), we decompose CSR net scores into CSR strengths scores and concerns scores separately and re-run the regressions. Robust standard errors are corrected for firm-level clustering and heteroskedasticity

*,**, and*** marks denote significance at the 10%, 5%, and 1% levels, respectively

Table 6.4 The dependent variables in model (1) to model (12) are two liquidity risk betas, Beta_A and Beta_PS: We regress liquidity risk on each of the six individual categories including community, diversity, employee relations, environment, human rights, and products

	Dependent Variable:											
	Beta_A	Beta_PS	Beta_A	Beta_PS	Beta_A	Beta_PS	Beta_A	Beta_PS	Beta_A	Beta_PS	Beta_A	Beta_PS
	(1)	(2)	(3)	(4)	(5)	(6)	(7)	(8)	(9)	(10)	(11)	(12)
Intercept	0.083	0.078	0.058	0.06	0.079	0.07	0.08	0.066	0.087	0.08	0.079	0.072
	[−0.137]	[−0.088]	[−0.137]	[−0.088]	[−0.137]	[−0.088]	[−0.137]	[−0.088]	[−0.137]	[−0.088]	[−0.137]	[−0.088]
COM(t − 1)	− 0.022***	− 0.008**										
	[−0.005]	[−0.003]										
DIV(t − 1)			− 0.008***	− 0.006***								
			[−0.002]	[−0.002]								
EMP(t − 1)					− 0.006**	− 0.007***						
					[−0.003]	[−0.002]						
ENV(t − 1)							− 0.006*	− 0.012***				
							[−0.003]	[−0.002]				
HUM(t − 1)									− 0.0002	− 0.001		
									[−0.009]	[−0.006]		
PRO(t − 1)											0.007	0.008***
											[−0.004]	[−0.003]
Industry FE	Yes	Yes	Yes	Yes	Yes	Yes	Yes	Yes	Yes	Yes	Yes	Yes

(continued)

Table 6.4 (continued)

	Dependent Variable:											
	Beta_A	Beta_PS	Beta_A	Beta_PS	Beta_A	Beta_PS	Beta_A	Beta_PS	Beta_A	Beta_PS	Beta_A	Beta_PS
	(1)	(2)	(3)	(4)	(5)	(6)	(7)	(8)	(9)	(10)	(11)	(12)
Year FE	Yes	Yes	Yes	Yes	Yes	Yes	Yes	Yes	Yes	Yes	Yes	Yes
Other controls	Yes	Yes	Yes	Yes	Yes	Yes	Yes	Yes	Yes	Yes	Yes	Yes
Observations	27,096	27,096	27,096	27,096	27,096	27,096	27,096	27,096	27,096	27,096	27,096	27,096
R^2	0.482	0.055	0.482	0.056	0.482	0.056	0.482	0.056	0.482	0.055	0.482	0.055
Adjusted R^2	0.48	0.052	0.48	0.052	0.48	0.052	0.48	0.053	0.48	0.052	0.48	0.052

We include all control variables, same as in Table 6.3. Robust standard errors are corrected for firm-level clustering and heteroskedasticity
The*,**, and*** marks denote significance at the 10%, 5%, and 1% levels, respectively.

control for the liquidity level, we add quote spread, effective spread, price impact, and share turnover in the control group. Table 6.5 reports the results with the controls of liquidity risk. We find the coefficients remain significantly negative when controlling for liquidity level separately and together.

We next apply a two-stage least square method. Following prior study (Cai et al., 2016), we use the CSR net score lagged by two years as the instrumental variable of the CSR scores. We report results in columns (1) and (2) of Table 6.6. The coefficients on the fitted value of CSR net score are still significantly negative for both liquidity risk betas, suggesting our observed negative relationship in our baseline regressions holds when addressing possible endogeneity. We also use the average CSR net score of other firms in the same Fama–French 48 industry as the instrumental variable (El Ghoul et al., 2018; Johnson, 2008), and the results are less but still significant (results untabulated).

Second, to mitigate the issue of reverse causality, we conduct the dynamic panel system GMM model (Bekaert et al., 2007; Watanabe & Watanabe, 2008). We employ the first two lags of the liquidity risk because including past liquidity risk levels enables us to account for the dynamic aspect of the CSR–liquidity risk relationship. The results in columns (3) and (4) of Table 6.6 suggest that we continue to find a significantly negative relationship. Overall, these analyses reinforce our previous findings of a negative association between CSR and liquidity risk. Collectively, these results indicate that our core results are not driven by an endogeneity issue.

6.2.4.3 Exploring the Underlying Mechanism

In this section, we explore the underlying economic channel through which CSR affects liquidity risk. When market-wide liquidity experiences a negative shock, the unexpected shortage in market liquidity has a detrimental effect on firm's operation. Insufficient access to capital has an adverse effect on firms, exhausting their internal capital and deteriorating their operating performance, both of which may drive down the stock price. This is how firms' stock returns covary with market-wide liquidity shocks.

Many empirical evidences (Becchetti et al., 2015; Deng et al., 2013) favor a stakeholder maximization view suggesting that CSR firms pay special attention to stakeholders' interest and satisfaction. Focusing on the well-being of stakeholders increases stakeholders' willingness to offer the firms critical resources or effort to support firms' operation. Banks and investors serve as important stakeholders of firms and they provide capital for firm's operation. During the liquidity crisis, banks and investors are more likely to supply capital to socially responsible firms as these firms used to be kind to them and care about their well-being. In addition, firms with intensive CSR engagement tend to have financial and operational transparency. CSR serves as a tool for banks and investors to build trust, especially during a liquidity crisis. Combining both factors that contribute to access to capital, socially responsible firms are more likely to be supplied with capital by such stakeholders to support operations and prevent their stock prices from going down. Under this scenario, we expect the returns of socially responsible firms will

Table 6.5 The dependent variables in model (1) to model (10) are two liquidity risk betas, Beta_A and Beta_PS: In models (1) to (8), we re-run our baseline regressions controlling for each of liquidity level measures: quoted spread, effective spread, price impact, and share turnover

	Dependent Variable									
	Beta_A	Beta_PS	Beta_A	Beta_PS	Beta_A	Beta_PS	Beta_A	Beta_PS	Beta_A	Beta_PS
	(1)	(2)	(3)	(4)	(5)	(6)	(7)	(8)	(9)	(10)
Intercept	− 0.258 [−0.136]	0.04 [−0.089]	− 0.206 [−0.137]	0.044 [−0.089]	0.071 [−0.137]	0.048 [−0.088]	0.041 [−0.136]	0.058 [−0.088]	− 0.214 [−0.136]	0.044 [−0.089]
CSR_net(t − 1)	− 0.004*** [−0.001]	− 0.004*** [−0.001]	− 0.004*** [−0.001]	− 0.004*** [−0.001]	− 0.004*** [−0.001]	− 0.004*** [−0.001]	− 0.005*** [−0.001]	− 0.004*** [−0.001]	− 0.004*** [−0.001]	− 0.004*** [−0.001]
Q_spread(t − 1)	6.992*** [−0.290]	0.403** [−0.188]							9.969*** [−0.809]	0.792 [−0.527]
E_spread(t − 1)			18.828*** [−0.945]	1.028* [−0.611]					− 12.481*** [−2.596]	− 2.323 [−1.690]
Price_ impact(t − 1)					− 0.074* [−0.038]	0.124*** [−0.024]			− 0.188*** [−0.039]	0.127*** [−0.026]
Turnover(t − 1)							0.007*** [−0.000]	0.0002 [−0.000]	0.004*** [−0.000]	0.0003 [−0.000]
Industry FE	Yes	Yes	Yes	Yes	Yes	Yes	Yes	Yes	Yes	Yes
Year FE	Yes	Yes	Yes	Yes	Yes	Yes	Yes	Yes	Yes	Yes
Other controls	Yes	Yes	Yes	Yes	Yes	Yes	Yes	Yes	Yes	Yes
Observations	27,088	27,088	27,088	27,088	27,088	27,088	27,088	27,088	27,088	27,088
R^2	0.493	0.056	0.49	0.056	0.482	0.057	0.489	0.056	0.497	0.057
Adjusted R^2	0.491	0.053	0.488	0.053	0.48	0.054	0.487	0.053	0.495	0.054

In models (9) and (10), we include all above liquidity-level measures. We include all control variables, same as in Table 6.3. Robust standard errors are corrected for firm-level clustering and heteroskedasticity

Table 6.6 The dependent variables in model (1) to model (4) are two liquidity risk betas, Beta_A and Beta_PS: In models (1) and (2), we apply a two-state lease square method and we use the CSR net score lagged by 2 years as the instruments following prior studies (e.g., Cai et al., 2016)

	Dependent Variable			
	Beta_A	Beta_PS	Beta_A	Beta_PS
	(1)	(2)	(3)	(4)
Constant	0.019 [−0.135]	0.078 [−0.088]	– 0.038 [−0.139]	0.117 [−0.091]
CSR_net fitted(t – 1)	– 0.005*** [−0.001]	– 0.004*** [−0.001]		
CSR_net(t – 1)			– 0.004*** [−0.001]	– 0.003*** [−0.001]
Beta_A (t – 1)			– 0.033** [−0.015]	
Beta_A (t – 2)			0.008 [−0.015]	
Beta_PS (t – 1)				– 0.022*** [−0.007]
Beta_PS (t – 2)				0.005 [−0.006]
Industry FE	Yes	Yes	Yes	Yes
Year FE	Yes	Yes	Yes	Yes
Other controls	Yes	Yes	Yes	Yes
Observations	27,096	27,096	26,219	26,219
R^2	0.5	0.058	0.5	0.06
Adjusted R^2	0.498	0.055	0.498	0.056

In models (3) and (4), we employ dynamic GMM method and use the first two lags of the liquidity risk to account for the dynamic aspects of the CSR–liquidity risk relation. We include all control variables same as in Table 6.3. Robust standard errors are corrected for firm-level clustering and heteroskedasticity

*,**, and*** marks denote significance at the 10%, 5%, and 1% levels, respectively

be less affected by market liquidity shocks and hence they have a lower liquidity risk represented by liquidity risk betas.

In order to test the above hypothesized mechanism, we argue that the negative relationship between CSR and the liquidity risk is more pronounced for firms with higher external capital reliance. This is because firms with higher external capital reliance have less internal capital during liquidity shortage periods. Therefore, the benefits associated with CSR engagements are pronounced for them. We expect the negative relationship between CSR and the liquidity risk is more prominent for firms that heavily rely on external financing.

Following Moshirian et al. (2021), we measure external capital finance reliance using the sum of net equity issuance and net debt issuance divided by capital expenditure. We rerun our baseline regression after partitioning the sample based

Table 6.7 This table presents the regression results of subsample analysis on the effect of CSR scores on firm-level liquidity risk: We partition the sample based on the median value of external capital finance dependence (CapDep), calculated as sum of net equity issuance and net debt issuance divided by capital expenditure

	Dependent Variable			
	High Reliance	Low Reliance	High Reliance	Low Reliance
	(CapDep ≥ median)	(CapDep < median)	(CapDep ≥ median)	(CapDep < median)
	(1)	(2)	(3)	(4)
Intercept	– 0.075 [−0.194]	0.338* [−0.199]	– 0.158 [−0.133]	0.324*** [−0.124]
CSR_net (t−1)	– 0.011*** [−0.002]	– 0.002 [−0.002]	– 0.005*** [−0.001]	– 0.003* [−0.001]
Industry FE	Yes	Yes	Yes	Yes
Year FE	Yes	Yes	Yes	Yes
Other controls	Yes	Yes	Yes	Yes
Observations	11,654	11,479	11,479	11,654
R^2	0.53	0.499	0.062	0.088
Adjusted R^2	0.526	0.495	0.054	0.08

We include all control variables same as in Table 6.3. Robust standard errors are corrected for firm-level clustering and heteroskedasticity

on the median values of external capital finance reliance. We report the results in Table 6.7. We find significantly negative coefficients on the CSR net score for both of the liquidity risk betas when firms have high external capital finance reliance. In contrast, when firms have low external capital finance reliance, the coefficient is insignificant for Beta_A and the coefficient is less statistically negative for Beta_PS compared with its counterpart when firms have high external capital finance reliance.

We further focus on the regional trust level to present a contextual background and investigate the differential effect of CSR on liquidity risk at regions with different trust levels. Firms located at trustworthy regions enjoy advantages in access to finance, obtaining capital at lower price and withstanding risk. When the trustworthy appear-ance of a region is lacking, the moral capital accumulated by the individual firms should be valued more by outsiders. In the context of our study, the effect of individual firm's CSR performance on the liquidity risk should be more pronounced when the re-gional trust level is low.

We obtain the state-level trust data from the US section of World Values Survey data. In the survey, the trust-related questions (V24, V103, V104, V105, and V160B) ask about interviewees' trust level towards their family, neighborhood, and various types of people. We recode the answer variables so that lower values would reflect lower trustworthiness. Then, we calculate the mean of the scores across the five questions as the social trust score for a particular respondent. We obtain the mean value of each variable by state (V246B) as the trust measures. We

Table 6.8 This table presents the results of the differential effect of CSR on liquidity risk at the regions with different trust level: We partition the sample based on the median value of state-level trust score

	Dependent Variable			
	High Trust	Low Trust	High Trust	Low Trust
	Beta_A	Beta_A	Beta_P	Beta_PS
	(1)	(2)	(3)	(4)
Intercept	– 0.142 [0.418]	0.348 [0.101]	0.223 [0.112]	– 0.038 [0.738]
CSR_net (t – 1)	– 0.004* [0.024]	– 0.005** [0.003]	– 0.003** [0.009]	– 0.004*** [0.000]
Industry FE	Yes	Yes	Yes	Yes
Year FE	Yes	Yes	Yes	Yes
Other controls	Yes	Yes	Yes	Yes
Observations	15,774	10,962	15,774	10,962
R^2	0.50	0.52	0.07	0.07

We include all control variables same as in Table 6.3. Robust standard errors are corrected for firm-level clustering and heteroskedasticity

merge the trust data with the sample based on firm's location (state) and perform the regression after portioning the sample according to the median values of trust score. We report the results in Table 6.8. Consistent with our prediction, we find more statistically significant negative coefficients on the CSR net score for both liquidity risk measures when firms operate in low-trust areas.

6.3 Summary and Conclusions

In this paper, we investigate the influence of CSR on firm liquidity risk using a comprehensive sample of U.S. firms from 1993 to 2018. We find a significantly negative association between firm's CSR performance and the liquidity risk after control-ling for various firm-specific determinants, as well as industry and year fixed effects. Our results remain intact when addressing for endogeneity issues by adding liquidity level to the model and employing the two-stage least square method and the dynamic GMM method. Furthermore, we find that external capital finance is the economic channel through which CSR could affect a firm's liquidity risk as the negative relationship between CSR and the liquidity risk is more prominent when firms heavily rely on external capital finance. The rationale behind this observation is that investors and banks are more likely to supply capital to firms with previously intensive CSR engagements during market liquidity shocks because of the "payback" effect and the trust-building resulted from previous CSR engagements. The results also suggest that the effect of CSR on liquidity risk is more pronounced when the firms operate in the states with low trust level.

Our study makes several contributions. Our findings lend strong support for the argument that firms could invest in CSR for risk mitigation. We extend the study of the relation between CSR and systematic risk and show that the risk-reducing effect of CSR is in line with the current studies between CSR and firm risk. This paper fills a gap in the literature of risk management by formalizing and testing whether and to what extent CSR policies affect the critical component of systematic risk, liquidity risk, which has been widely accepted as a prominent systematic risk across stocks. We also contribute to the stream of literature on the determinant of systemic risk given that the recent financial crisis and pandemic crisis have demonstrated that market liquidity is a prominent systematic risk globally. Our study indicates that CSR investment could serve as an instrument in the systemic risk mitigation. The paper also contributes to the literature by offering the dynamic GMM method that attempts to deal with the potential endogeneity of CSR.

Our findings shed light on investment decisions and risk management and therefore are very important for firms and investors. From the firm's perspective, with the mechanism explained in the previous section, corporate managers can identify the im-plications of active CSR management. They may make strategic decisions on CSR engagement, which will affect their trustworthiness with stakeholders and the capital-raising ability during market liquidity shortage periods. These strategic decisions on CSR engagement will serve as a tool to manage firm's liquidity risk. From an investor's perspective, our findings between CSR and liquidity risk have implications for portfolio construction and investment decisions. For example, CAPM predicts that any systematic fluctuation of asset prices is captured solely by market risk. Therefore, the covariance of stock returns with market returns is the key to the success of portfolio diversification. This liquidity risk, which is independent of market risk, provides an additional layer to consider when investors seek to diversify away risks. Therefore, CSR performance can be used to evaluate individual stocks' or portfolios' liquidity risk exposure or even to predict liquidity risk and the change in the liquidity risk of the underlying investments.

Although our research provided novel evidence and generated critical implications for both academic researchers and practitioners, we recognize that this article is not without weakness. We limit our study to the firms in the US. We believe that ex-tending our study on a global basis may enrich and contribute the documented mitigating effect of CSR on firm's liquidity risk. In addition, though the existing studies suggest that CSR is more prominent in developed countries, the developing countries also require elaborate efforts. We notice that there are some extended studies that focus on the CSR effect in developing countries (Ali & Kaur, 2021). We believe our findings also have academic implications for developing countries. Further studies regarding the impact of sustainability issues including CSR implementation on risk management could be undertaken in developing countries. Noteworthy CSR performance induces moral capital, but the effect of CSR may differ in culturally heterogeneous nations. In addition, the legal and regulation systems in financial markets may also differ; this is especially distinct between developed and developing nations. Hence, investors in each market may perceive liquidity risk differently, which also influence the CSR effect on liquidity risk. Extending the study on a global basis would confirm the robustness of the documented relationship. It would be also rewarding to investigate how this documented relationship will vary across countries, especially the difference between developed and developing countries. We encourage scholars to answer these questions in the future.

Acknowledgements This chapter is based on the article previously published as: Zhao, H., Jiao, Z., Wang, J., & Kamar, A. (2021). Corporate Social Responsibility and Firm Liquidity Risk: US Evidence. *Sustainability, 13*(22), 12894. The citation style in this version has been updated from the original numeric format to the author–year format to ensure consistency

References

Acharya, V., & Pedersen, L. H. (2005). Asset pricing with liquidity risk. *Journal of Financial Economics, 77*, 375–410. https://doi.org/10.1016/j.jfineco.2004.06.007

Albuquerque, R. A., Durnev, A., & Koskinen, Y. (2014). *Corporate social responsibility and firm risk: Theory and empirical evidence*. SSRN Working Paper 1961971.

Albuquerque, R., Koskinen, Y., & Zhang, C. (2019). Corporate social responsibility and firm risk: Theory and empirical evidence. *Management Science, 65*, 4451–4469. https://doi.org/10.1287/mnsc.2018.3043

Ali, S. S., & Kaur, R. (2021). Effectiveness of corporate social responsibility in implementation of social sustainability in warehousing of developing countries: A hybrid approach. *Journal of Cleaner Production, 324*, Article 129154. https://doi.org/10.1016/j.jclepro.2021.129154

Amihud, Y. (2002). Illiquidity and stock returns: Cross-section and time-series effects. *Journal of Financial Markets, 5*, 31–56. https://doi.org/10.1016/S1386-4181(01)00024-6

Amihud, Y., & Noh, J. (2021). Illiquidity and stock returns II: Cross-section and time-series effects. *Review of Financial Studies, 34*, 2101–2123. https://doi.org/10.1093/rfs/hhaa080

Bae, K.-H., El Ghoul, S., Gong, Z. J., & Guedhami, O. (2021). Does CSR matter in times of crisis? Evidence from the COVID-19 pandemic. *Journal of Corporate Finance, 67*, Article 101876.

Becchetti, L., Ciciretti, R., & Hasan, I. (2015). Corporate social responsibility, stakeholder risk, and idiosyncratic volatility. *Journal of Corporate Finance, 35*, 297–309. https://doi.org/10.1016/j.jcorpfin.2015.09.007

Bekaert, G., Harvey, C. R., & Lundblad, C. (2007). Liquidity and expected returns: Lessons from emerging markets. *Review of Financial Studies, 20*, 1783–1831. https://doi.org/10.1093/rfs/hhm030

Blundell, R., & Bond, S. (1998). Initial conditions and moment restrictions in dynamic panel data models. *Journal of Econometrics, 87*, 115–143. https://doi.org/10.1016/S0304-4076(98)00009-8

Brennan, M. J., Chordia, T., & Subrahmanyam, A. (1998). Alternative factor specifications, security characteristics, and the cross-section of expected stock returns. *Journal of Financial Economics, 49*, 345–373.

Brockman, P., & Chung, D. Y. (2003). Investor protection and firm liquidity. *Journal of Finance, 58*, 921–937. https://doi.org/10.1111/1540-6261.00551

Cai, L., Cui, J., & Jo, H. (2016). Corporate environmental responsibility and firm risk. *Journal of Business Ethics, 139*(3), 563–594. https://doi.org/10.1007/s10551-015-2630-4

Chang, K., Kim, I., & Li, Y. (2014). The heterogeneous impact of corporate social responsibility activities that target different stakeholders. *Journal of Business Ethics, 125*(2), 211–234.

Cheng, B., Ioannou, I., & Serafeim, G. (2014). Corporate social responsibility and access to finance. *Strategic Management Journal, 35*, 1–23. https://doi.org/10.1002/smj.2131

Cheung, A. W. K. (2016a). Corporate social responsibility and corporate risk-taking: Theory and evidence. *Journal of Business Ethics, 136*(3), 431–448.
Cheung, A. W. K. (2016b). Corporate social responsibility and corporate cash holdings. *Journal of Corporate Finance, 37*, 412–430.
Chiyachantana, C. N., Jain, P. K., Jiang, C., & Wood, R. A. (2004). International evidence on institutional trading behavior and price impact. *Journal of Finance, 59*, 869–898. https://doi.org/10.1111/j.1540-621.2004.00651.x
D'Adamo, I., Morone, P., & Huisingh, D. (2021). Bioenergy: A sustainable shift. *Energies, 14*, 5661. https://doi.org/10.3390/en14185661
Datar, V. T., Naik, N. Y., & Radcliffe, R. (1998). Liquidity and stock returns: An alternative test. *Journal of Financial Markets, 1*, 203–219. https://doi.org/10.1016/S1386-4181(97)00004-9
Deng, X., Kang, J.-K., & Low, B. S. (2013). Corporate social responsibility and stakeholder value maximization: Evidence from mergers. *Journal of Financial Economics, 110*, 87–109. https://doi.org/10.1016/j.jfineco.2013.04.014
Egginton, J. F., & McBrayer, G. A. (2019). Does it pay to be forthcoming? Evidence from CSR disclosure and equity market liquidity. *Corporate Social Responsibility and Environmental Management, 26*, 396–407. https://doi.org/10.1002/csr.1691
El Ghoul, S., Guedhami, O., Kwok, C. C., & Mishra, D. R. (2011). Does corporate social responsibility affect the cost of capital? *Journal of Banking & Finance, 35*, 2388–2406. https://doi.org/10.1016/j.jbankfin.2011.02.007
El Ghoul, S., Guedhami, O., Kim, H., & Park, K. (2018). Corporate environmental responsibility and the cost of capital: International evidence. *Journal of Business Ethics, 149*, 335–361. https://doi.org/10.1007/s10551-015-3005-6
Eleswarapu, V. R., & Venkataraman, K. (2006). The impact of legal and political institutions on equity trading costs: A cross-country analysis. *Review of Financial Studies, 19*, 1081–1111. https://doi.org/10.1093/rfs/hhj026
Fama, E. F., & French, K. R. (1993). Common risk factors in the returns on stocks and bonds. *Journal of Financial Economics, 33*, 3–56. https://doi.org/10.1016/0304-405X(93)90023-5
Frazzini, A., & Pedersen, L. H. (2014). Betting against beta. *Journal of Financial Economics, 111*, 1–25. https://doi.org/10.1016/j.jfineco.2013.10.005
Friede, G., Busch, T., & Bassen, A. (2015). ESG and financial performance: Aggregated evidence from more than 2000 empirical studies. *Journal of Sustainable Finance & Investment, 5*, 210–233. https://doi.org/10.1080/20430795.2015.1118917
Godfrey, P. C. (2005). The relationship between corporate philanthropy and shareholder wealth: A risk management perspective. *Academy of Management Review, 30*, 777–798. https://doi.org/10.5465/amr.2005.18378878
Harjoto, M., & Jo, H. (2015). Legal vs. normative CSR: Differential impact on analyst dispersion, stock return volatility, cost of capital, and firm value. *Journal of Business Ethics, 128*, 1–20.
Harjoto, M., & Laksmana, I. (2016). The impact of corporate social responsibility on risk taking and firm value. *Journal of Business Ethics, 1*, 1–21.
Harjoto, M., & Laksmana, I. (2018). The impact of corporate social responsibility on risk taking and firm value. *Journal of Business Ethics, 151*, 353–373.
Harvey, C. R., & Siddique, A. (2000). Conditional skewness in asset pricing tests. *Journal of Finance, 55*, 1263–1295. https://doi.org/10.1111/0022-1082.00247
Hsu, F. J., & Chen, Y.-C. (2015). Is a firm's financial risk associated with corporate social responsibility? *Management Decision, 53*, 2175–2199.
Husted, B. W. (2005). Risk management, real options, corporate social responsibility. *Journal of Business Ethics, 60*, 175–183. https://doi.org/10.1007/s10551-005-3777-1
Jo, H., & Harjoto, M. A. (2011). Corporate governance and firm value: The impact of corporate social responsibility. *Journal of Business Ethics, 103*, 351–383. https://doi.org/10.1007/s10551-011-0869-y
Johnson, T. (2008). Volume, liquidity, and liquidity risk. *Journal of Financial Economics, 87*, 388–417. https://doi.org/10.1016/j.jfineco.2007.03.006

Kim, Y., Li, H., & Li, S. (2014). Corporate social responsibility and stock price crash risk. *Journal of Banking & Finance, 43*, 1–13. https://doi.org/10.1016/j.jbankfin.2014.02.013

Kotler, P., & Lee, N. (2005). Best of breed: When it comes to gaining a market edge while supporting a social cause, "corporate social marketing" leads the pack. *Social Marketing Quarterly, 11*, 91–103. https://doi.org/10.1080/15245000500414480

Lee, K.-H. (2011). The world price of liquidity risk. *Journal of Financial Economics, 99*, 136–161. https://doi.org/10.1016/j.jfineco.2010.08.003

Lesmond, D. A. (2005). Liquidity of emerging markets. *Journal of Financial Economics, 77*, 411–452. https://doi.org/10.1016/j.jfineco.2004.01.005

Liang, S. X., & Wei, J. K. (2012). Liquidity risk and stock returns around the world. *Journal of Banking & Finance, 36*, 3274–3288. https://doi.org/10.1016/j.jbankfin.2012.07.021

Lins, K. V., Servaes, H., & Tamayo, A. (2017). Social capital, trust, and firm performance: The value of corporate social responsibility during the financial crisis. *Journal of Finance, 72*, 1785–1824. https://doi.org/10.1111/jofi.12505

Liu, W. (2006). A liquidity-augmented capital asset pricing model. *Journal of Financial Economics, 82*, 631–671. https://doi.org/10.1016/j.jfineco.2005.10.001

Luo, X., & Bhattacharya, C. B. (2009). The debate over doing good: Corporate social performance, strategic marketing levers, and firm-idiosyncratic risk. *Journal of Marketing, 73*(6), 198–213.

McAlister, L., Srinivasan, R., & Kim, M. (2007). Advertising, research and development, and systematic risk of the firm. *Journal of Marketing, 71*, 35–48. https://doi.org/10.1509/jmkg.71.1.035

Meseguer-Sánchez, V., Gálvez-Sánchez, F. J., López-Martínez, G., & Molina-Moreno, V. (2021). Corporate social responsibility and sustainability: A bibliometric analysis of their interrelations. *Sustainability, 13*, 1636. https://doi.org/10.3390/su13041636

Mishra, S., & Modi, S. B. (2013). Positive and negative corporate social responsibility, financial leverage, and idiosyncratic risk. *Journal of Business Ethics, 117*, 431–448. https://doi.org/10.1007/s10551-012-1526-9

Molina-Azorín, J. F., Claver-Cortés, E., López-Gamero, M. D., & Tarí, J. J. (2009). Green management and financial performance: A literature review. *Management Decision, 47*, 1080–1100. https://doi.org/10.1108/00251740910978313

Moshirian, F., Tian, X., Zhang, B., & Zhang, W. (2021). Stock market liberalization and innovation. *Journal of Financial Economics, 139*, 985–1014. https://doi.org/10.1016/j.jfineco.2020.08.018

Pástor, Ľ, & Stambaugh, R. F. (2003). Liquidity risk and expected stock returns. *Journal of Political Economy, 111*, 642–685. https://doi.org/10.1086/374184

Pástor, Ľ., & Stambaugh, R. F. (2019). *Liquidity risk after 20 years*. NBER Working Paper.

Sadka, R. (2006). Momentum and post-earnings-announcement drift anomalies: The role of liquidity risk. *Journal of Financial Economics, 80*, 309–349. https://doi.org/10.1016/j.jfineco.2005.04.005

Servaes, H., & Tamayo, A. (2013). The impact of corporate social responsibility on firm value: The role of customer awareness. *Management Science, 59*, 1045–1061. https://doi.org/10.1287/mnsc.1120.1630

Sharfman, M. P., & Fernando, C. S. (2008). Environmental risk management and the cost of capital. *Strategic Management Journal, 29*, 569–592. https://doi.org/10.1002/smj.678

Watanabe, A., & Watanabe, M. (2008). Time-varying liquidity risk and the cross section of stock returns. *Review of Financial Studies, 21*, 2449–2486. https://doi.org/10.1093/rfs/hhm054

Wintoki, M. B., Linck, J. S., & Netter, J. M. (2012). Endogeneity and the dynamics of internal corporate governance. *Journal of Financial Economics, 105*, 581–606. https://doi.org/10.1016/j.jfineco.2012.03.005

ESG, Cost of Capital, and Access to Financing

7

7.1 ESG and Access to Finance

The cost of capital is a cornerstone of modern corporate finance. It serves as the minimum threshold rate of return that firms must exceed to justify investments and capital expenditures. Whether in the context of project appraisal, valuation, or capital budgeting, the cost of capital reflects the opportunity cost of funds and the compensation required by investors—both equity holders and creditors—for bearing financial risk. As such, it plays a critical role in determining the firm's value, capital structure decisions, financing strategies, and overall market competitiveness.

Traditionally, financial economists have explained variations in cost of capital through a well-established set of firm-specific, market-level, and institutional factors. In frictionless markets, as posited by Modigliani and Miller (1958), the firm's value is independent of its capital structure. Yet, real-world frictions such as taxes, bankruptcy costs, asymmetric information, and agency conflicts make capital structure highly relevant. The trade-off theory, for instance, suggests that firms balance the tax shields provided by debt against the probability and cost of financial distress (Kraus & Litzenberger, 1973). The pecking-order theory (Myers & Majluf, 1984) further proposes that information asymmetry leads firms to prioritize internal financing, followed by debt, and consider external equity as a last resort.

Empirical evidence supports these theories. Large firms with high profitability, low leverage, and substantial tangible assets typically enjoy better access to external capital and benefit from lower borrowing costs. Smaller or riskier firms often face capital rationing and must pay higher risk premia. Studies such as those by Titman and Wessels (1988) and Rajan and Zingales (1995) underscore the roles of firm fundamentals in explaining financing costs, while macroeconomic factors—interest rates, inflation expectations, investor sentiment, and global liquidity—add another layer of variability (Fama & French, 1993; Pastor & Stambaugh, 2003).

J. Wang, *ESG Strategies and Financial Markets*, Management for Professionals,
https://doi.org/10.1007/978-981-95-5620-5_7

Legal institutions and governance mechanisms also shape the risk-return calculus. The quality of investor protection, efficiency of legal systems, and strength of enforcement regimes all influence how creditors and shareholders price risk (La Porta et al., 2000). Where investor rights are protected, agency costs decline, and both the availability and pricing of capital improve. Bondholders, in particular, are sensitive to bankruptcy resolution efficiency and creditor rights, which affect recovery rates in distress scenarios (Djankov et al., 2008).

Another critical dimension is transparency. Information asymmetry between insiders and external financiers creates a wedge that raises the required rate of return. Higher-quality financial disclosure, analyst coverage, and institutional monitoring help reduce this wedge. The foundational work by Botosan (1997) and Francis et al. (2004) shows that firms with better accounting quality face lower costs of capital, and that information environments significantly influence equity and debt pricing.

These traditional determinants have long served as the dominant paradigm in understanding capital market pricing. However, as global financial systems evolve in response to broader socio-economic trends—including climate change, social justice movements, and governance reform—so too has the definition of what constitutes relevant information for investors. In this context, a growing stream of research in recent decades has introduced Environmental, Social, and Governance (ESG) factors as an emergent and increasingly material dimension of corporate financial decision-making. Initially seen as peripheral or ethical concerns, ESG considerations are now widely acknowledged as financially relevant, impacting firm risk, investor perception, and ultimately, the cost and availability of capital.

Environmental exposures such as carbon intensity, water usage, waste disposal, and climate change liabilities can have direct and indirect effects on a firm's cash flows and risk profile. Social risks—including labor relations, occupational safety, human rights in the supply chain, and data privacy—shape operational continuity and stakeholder trust. Governance variables—board structure, executive compensation, shareholder rights, and anti-corruption policies—directly influence internal control quality and fraud risk. Together, these ESG dimensions contribute to a more comprehensive picture of a firm's risk-return structure and long-term sustainability.

From a capital provider's perspective, strong ESG performance signals lower downside risk and better overall management quality. Investors increasingly view ESG indicators as proxies for long-term strategic thinking, operational resilience, and ethical leadership. As a result, institutional investors, particularly those with long-term horizons—such as pension funds, sovereign wealth funds, and endowments—are incorporating ESG metrics into their investment mandates, risk screening protocols, and engagement strategies. For debt providers, ESG profiles influence both initial credit assessments and ongoing risk monitoring, affecting everything from loan pricing to covenant structures.

Moreover, ESG contributes to reducing information asymmetry. Firms that disclose ESG metrics and issue sustainability reports signal transparency and long-term orientation, narrowing the gap between insiders and outsiders. ESG disclosure also aligns with the growing due diligence practices of institutional investors, who integrate ESG metrics into their screening and stewardship frameworks. In this regard, ESG is both a risk mitigant and a transparency enhancer, directly affecting pricing in both equity and debt markets.

A rich body of empirical research supports these claims. Dhaliwal et al. (2011) show that the initiation of voluntary CSR disclosure is associated with reductions in the cost of equity. Goss and Roberts (2011) find that banks charge higher spreads to firms with poor social responsibility performance. Chava (2014) demonstrates that firms with weak environmental records face higher borrowing costs. Flammer (2021) reveals that green bond issuers enjoy yield advantages compared to traditional bond issuers, as investors reward environmental stewardship.

Taken together, these studies suggest that ESG performance has become a financially material factor—an intangible asset that shapes how capital providers assess risk, reward, and credibility. This reframing of ESG from a "soft" reputational variable to a "hard" financial driver marks a pivotal evolution in corporate finance theory and practice.

At the same time, researchers have begun to explore how ESG affects access to different types of capital markets—not just public equity or rated bond markets, but also private placements and alternative financing mechanisms. One such mechanism is the Rule 144A debt market, a critical channel through which firms raise funds without undergoing the full rigor of SEC registration.

Rule 144A, adopted by the SEC in 1990, facilitates the private resale of securities to Qualified Institutional Buyers (QIBs). It has become especially important for firms with limited public track records, foreign issuers seeking access to U.S. capital, and companies aiming to expedite fundraising without extensive disclosure. However, the lower regulatory scrutiny and disclosure requirements of Rule 144A markets create elevated information asymmetry, making investor trust and firm reputation paramount.

This institutional feature makes Rule 144A an ideal setting to examine whether ESG performance—particularly through its social responsibility (CSR) dimension—can substitute for regulatory disclosure and reduce financing frictions. If CSR practices help firms signal trustworthiness and lower perceived risk, then we should observe more favorable financing terms for CSR-aligned firms in Rule 144A offerings. If not, the value of ESG may be confined to contexts where disclosure is mandatory and visibility is high.

Against this backdrop, the remainder of this chapter presents the paper titled "CSR and Rule 144A Debt Offering: Empirical Evidence" (Dbouk et al., 2018), which empirically explores how CSR affects firms' access to and pricing in Rule 144A markets. The study leverages a rich dataset of private debt offerings to investigate whether CSR performance influences yield spreads, investor participation, and overall capital access. In doing so, it contributes to both corporate finance and ESG literatures by highlighting the importance of sustainability strategies in shaping capital market outcomes—particularly in less transparent, institutionally complex settings.

By situating CSR within the Rule 144A context, the chapter offers valuable insight into how firms can leverage sustainability strategies to reduce financing costs even in markets with limited disclosure. This not only reinforces the financial materiality of ESG but also provides practical implications for corporate managers, institutional investors, and policymakers seeking to align capital allocation with long-term value creation and sustainable development goals.

7.2 Corporate Social Responsibility and Rule 144A Debt Offerings: Empirical Evidence

Abstract

Rule 144A allows a firm to issue securities without a public registration statement with the Securities and Exchange Commission, and only qualified institutional investors can purchase such securities. In this study, focusing on corporate bonds issued under Rule 144A, we empirically investigate the relationship between the corporate social responsibility (CSR) of issuing firms and the bond yield spread at issuance. We document a significant and positive relation between CSR concerns, whereas CSR strengths seem to play an insignificant role in determining bond yield spread. Our main findings are robust to the instrumental variable approach and simultaneous equation estimation to address the potential endogeneity issues. We further explore the time-series changes in issuing firms' CSR profiles, and report that institutional investors demand a higher bond yield spread when issuing firms' exposure to higher social, environmental, and stakeholder concerns. Our analyses reveal that the main sources of such risk exposure are stakeholder conflict and concerns from primary stakeholder groups.

Keywords: Private placement; Rule 144A; Bond yield spread; Corporate social responsibility.

7.2.1 Introduction

The Securities and Exchange Commission (SEC) has institutionalized regulation regarding security issuances under Rule 144A since 1990. Firms can privately place their securities under Rule 144A without filing a public registration statement, and only qualified institutional investors can purchase such securities (Arena, 2011; Chaplinsky & Ramchand, 2004). Although firms can issue both equity and debt under Rule 144A, the volume of debt issuance is nearly eight times the amount of equity raised (Chaplinsky & Ramchand, 2004). Rule 144A allows for a fast issuing procedure with less information disclosure burden. Nonetheless, the lack of registration results in insufficient time for potential investors to conduct due diligence (Fenn, 2000) to fully understand the issuing firms' financial conditions. As a result, investors purchasing privately placed securities may render themselves to exploitation by issuers because of increased asymmetric information. Therefore, in order to reach efficient contracts, investors may resort to other reference points to obtain extra information and assess the creditworthiness of issuing firms. Such information will then be factored into the price formation process of securities placed under Rule 144A.

Recent studies have stressed the prevalence of firms to engage in corporate social responsibility (CSR), because firms increasingly face demands from external stakeholders to address social and environmental issues. CSR activities help firms enhance their corporate social performance, and in turn improve their financial performance (Hasan et al., 2018; Li et al., 2016). More important, the existing literature has documented that CSR activities can effectively reduce firm risk and build social capital to facilitate efficient contracting with other economic agents in the capital market (Amiraslani et al., 2018; Orlitzky & Benjamin, 2001). In parallel, for the last two decades, institutional investors have been involved in socially responsible investing in which the institutional investors screen firms based on desirable or undesirable characteristics in the profile of firm social performance (Chava, 2014).

In this study, focusing on the bonds issued under Rule 144A by United States (U.S.) firms, we examine the relation between issuing firms' CSR profiles and the bond yield spread at issuance. Firm investments in CSR activities incur significant cost and divert scarce resources away from productive activities (Goss & Roberts, 2011). The corporate decision-making process becomes more complicated than simply maximizing shareholder value (Amit & Wernerfelt, 1990; Bettis, 1983; Orlitzky & Benjamin, 2001; Stulz, 1996). As such, the information content in a particular firm's CSR profile is opaque and hard to evaluate. Investors purchasing securities under Rule 144A are typically sophisticated institutional investors with great experience and expertise assessing complicated financial claims. Therefore, the institutional features of Rule 144A debt offerings present an ideal context to investigate whether and to what extent sophisticated institutional investors extract information from issuing firms CSR profiles and incorporate that information in the bond contracting under Rule 144A.

One strand of research generally confirms that CSR involvement reduces firm risk in various contexts. For example, using different measures of CSR activities, researchers report that CSR involvement can effectively reduce the vulnerability of future cash flows, lower market-based risk (Albuquerque et al., 2014; Cai et al., 2016; Chang et al., 2014; Cheung, 2016; Godfrey et al., 2009; Harjoto & Jo, 2015; Lee & Faff, 2009; Luo & Bhattacharya, 2009), and induce safer profit-seeking incentives (Bae et al., 2011). Other empirical studies have shown that good CSR relationships are negatively correlated with firm credit risk and bankruptcy risk (Godfrey, 2005; Hsu & Chen, 2015; Kytle & Ruggie, 2005), and they prevent firms from taking excessive risks (Harjoto & Laksmana, 2016). Therefore, the risk mitigation view of CSR suggests that investors will demand a lower yield spread of privately placed bonds by firms with better corporate social performance.

Nonetheless, another line of research has posited that firm resources may be misallocated or appropriated (Becchetti et al., 2013; Garriga & Melé, 2004; Margolis & Walsh, 2003). In this sense, CSR activities are controversial mainly because of their voluntary nature beyond regulatory compliance (McWilliams & Siegel, 2001). It is plausible that firm managers allocate resources to improve firm social conditions and stakeholder welfare, but not necessarily maximize shareholder value. Barnea and Rubin (2005) contended that firm management has the incentive to make excessive investments in CSR at the cost of shareholders and take the credit for CSR initiatives. Investment in CSR may negatively affect the productive operation and expose firms to higher credit risk. Therefore, firms overinvesting in CSR may have to pay a higher premium to raise external funds.

In the context of security issuance through private placement (i.e., Rule 144A), issuing firms tend to have low credit quality (Arena, 2011), and are subject to significant information asymmetry (Chandra & Nayar, 2008). Issuing firms' CSR profiles may provide additional information for institutional investors to assess their credit risk and determine the cost of capital (Cheng et al., 2014; El Ghoul et al., 2011; Oikonomou et al., 2014). Do investments in CSR activities really reduce firm risk, thus lead to a lower cost of financing? Does incompliance with regulations (Salama et al., 2011) and potential stakeholder conflicts (Becchetti et al., 2012) result in a higher credit risk? Investigating the relation between the CSR profiles of issuing firms and bond yield spread at issuance under Rule 144A can shed further light on this important research question, and further advance our understanding regarding the CSR policy and its relationship with firm financial decisions and outcomes.

In this study, we retrieve information on bonds issued under Rule 144A from the Thomson Reuters SDC Platinum New Issue Database (SDC) in the period from 1998 to 2013. We use information from the KLD Research & Analytics database (KLD) to measure the corporate social performance of our sample-issuing firms. We document a significantly positive relation between the CSR concerns and bond yield spread at issuance under Rule 144A. In addition, CSR strengths seem to play an insignificant role in determining bond yield spread. Endogeneity issues arise because firms voluntarily engage in CSR-related activities, and the price term and non-price term in loan contracts can be simultaneously determined. Our results are robust to the instrument variable approach and simultaneous equation estimation to address the potential endogeneity issues.

We further investigate whether institutional investors extract information from the time-series changes of corporate social performance of issuing firms. We examine the changes in CSR strengths and concerns for three, four, and five-year windows before bond issuance. Our results indicate that indeed, investors incorporate the dynamic changes of CSR scores into the pricing of Rule 144A debt offerings. Specifically, the time-series changes of CSR concerns result in higher bond yield spread if such changes expose the issuing firms to higher environmental, social, and stakeholder risk. We also investigate the sources of the potential credit risk stemming from issuing firms' CSR concerns. We find that if an issuing firm's CSR policy is associated with more stakeholder conflicts, or higher concerns from primary stakeholders, institutional investors tend to demand higher bond yield spread.

We believe that our study contributes to the existing research in several ways. First, focusing on privately placed bonds, we establish a robust link between a firm's CSR profile and its cost of debt, and add to the literature (Chava, 2014; Ghoul et al., 2011; Goss & Roberts, 2011) by providing additional and novel evidence that is consistent with externalities of socially irresponsible activities. Second, in a closely related research study by Amiraslani et al. (2018), they reported an insignificant relation between CSR and bond yield spread. We posit that the effect of social capital and trust generated from CSR involvement on the firm cost of capital is context-dependent. The complexity in CSR strategies makes it difficult to interpret the information content in CSR profiles, and sophisticated investors (e.g., banks and qualified institutional investors) are better equipped with the necessary expertise to do so. The investigation in the context of Rule 144A debt offerings manifests our conjecture. Third, we further show that institutional investors can extract information from both the cross-sectional variations and time-series changes of issuers' CSR profiles. Last, we show that institutional investors are more sensitive when CSR externalities lead to stakeholder conflicts and concerns from primary stakeholders.

The rest of our paper is organized as follows. Section 2 reviews the related literature, and Sect. 3 details the data, sample, and measures. In Sect. 4, we discuss our identification strategies and report empirical results. Section 5 summarizes and concludes.

7.2.2 Related Literature

In this study, we focus on debt offerings under Rule 144A, and highlight a few distinct features of Rule 144A debt offerings compared with public debt. Rule 144A is adopted in 1990 by the SEC to improve the liquidity of private placement of both equity and debt. Securities offered under Rule 144A are not required to be registered with the SEC, and are not allowed to be traded among individual investors, but may be traded immediately among qualified institutional buyers. Domestic firms in the U.S. tend to sell securities that are eligible to be subsequently registered in a short period of time (Huang & Ramirez, 2010). Rule 144A permits a minimum level of public-accessible information and a rapid issuance without registration with the SEC (Fenn, 2000). When the Rule 144A debt is subsequently registered, the debt carries the nature of public market debt, and the investors enjoy the benefit of public market liquidity (Fenn, 2000).

Institutional investors have limited legal protection in Rule 144A debt offerings, because they are typically sophisticated investors (Arena, 2011). Institutional investors tend to demand a higher premium on the issued securities, and are likely to explore various sources of information, including issuing firms' CSR profiles to assess the riskiness of the issuances. A firm managing for stakeholders has to allocate resources to fulfill the demands of important stakeholders by engaging in various CSR activities (Harrison & Bosse, 2013; McWilliams & Siegel, 2001; Waddock & Graves, 1997). Therefore, firms engaging in CSR activities are often confronted with the question of whether "doing good and doing well" converge (Peterson, 2004). Numerous empirical studies have tried to confirm the existence of shareholder wealth creation through socially desirable decisions to legitimize CSR on a sound economic ground. However, research that examines the link between CSR and firm performance from the perspective of debt is scant. Given the distinct features of Rule 144A debt offerings, it is important to understand how investors make use of issuing firms' CSR profiles to extract information and incorporate their assessments to price the debt.

Three major views exist regarding the relation between CSR involvement and the cost of debt. For example, the risk mitigation view posits that a well-balanced CSR strategy can enhance firm performance and reduce potential risks, thus stabilizing income streams, as well as ensuring a firm's solvency. CSR strategy is widely adopted as a risk-management tool in corporate decisions (Benlemlih & Girerd-Potin, 2017; Jo & Na, 2012; Orlitzky & Benjamin, 2001). The voluntary nature of CSR activities (Godfrey et al., 2009) can signal to important stakeholder groups that socially responsible firms are willing to act altruistically (Mackey et al., 2007). Consequently, CSR involvement can produce social capital that offers "insurance-like" protection (Godfrey et al., 2009; Lins et al., 2017; Minor & Morgan, 2011) against adverse events, and even results in better firm performance. The existing literature provides evidence that the socially responsible firms are rewarded in financing by experiencing more favorable credit ratings, the ease of access to the finance, and a lower cost of equity and debt financing (Cheng et al., 2014; El Ghoul et al., 2011; Jiraporn et al., 2014). Therefore, better corporate social performance should correlate with a lower cost of debt.

Another stream of research views CSR as a form of investment (McWilliams & Siegel, 2001). As such, the value of CSR can be evaluated through the principle of the net present value (NPV) approach (Harris & Raviv, 1996). The NPV rule states that a firm should undertake projects with positive NPVs when the value of the discounted cash that flows from its future income streams outweighs the cost of conducting such investment (Hirshleifer, 1961; Ross, 1978). Numerous empirical studies attempt to identify the financial consequences of CSR investments (Barnett & Salomon, 2006; Brammer & Millington, 2008; Surroca et al., 2010; Waddock & Graves, 1997). For example, one perspective (McWilliams & Siegel, 2001) stresses that the costs of CSR-related investments may offset the potential benefits (i.e., zero NPV). Another perspective (Barnea & Rubin, 2005) based on agency theory suggests that a firm manager may overinvest in CSR activities to pursue private benefit at the expense of shareholders (i.e., negative NPV). Nonetheless, recent research by Li et al. (2016) documented that firms with powerful CEOs do not necessarily engage more in CSR activities, which is contrary to what agency theory suggests. Therefore, although there is some evidence that firms integrating various stakeholders' interests in their business operations make better CSR investments, the positive relation between CSR activities and firm performance is not guaranteed. In other words, under certain circumstances, we may observe an insignificant or even positive relation between a firm's CSR profile and the cost of debt.

A third view highlights the potential externalities of socially irresponsible activities (Chava, 2014). Instead of making investments in CSR activities to develop strengths in certain dimensions of socially desirable outcomes, some firms experience significant concerns due to socially irresponsible actions. For example, firms may have inferior performance in their environmental management by the emission of toxic chemicals and hazardous waste. In another instance, firms may have a bad reputation in committing to fair employee treatment. Concerns regarding a firm's CSR profile may expose a firm to higher risk such as an increased likelihood of litigation. Debt holders may view CSR concerns as an indicator of heightened uncertainty of repaying the debt, and thus demand a higher premium to compensate for bearing more risk.

In summary, the relation between borrowing firms' CSR profiles and the cost of debt is ambiguous, and is thereby an empirical question. Despite the limited research along this line, investigating how institutional investors assess issuing firms' corporate social performance in the context of privately placed bonds allows us to offer new insights into the existing literature. For example, should firms devote more resources to satisfy stakeholder demands through CSR initiatives, so that "more is always better" (Harrison & Bosse, 2013)? If not, how much is too much? Moreover, firms issuing securities under Rule 144A are likely to be financially constrained, and the benefits of allocating resources to CSR activities may not justify the cost. It is plausible that these firms may have limited resources to manage stakeholder relationships, and thus result in significant concerns for important stakeholder groups. Will the externalities of socially irresponsible actions adversely affect the cost of debt issued under Rule 144A? In this study, we tend to conduct an empirical investigation to shed some further light on these important issues.

7.2.3 Data, Sample, and Measures

7.2.3.1 Data and Sample

We rely on various data sources to construct our sample. We retrieve information on bond issuances under Rule 144A from the Thomson Reuters SDC Platinum New Issue Database (SDC). We focus on bonds issued by publicly traded firms in the United States, and require our sample bonds to be non-convertible, with a fixed coupon rate and maturity longer than one year. We collect data items such as the issuing company's identity, bond yield, maturity, issue size, and credit rating from the SDC database (Albring et al., 2011; Arena, 2011; Chandra & Nayar, 2008; Chou & Chen, 2014).

We match the bond issuance data from the SDC with the KLD Research & Analytics (KLD) database according to the issuers' names, IDs, and ticker symbols. We further supplement our matched sample with the Compustat database to retrieve necessary financial information. Following the convention, we eliminate financial firms (SIC codes 6000–6999) and utility firms (SIC codes 4900–4999), because firms in these industry segments are highly regulated. Our sampling procedure yields 899 bond issuances under Rule144A by 645 unique firms in the period from 1998 to 2013.

7.2.3.2 Measures

The dependent measure is the cost of bond (i.e., yield spread expressed as basis points) at issuance, which is calculated as the bond yield over the yield of a treasury bond with a similar issuing date and maturity. We further take the natural logarithm of yield spread to normalize the distribution and ease the interpretation of our results.

In line with the existing literature (Becchetti et al., 2013; Deng et al., 2013Greg et al. 2009), we reply on the KLD database to calculate our main explanatory variables. While the KLD dataset is subject to various critics, it is widely adopted by practitioners and academics to obtain objective measures of CSR-related activities and corporate social performance. KLD uses multiple information sources to rate firms across seven broad categories including the environment, community, corporate governance, human rights, employee relations, diversity, and product quality and safety (Goss & Roberts, 2011; Hillman & Keim, 2001). For each category, KLD assigns scores (1/0) for different items according to whether a firm has a concern or a strength along that dimension. We sum up all of the strengths (concerns) for the six dimensions, excluding corporate governance, to obtain CSR_strengths score (CSR_concerns score). Considering that KLD claims that the rating reflects CSR activities at the calendar year-end, we measure CSR_strengths and CSR_Concern with a one-year lag. In the regression analysis, we take the natural logarithm of CSR variables to normalize the distributions (Chan et al., 2014).

In the regression analysis, we control for two sets of variables capturing various aspects of firm characteristics and bond contractual features. We include firm size, Tobin's Q, book leverage, profitability, and sales growth rate as the first set of variables. Specifically, firm size is measured as the natural logarithm of the book value of firm assets. We include Tobin's Q as a proxy for firm growth potential, which is calculated as the firm market capitalization divided by the book value of the asset. We measure firm book leverage as total debt divided by the book value of firm assets. We use return on assets (ROA) as the proxy for firm profitability. In addition, we measure the firm sales growth rate as the percentage change of firm net sales from year $t - 1$ to year t. In the second set of variables, we calculate the issuing size as the natural logarithm of bond proceeds at issuance. Debt maturity is measured as the natural logarithm of the number of years from issuance to maturity. Following Arena (2011), we include a numerical variable to reflect the debt rating of bond issuers, with 22 for grade AAA rating and one for grade D rating.

Table 7.1 Summary statistics

Variables	*N*	Mean	SD	p50
Yield spread (bps)	892	379.956	232.071	334.000
CSR_strengths	892	1.303	2.154	0.000
CSR_concerns	892	1.789	1.714	1.000
Firm size	892	8.228	1.196	8.119
Tobin's Q	892	1.563	0.829	1.324
Profitability	892	0.128	0.073	0.120
Sales growth rate	892	0.622	7.031	0.106
Book leverage	892	0.384	0.157	0.367
Maturity (years)	892	9.214	4.764	8.181
Debt rating	892	10.920	3.293	10.000
Issuing size ($ mil)	892	631.553	1048.566	321.088

7.2.4 Summary Statistics and Univariate Test

Table 7.1 reports the summary statistics of our sample. The Rule 144A bond issuances in our sample have a mean yield spread of 380 basis points and with an average maturity of 9.2 years. The means of CSR_strengths and CSR_concerns are 1.303 and 1.789, respectively. Preliminarily, the results indicate for our sample bond issuances that the concerns in CSR-related activities is more of an issue, because CSR_strengths' scores net of CSR_concerns scores are on average negative. It is worth noting that the mean difference between CSR_strengths and CSR_concerns for issuers of Rule 144A debt offerings is – 0.486, whereas the mean difference of CSR_strengths and CSR_concerns for issuers of public bonds is 1.798 as shown in Table 7.2.

This paper provides descriptive statistics for variables used in regression analyses. Yield spread is the bond yield in basis points at the issuance subtracting the yield of treasure bond with similar issuing date and maturity. CSR_stengths (CSR_conerns) is the sum of all of the scores in different categories, capturing the strengths (concerns) of a firm's corporate social responsibility (CSR) activities in the KLD database. Firm size refers to the natural logarithm of book assets. Tobin's Q is measured as firm market capitalization divided by the book value of firm assets. Profitability is measured as firm return on assets. Sales growth rate is measured as the percentage change of firm net sales from year t – 1 to year t. Book leverage is the ratio of total debt over the book value of firm assets. Maturity is the number of years from bond issuance to maturity. Debt rating is the Standard & Poor's (S&P) long-term debt rating with 22 for grade AAA and 1 for grade D. Issuing size is the bond proceeds.

To reveal some of the uniqueness of our sample bonds, we conducted a univariate analysis to compare bonds issued under Rule 144A and bonds issued to public markets. We chose a matching group of public bonds (N = 3112) issued in the

Table 7.2 Univariate tests

Variables	Rule 144A Bonds (*N* = 892)	Public Bonds (*N* = 3112)	Mean Difference	*t* Statistics
Yield spread	379.956	173.503	206.5***	33.202
CSR strength	1.303	4.816	−3.513***	−24.450
CSR concern	1.789	3.018	−1.229***	−12.790
Firm size	8.230	9.733	−1.504***	−32.712
Tobin's Q	1.562	1.958	−0.396***	−11.076
Profitability	0.128	0.158	−0.0294***	−11.409
Sales growth rate	0.623	5.515	−4.892	−1.205
Book leverage	0.384	0.301	0.0828***	16.999
Years to maturity	9.213	11.596	−2.383***	−7.283
Debt rating	10.920	15.735	−4.816***	−41.981
Issue size	632.010	1218.347	−586.3***	−6.620

***$p < 0.01$. This table reports the univariate tests of key variables for firms issuing bonds issued under Rule 144A and firms issuing bonds in the public market. CSR_stengths (CSR_conerns) is the sum of all of the scores in different categories, capturing the strengths (concerns) of a firm's CSR activities in the KLD database. Firm size is measured as the natural logarithm of book assets. Tobin's Q is measured as firm market capitalization divided by the book value of firm assets. Profitability is measured as firm return on assets. Sales growth rate is measured as the percentage change of firm net sales from year t − 1 to year t. Book leverage is the ratio of total debt over book value of firm assets. Maturity is the number of years from bond issuance to maturity. Debt rating is the S&P long-term debt rating with 22 for grade AAA and one for grade D. Issuing size is the bond proceeds

same year and with similar bond contractual features, including the size of issuance and maturity. As shown in the table, on average, the yield spread of bonds issued under Rule 144A is higher than that of public bonds by 206 basis points. Consistent with previous studies (Denis & Mihov, 2003; Livingston & Zhou, 2002), bond issuers under Rule 144A tend to have lower credit quality in terms of debt rating. Bonds issued under Rule 144A have short maturity and a smaller issuing size. Firms issuing bonds under Rule 144A tend to engage less in CSR-related activities, have less growth potential, and be less profitable. Overall, the results reported in Table 7.2 indicate that bond issuances as well as bond issuers are quite different from those made through public offerings (Denis & Mihov, 2003).

7.2.4.1 Results

Regression Analyses Relating Bond Yield Spread at Issuance to Firm CSR Scores

Table 7.3 reports the baseline regression results relating bond yield spread at issuance under Rule 144A to the CSR involvement of bond issuers. Specifically, we model the bond yield spread as a function of firm CSR scores along with variables capturing various aspects of firm characteristics and bond contractual features (Eq. 7.1). We use the Stata software package to perform our regression analyses.

In all of the model specifications, we include year fixed effects (θ_t) to control for the timely trend and economy-wide shocks. We also add industry fixed effects at the two-digit SIC level (η_j) to absorb all of the industry-level unobservable but time-invariant factors. In addition, we cluster the standard error by firm to control for the possibility that the errors may correlate for the bonds issued by the same firm over time (Petersen, 2009).

$$Bondyieldspreadatissuance = \alpha + \beta * CSRscore + \gamma * Firmcharacteristics + \phi * Bondcharacteristics + \eta_j + \theta_t + \varepsilon \quad (7.1)$$

In columns 1 and 2, we enter CSR_strengths and CSR_concerns separately with controls only for firm characteristics. It appears that CSR_strengths is insignificant in determining bond yield spread (column 1). The results cannot reject neither a risk mitigation hypothesis nor an overinvestment hypothesis. Note that our sample issuing firms have lower credit quality, less profitability, and engage less in CSR-related activities. It is plausible that investors view investments in CSR activities by our sample firms as less attractive because such investments divert scarce resources to non-productive activities. Even if investments in CSR can mitigate firm risk exposure, the benefit can be offset by excessive engagement in CSR-related activities. Strikingly, we document a significant and negative coefficient on CSR_concerns (column 2). It appears that the externalities of CSR activities expose issuing firms to environmental, social, or stakeholder concerns, which result in a higher bond yield spread demanded by investors (Chava, 2014; Goss & Roberts, 2011). We replicate our regression analyses in columns 3 and 4 by adding controls for the debt contractual features, and we generally find consistent results. Overall, the results in Table 7.3 indicate that the qualified institutional investors do assess information in a firm's CSR policy, and demand higher spreads for higher CSR concerns (Goss & Roberts, 2011).

In a similar study, Amiraslani et al. (2018) reported an insignificant relation between CSR and bond spreads in the period 2005–2013, and argued that CSR activities only help reduce the bond spreads in the financial crisis (i.e., 2008–2009). Goss and Roberts (2011) documented that the CSR scores related to concerns have a significantly positive effect on the cost of bank loans. It seems that the effects of CSR on the firm cost of debt vary in different contexts. It is plausible that banks as delegated monitors and inside lenders have the expertise to extract information from borrowers' CSR profiles to facilitate the lending decisions. However, as a means of arm's length financing, investors of public bonds rely more on rating agencies' assessment to gauge the riskiness of the issuance and price the bond accordingly. In the context of private placement under Rule 144A, the bond investors are sophisticated institutional investors, and they resemble the banks in loan contracts in terms of their ability to interpret the information content of issuing firms' CSR profiles (Goss & Roberts, 2011).

Table 7.3 Baseline regressions relating CSR to bond yield spread at issuance under Rule 144A

Independent Variables	Dependent Variable: Yield Spread (in logs)			
	(1)	(2)	(3)	(4)
CSR_strengths	−0.033 (0.039)		−0.011 (0.039)	
CSR_concerns		0.110*** (0.037)		0.129*** (0.036)
Firm size	− 0.182*** (0.023)	−0.216*** (0.021)	−0.156*** (0.027)	−0.180*** (0.025)
Tobin's Q	−0.178*** (0.035)	−0.175*** (0.035)	−0.121*** (0.034)	−0.110*** (0.034)
Profitability	−1.079*** (0.346)	−1.084*** (0.335)	−1.021*** (0.352)	−1.014*** (0.337)
Sales growth rate	−0.002*** (0.001)	−0.002*** (0.001)	−0.002*** (0.001)	−0.002*** (0.001)
Book leverage	0.890*** (0.145)	0.901*** (0.144)	0.864*** (0.142)	0.881*** (0.141)
Maturity			0.003 (0.004)	0.004 (0.004)
Issuing size			−0.000 (0.000)	−0.000** (0.000)
Debt rating			−0.475*** (0.104)	−0.495*** (0.101)
Constant	6.984*** (0.241)	7.137*** (0.236)	6.780*** (0.244)	6.839*** (0.238)
Year fixed effect	Yes	Yes	Yes	Yes
Industry fixed effect	Yes	Yes	Yes	Yes
Observations	892	892	892	892
Adjusted R-squared	0.627	0.633	0.648	0.657

***$p < 0.01$,**$p < 0.05$,*$p < 0.1$. Note the CSR-related activities are a voluntary business decision. In this table, we report the baseline regression rating issuing firms' CSR profiles to the bond yield spread at issuance under Rule 144A. The dependent variable is the natural logarithm of yield spread at issuance. CSR_stengths (CSR_conerns) is the sum of all of the scores in different categories capturing the strengths (concerns) of a firm's CSR activities in the KLD database. Firm size indicates the natural logarithm of book assets. Tobin's Q is measured as firm market capitalization divided by book value of firm assets. Profitability is measured as firm return on assets. Sales growth rate is measured as the percentage change of firm net sales from year t − 1 to year t. Book leverage is the ratio of total debt over the book value of firm assets. Maturity is the number of years from bond issuance to maturity. Debt rating is the S&P long-term debt rating with 22 for grade AAA and one for grade D. Issuing size is the bond proceeds. Clustered standard errors by issuers are reported in parentheses

Regarding other control variables, our results are generally consistent with the existing literature (Francis et al., 2018; Goss & Roberts, 2011). For example, issuing firms experience a lower bond yield spread at issuance when they are larger, more profitable, have a lower debt ratio, and have a higher sales growth rate.

Therefore, the endogeneity issue arises in the baseline regression analysis and can potentially bias the estimation. As Li et al. (2016) suggested, several approaches exist to address the endogeneity issue, which include general method of moments (GMM) estimation, the instrumental variable approach, fixed effect analysis, dynamic panel with lagged dependent variable, and the inclusion of more controls to alleviate omitted variable problems. GMM estimation, fixed effects, and dynamic panel estimation require a panel data structure to obtain consistent estimation. However, our sample consisting of 899 bond issuances by 645 unique issuers is closer to the cross-sectional data, and makes it difficult to implement the above-mentioned three approaches. Therefore, we adopted an instrument variable approach in our estimation (El Ghoul et al., 2011; Goss & Roberts, 2011). In particular, following Rubin (2008) and Di Giuli and Kostovetsky (2014), we used the state voting records as the instrument variable of the firm's CSR involvement. Rubin (2008) found that companies with a high CSR rating tend to be located in democratic states, whereas companies with a low CSR rating tend to be located in republican states. We use state-level voting record for Republican or Democratic as a valid instrument, because the preference in state voting is likely to influence a firm's CSR involvement, but is unlikely to have a direct effect on the cost of bond issuance. Specifically, for each state, we calculated the percentage of votes for Republican as our instrument. Since voting records are only available for the election years, for non-election years, we used voting records in the immediately following election year to calculate the instrument variable.

Table 7.4 reports the second stage regression results with CSR_strengths and CSR_concerns being instrumented by the state voting record of voting Republican, as detailed above. We only control for firm characteristics in columns 1 and 3, and add additional controls for bond contractual features in columns 2 and 4. We document significant and positive coefficients on instrumented CSR_concerns in both columns 3 and 4. The findings based on the instrument variable approach are generally consistent with our findings reported in Table 7.3. We also documented a significant and negative coefficient on CSR_strengths, although the significance is only marginal ($p < 0.10$). In addition, we note that the coefficients of firm size in columns 1 and 2 become insignificant. A recent research by Dang et al. (2018) did a comprehensive investigation regarding the effects of various measures of firm size on empirical corporate finance, and concluded that the choices of measures of firm size matter. Therefore, in order to ensure the robustness of our findings, we used firm market capitalization (logged) as an alternative measure of firm size, and found qualitatively similar results (results not reported). Moreover, we found a relatively high correlation between CSR_strengths and firm size, which reflects that large firms may engage more in CSR activities to build their strengths in fulfilling the demand of multiple stakeholder groups. It is plausible that firm size takes away the significance of CSR_strengths in Table 7.3. As evidenced in columns 1 and 2 in Table 7.4, once the CSR_strengths factor is instrumented, the coefficients of CSR_strengths become marginally significant and negative, and the significance of firm size vanishes.

Moreover, for IV estimations, we conduct several post-estimation diagnostic tests to ensure the appropriateness of our choice of IVs. The significant Durbin–Wu–Hausman test statistics that are reported in Table 7.4 indicate that the CSR variables are indeed endogenous, and other unobservable variables exist and have a strong influence on firms' decision to engage in CSR activities. Therefore, it is appropriate to treat CSR variables as endogenous, and adopt the IV approach to address the issue. We further report the coefficients for the IVs in the first-stage regression and Kleibergen–Paaprk Wald F-statistics for the weak identification test. The significant coefficients of our IVs and large F-values indicate that the chosen instruments are strongly relevant. Additionally, the Kleibergen–Paaprk Lagrange multiplier (LM) statistics suggest that our regression models are well specified and not subject to the under-identification problem (Kleibergen & Paap, 2006). After controlling for the endogeneity issue, we still found a significant and positive relation between CSR_concerns and bond yield spread at issuance. We also note that the effects of CSR_strengths on bond yield spread at issuance turns out to be negative ($p < 0.10$), which further manifests the necessity to address the endogeneity issue in order to obtain consistent estimation.

It is also plausible that price term (i.e., bond yield spread at issuance) and non-price term (maturity) are simultaneously determined. Our estimate can be biased if we fail to control for the simultaneity in the design of bond contracts (Dennis et al., 2000; Goss & Roberts, 2011). We adopt a structural framework to accommodate the simultaneous determination of bond yield spreads and maturity (Bharath et al., 2011; Degryse & Ongena, 2001). Specifically, we assume that bond maturity affects bond yield, and bond maturity can also be separately determined. Following the existing literature (Bharath et al., 2011), we estimate a system of equations through a three-stage least squares (3SLS) estimator, and report the estimation results in Table 7.5.

In Table 7.5, we focus on CSR_strengths and CSR_concerns in columns 1–2 and columns 3–4, respectively. Generally, we find that maturity is positively correlated with bond yield spread at issuance. It is plausible that investors may demand a higher yield for bonds with longer maturity because the associated risk exposure will be higher. Nonetheless, this model specification does not take away our main findings. Taken as a whole, results reported in Tables 7.3, 7.4, 7.5 indicate that higher CSR concerns are associated with higher bond spreads. Moreover, across different model specifications, CSR strengths are generally insignificant.

Additional Robustness Checks

In this section, we examine whether institutional investors also make use of information in the time-series changes of the firm CSR scores of our sample issuers. Over time, firms can invest in CSR activities to improve their corporate social performance. By doing so, firms can either increase their CSR profiles or limit their expose themselves to more social, environmental, or stakeholder issues. In

Table 7.4 Addressing the endogeneity issue: an instrumental variable approach

Independent Variables	Dependent Variable: Yield Spread (in logs)			
	(1)	(2)	(3)	(4)
CSR_strengths (Instrumented)	−1.203* (0.633)	−1.067* (0.544)		
CSR_concerns (Instrumented)			0.971** (0.393)	0.984** (0.408)
Firm size	0.178 (0.196)	0.086 (0.126)	−0.400*** (0.084)	−0.326*** (0.071)
Tobin's Q	0.003 (0.106)	0.011 (0.075)	−0.109** (0.044)	−0.030 (0.050)
Profitability	−0.849* (0.462)	−0.911** (0.420)	−1.074*** (0.305)	−0.963*** (0.295)
Sales growth rate	−0.001* (0.001)	−0.002*** (0.001)	−0.002** (0.001)	−0.002*** (0.001)
Book leverage	0.717*** (0.212)	0.601*** (0.223)	0.946*** (0.150)	0.979*** (0.156)
Maturity		−0.005 (0.007)		0.009 (0.006)
Issuing size		0.000 (0.000)		−0.000*** (0.000)
Debt rating		−0.226 (0.195)		−0.610*** (0.121)
Constant	5.018*** (1.381)	5.643*** (0.846)	8.218*** (0.315)	7.504*** (0.238)
Year fixed effect	Yes	Yes	Yes	Yes
Industry fixed effect	Yes	Yes	Yes	Yes
Observations	892	892	892	892
Adjusted R-squared	0.167	0.196	0.193	0.231
Durbin–Wu–Hausman (endogeneity test)	10.007	9.984	8.228	7.68
	($p < 0.01$)	($p < 0.01$)	($p < 0.01$)	($p < 0.01$)
Kleibergen–Paaprk LM statistic (under-identification test)	5.98	7.394	10.501	10.398
	($p < 0.05$)	($p < 0.01$)	($p < 0.01$)	($p < 0.01$)
First-stage coefficient of instrument	−2.191	−2.443	3.14	2.98
	($p < 0.05$)	($p < 0.01$)	($p < 0.01$)	($p < 0.01$)
Kleibergen–Paaprk Wald F statistic (weak identification test)	4.804	5.963	9.894	8.911
	($p < 0.05$)	($p < 0.01$)	($p < 0.01$)	($p < 0.01$)

***$p < 0.01$,**$p < 0.05$,*$p < 0.1$. In this table, we used the instrumental variable approach to address the endogeneity issue. The dependent variable is the natural logarithm of yield spread at issuance. CSR_stengths (CSR_conerns) is the sum of all of the scores in different categories capturing the strengths (concerns) of a firm's CSR activities in the KLD database. We use the state voting records in the presidential election as the instrument variable of the firm's CSR involvement. Firm size is measured as the natural logarithm of book assets. Tobin's Q is measured as firm market capitalization divided by the book value of firm assets. Profitability is measured as firm return on assets. Sales growth rate is measured as the percentage change of firm net sales from year t − 1 to year t. Book leverage is the ratio of total debt over the book value of firm assets. Maturity is the number of years from bond issuance to maturity. Debt rating is the S&P long-term debt rating, with 22 for grade AAA and one for grade D. Issuing size is the bond proceeds. Clustered standard errors by issuers are reported in parentheses

Table 7.5 Simultaneous determination of bond yield spread and maturity: three-stage least squares (3SLS) estimation

Independent Variables	Dependent Variables			
	Yield Spread	Maturity	Yield Spread	Maturity
	(1)	(2)	(3)	(4)
Maturity	0.045** (0.018)		0.056** −0.028	
CSR strengths	0.011 (0.029)	−0.249 (0.607)		
CSR concerns			0.118*** −0.03	−1.970* −1.094
Firm size	−0.171*** (0.020)	3.747** (1.662)	−0.195*** −0.021	3.237* −1.777
Tobin's Q	−0.137*** (0.021)	2.986* (1.546)	−0.124*** −0.021	2.026 −1.346
Profitability	−1.497*** (0.230)	32.738** (15.376)	−1.530*** −0.241	25.353* −14.065
Sales growth rate	−0.001 (0.002)	0.032 (0.046)	−0.001 −0.002	0.018 −0.036
Book leverage	1.035*** (0.110)	−22.626** (11.023)	1.042*** −0.112	−17.177* −10.2
Issue size	−0.000*** (0.000)	0.002** (0.001)	−0.000*** 0	0.002** −0.001
Debt rating	−0.440*** (0.070)	9.620* (5.077)	−0.453*** −0.069	7.424 −4.836
Constant	6.812*** (0.332)	−148.737* (79.230)	6.718*** −0.375	−109.556 −74.006
Year fixed effect	Yes	Yes	Yes	Yes
Industry fixed effect	Yes	Yes	Yes	Yes
Observations	892	892	892	892
Adjusted R-squared	0.633	0.756	0.597	0.492

***$p < 0.01$,**$p < 0.05$,*$p < 0.1$. This table reports regression results using 3SLS estimator to estimate a system of two equations. The dependent variables are the natural logarithm of yield spread at issuance and bond maturity. CSR_stengths (CSR_conerns) is the sum of all of the scores in different categories capturing the strengths (concerns) of a firm's CSR activities in the KLD database. Firm size is measured as the natural logarithm of book assets. Tobin's Q is measured as firm market capitalization divided by the book value of firm assets. Profitability is measured as firm return on assets. Sales growth rate is measured as the percentage change of firm net sales from year t − 1 to year t. Book leverage is the ratio of total debt over book value of firm assets. Maturity is the number of years from bond issuance to maturity. Debt rating is the S&P long-term debt rating, with 22 for grade AAA and one for grade D. Issuing size is the bond proceeds. Clustered standard errors by issuers are reported in parentheses

Table 7.6, we link bond yield spread at issuance to the changes of CSR strengths and concerns over time.

We adopt a three-year window to measure the changes of CSR strengths for year t− 4 to year t − 1, with year t being the year of bond issuance. In addition, we measure the changes with a four-year window and a five-year window. For CSR concerns, we follow the same approach to measure the changes in different time windows. In columns 1–3 of Table 7.6, we focus on the changes in CSR strengths, and in columns 4–6, we focus on the changes in CSR concerns. Our results indicate that the increased number of CSR concerns over the past three-year and four-year windows results in a higher bond yield spread at issuance. It appears that institutional investors tend to demand a higher premium on bonds issued under Rule 144A, if the issuing firms expose themselves to more environmental, social, and stakeholder risk due to socially irresponsible activities. In addition, we find that the improvement of CSR strengths is not significantly correlated with bond yield spread. It is plausible that, from institutional investors' point of view, the benefits of improved corporate social performance do not justify the incurred cost of allocating extra resources to CSR-related activities.

Given that institutional investors demand a higher bond yield spread for bonds issued by firms facing greater concerns for environmental, social, and stakeholder risks, we further explore the sources of increased risk exposure in this section, and report our results in Table 7.7.

Existing studies have found that stakeholder risk associated with CSR activities may negatively affect a firm's volatility and the cost of bank loans (Becchetti et al., 2015; Goss & Roberts, 2011). Firms engaging in CSR-related activities adopt a more complex strategy of stakeholder satisfaction. Firms taking socially responsible actions may set priorities on the demand of different stakeholder groups in order to retain their willful participation in productive operations (Harrison et al., 2010). Conflicts exist among various stakeholder groups when firms cannot fulfill their demands. Therefore, certain CSR concerns may indicate the level of stakeholder risk. Following Becchetti et al. (2015), we focus on the following KLD items: COM-con-A, COM-con-B, COM-con-C, COM-con-D, COM-con-X, DIV-con-A, DIV-con-X, EMP-con-B, EMP-con-X, ENV-con-X, HUM-con-D, HUM-con-F, HUM-con-G, HUM-con-X, PRO-con-A, PRO-con-D, and PRO-con-E, PRO-con-X. For each item, the KLD assigns a binary score (1/0), with one indicating that a particular firm has a concern for that time. We measured stakeholder risk as the sum of the scores for all of the items, and then scale the total number of concerns by the total number (18) of items.

In addition, we also made a distinction between a firm's primary stakeholder groups and secondary stakeholder groups. Managing relationships with primary stakeholders helps firms develop productive intangible assets, and thus create shareholder value (Hillman & Keim, 2001). Secondary stakeholders do not get directly involved in direct transactions with the firms (Jamali, 2008). We thereby classified CSR activities according to their target stakeholder groups (Buysse & Verbeke, 2003). The items for concerns for primary stakeholders (Concerns_primary stakeholders) are from the KLD categories including employee relations,

Table 7.6 Time-series changes in CSR profiles and bond yield spread at issuance under Rule 144A

Independent Variables	Dependent Variable: Yield Spread (in logs)					
	(1)	(2)	(3)	(4)	(5)	(6)
Δ CSR_ strengths (t− 3)	−0.003 (0.018)					
Δ CSR_ strengths (t− 4)		0.007 (0.022)				
Δ CSR_ strengths (t− 5)			0.000 (0.020)			
Δ CSR_ concerns (t− 3)				0.037** (0.016)		
Δ CSR_ concerns (t− 4)					0.0270** (0.014)	
Δ CSR_ concerns (t− 5)						0.025 (0.016)
Firm size	−0.121*** (0.031)	−0.110*** (0.032)	−0.123*** (0.036)	−0.114*** (0.030)	−0.128*** (0.035)	−0.123*** (0.030)
Tobin's Q	−0.098*** (0.035)	−0.091** (0.039)	−0.074* (0.044)	−0.087** (0.041)	−0.072 (0.044)	−0.097*** (0.036)
Profitability	−1.192*** (0.423)	−1.157** (0.493)	−1.206** (0.510)	−1.169** (0.499)	−1.216** (0.509)	−1.192*** (0.427)
Sales growth rate	0.034 (0.061)	0.007 (0.067)	−0.005 (0.082)	−0.003 (0.070)	−0.013 (0.084)	0.034 (0.064)
Book leverage	0.859*** (0.171)	0.904*** (0.186)	0.918*** (0.195)	0.896*** (0.183)	0.901*** (0.193)	0.854*** (0.170)
Maturity	0.004 (0.005)	0.003 (0.005)	0.001 (0.005)	0.003 (0.004)	0.001 (0.005)	0.004 (0.005)
Issue size	−0.000* (0.000)	−0.000** (0.000)	−0.000 (0.000)	−0.000* (0.000)	−0.000 (0.000)	−0.000* (0.000)
Debt rating	−0.494*** (0.114)	−0.544*** (0.116)	−0.566*** (0.130)	−0.540*** (0.114)	−0.563*** (0.128)	−0.493*** (0.114)
Constant	6.446*** (0.297)	6.351*** (0.313)	6.459*** (0.345)	6.343*** (0.294)	6.468*** (0.323)	6.443*** (0.289)
Year fixed effect	Yes	Yes	Yes	Yes	Yes	Yes
Firm fixed effect	Yes	Yes	Yes	Yes	Yes	Yes

(continued)

Table 7.6 (continued)

Independent Variables	Dependent Variable: Yield Spread (in logs)					
	(1)	(2)	(3)	(4)	(5)	(6)
Observations	590	512	460	590	512	460
Adjusted R-squared	0.682	0.698	0.705	0.702	0.707	0.684

$^{***}p < 0.01$,$^{**}p < 0.05$,$^{*}p < 0.1$. This table reports the regression results relating to the time-series changes in CSR profiles to bond yield spread at issuance under Rule 144A. The dependent variable is the natural logarithm of yield spread at issuance. CSR_stengths (CSR_conerns) is the sum of all of the scores in different categories capturing the strengths (concerns) of a firm's CSR activities in the KLD database. The main explanatory variables are the changes in CSR-strengths and CSR_concerns from year t − 5 to year t − 1, year t − 4 to year t − 1, and year t − 3 to year t − 1. We use the state voting records in presidential election as the instrument variable of the firm's CSR involvement. Firm size the natural logarithm of book assets. Tobin's Q is measured as firm market capitalization divided by the book value of firm assets. Profitability is measured as firm return on assets. Sales growth rate is measured as the percentage change of firm net sales from year t − 1 to year t. Book leverage is the ratio of total debt over the book value of firm assets. Maturity is the number of years from bond issuance to maturity. Debt rating is the S&P long-term debt rating with 22 for grade AAA and one for grade D. Issuing size is the bond proceeds. Clustered standard errors by issuers are reported in parentheses

diversity dimensions, and product relations. The items for concerns for secondary stakeholders (Concerns_secondary stakeholder) are from KLD categories including community relations, and environmental and human rights.

In columns 1–3 of Table 7.7, we separately examine stakeholder conflicts, concerns for primary stakeholders, and concerns for secondary stakeholders. We documented a significant and positive coefficient on stakeholder conflict in column 1. It appears that concerns for primary stakeholders have a significant and positive effect on bond yield spread at issuance under Rule 144A. However, the concerns for secondary stakeholders seem to have an insignificant effect on bond yield spread. Overall, the findings reported in Table 7.7 indicate that firms CSR strategies are not necessarily in line with the expectation of all of the stakeholder groups. Conflicts among various stakeholders may reflect the inefficient utilization of firm resources, which are more important for those firms that issue bonds under Rule 144A. More important, the stakeholder conflicts expose firms to higher risks, and consequently, investors demand higher bond yield spreads. Our results also reveal that the concerns for primary stakeholders are important. After all, primary stakeholders have a more salient footprint on a firm's business operation.

7.3 Summary and Conclusions

This study investigates the relationship between CSR and the firm cost of capital from the debt-holder perspective. Particularly, we focus on bonds issued under Rule 144A, because the issuing firms tend to have lower credit quality, and the investors are qualified and sophisticated institutional investors. Rule 144A bond

Table 7.7 Exploring sources of risk exposure in CSR profiles and bond yield spread

Independent Variables	Dependent Variable: Yield Spread (in logs)		
	(1)	(2)	(3)
Stakeholder conflict	0.049** (0.022)		
Concerns_primary stakeholders		0.038** (0.016)	
Concerns_secondary stakeholders			0.024 (0.028)
Firm size	−0.177*** (0.024)	−0.166*** (0.023)	−0.159*** (0.025)
Tobin's Q	−0.129*** (0.039)	−0.131*** (0.039)	−0.132*** (0.039)
Profitability	−1.327*** (0.365)	−1.298*** (0.372)	−1.353*** (0.373)
Sales growth rate	−0.002*** (0.001)	−0.002*** (0.001)	−0.002*** (0.001)
Book leverage	0.984*** (0.143)	0.983*** (0.143)	0.985*** (0.145)
Maturity	0.004 (0.004)	0.003 (0.004)	0.003 (0.004)

(continued)

Table 7.7 (continued)

Independent Variables	Dependent Variable: Yield Spread (in logs)		
	(1)	(2)	(3)
Issue size	−0.000** (0.000)	−0.000** (0.000)	−0.000** (0.000)
Debt rating	−0.461*** (0.091)	−0.455*** (0.091)	−0.445*** (0.090)
Constant	7.280*** (0.221)	7.183*** (0.220)	7.139*** (0.226)
Year fixed effect	Yes	Yes	Yes
Firm fixed effect	Yes	Yes	Yes
Observations	892	892	892
Adjusted R-squared	0.709	0.708	0.705

***$p < 0.01$,**$p < 0.05$,*$p < 0.1$. This table reports the regression results relating various aspects of CSR profiles to bond yield spread at issuance under Rule 144A. The dependent variable is the natural logarithm of yield spread at issuance. Stakeholder conflicts capture the complexity in CSR strategy and stakeholder risk. Concerns_primary stakeholder is the CSR_concerns related to primary stakeholders, including employee relations, diversity, and product relations. Concerns_secondary stakeholder is the CSR_concerns related to secondary stakeholders, including the community, and environmental and human rights. We use the state voting records in presidential elections as the instrument variable of the firm's CSR involvement. Firm size is measured as the natural logarithm of book assets. Tobin's Q is measured as firm market capitalization divided by the book value of firm assets. Profitability is measured as firm return on assets. Sales growth rate is measured as the percentage change of firm net sales from year t − 1 to year t. Book leverage is the ratio of total debt over the book value of firm assets. Maturity is the number of years from bond issuance to maturity. Debt rating is the S&P long-term debt rating, with a rating of 22 for grade AAA and one for grade D. Issuing size is the bond proceeds. Clustered standard errors by issuers are reported in parentheses issuances provide an ideal setting to investigate how institutional investors make use of the information in the CSR profiles of issuing firms. Moreover, given that issuing firms may have limited organizational slack and limited access to the public debt market, we may gain new insights regarding the effects of investments in CSR activities on firm financial outcomes.

Our empirical analyses reveal that the CSR concerns of issuing firms result in a higher bond yield spread at issuance. However, we only document an insignificant effect of CSR strengths on bond pricing. It is plausible that the benefits of engaging in CSR activities do not justify the cost of diverting productive resources to achieve socially desirable outcomes, at least for the issuing firms in our sample. Nevertheless, CSR concerns may expose issuing firms to higher risk (e.g., litigation risk) and have an adverse effect on the ability of issuing firms to repay the debt. Consequently, investors of Rule 144A bonds demand higher premiums for firms with higher CSR concerns. Additionally, institutional investors purchasing Rule 144A bonds indeed extract information from both cross-sectional and time-series variations in issuing firms' CSR profiles. Our empirical results indicate that the main sources of risk exposure due to externalities of CSR activities are stakeholder conflicts and concerns from primary stakeholders.

Our research has important managerial implications for practitioners as well. CSR strategies are not isolated decisions, and their instrumental value can only be evaluated in conjunction with other critical firm decisions. Since the effectiveness of CSR strategies is context-dependent, resource configuration and allocation to CSR activities has to be integrated with firm core business and operation. Moreover, corporate managers need to take into consideration the externalities of socially irresponsible activities, because those activities may expose the firms to significant risk and reduce firm value.

Nonetheless, our study is not without limitations. For example, because of the lack of information on the qualified institutional investors, we do not know who purchases the bonds issued under Rule 144A. Therefore, we are unable to further explore the dynamics regarding the interactions between the bond issuers and bond buyers, which hinders our understanding of the underlying mechanisms in the issuing process of Rule 144A debt offerings. Furthermore, we do not explicitly examine those issuers with experience related to both public issuances and private placements. It appears that the effects of CSR vary in different contexts, and not every economic agent interprets the information regarding CSR in the same way. These limitations also present future research opportunities to advance our understanding regarding the role played by corporate social responsibility in the capital markets.

Acknowledgements This chapter is based on the article previously published as: Dbouk, W., Jin, D., Wang, H., & Wang, J. (2018). Corporate social responsibility and rule 144A debt offerings: Empirical evidence. International Journal of Financial Studies, 6(4), 94. https://doi.org/https://doi.org/10.3390/ijfs6040094. Reprinted with permission from International Journal of Financial Studies.

References

Albring, S. M., Khurana, I. K., Nejadmalayeri, A., & Pereira, R. (2011). Managerial compensation and the debt placement decision. *Journal of Corporate Finance, 17*, 1445–1456.

Albuquerque, R. A., Durnev, A., & Koskinen, Y. (2014). *Corporate social responsibility and firm risk: Theory and empirical evidence*. CEPR.

Amit, R., & Wernerfelt, B. (1990). Why do firms reduce business risk? *Academy of Management Journal, 33*, 520–533.

Amiraslani, H., Lins, K., Servaes, H., & Tamayo, A. (2018). *The bond market benefits of corporate social capital.* ECGI Finance Working Paper.

Arena, M. P. (2011). The corporate choice between public debt, bank loans, traditional private debt placements, and 144A debt issues. *Review of Quantitative Finance and Accounting, 36*, 391–416.

Bae, K.-H., Kang, J.-K., & Wang, J. (2011). Employee treatment and firm leverage: A test of the stakeholder theory of capital structure. *Journal of Financial Economics, 100*, 130–153. https://doi.org/10.1016/j.jfineco.2010.10.019

Barnea, A., & Rubin, A. (2005). *Corporate social responsibility as a conflict between owners.* Working paper, Simon Fraser University.

Barnett, M. L., & Salomon, R. M. (2006). Beyond dichotomy: The curvilinear relationship between social responsibility and financial performance. *Strategic Management Journal, 27*, 1101–1122.

Becchetti, L., Ciciretti, R., Hasan, I., & Kobeissi, N. (2012). Corporate social responsibility and shareholder's value. *Journal of Business Research, 65*, 1628–1635. https://doi.org/10.1016/j.jbusres.2011.10.022

Becchetti, L., Ciciretti, R., & Giovannelli, A. (2013). Corporate social responsibility and earnings forecasting unbiasedness. *Journal of Banking & Finance, 37*, 3654–3668. https://doi.org/10.1016/j.jbankfin.2013.05.026

Becchetti, L., Ciciretti, R., & Hasan, I. (2015). Corporate social responsibility, stakeholder risk, and idiosyncratic volatility. *Journal of Corporate Finance, 35*, 297–309.

Benlemlih, M., & Girerd-Potin, I. (2017). Corporate social responsibility and firm financial risk reduction: On the moderating role of the legal environment. *Journal of Business Finance & Accounting, 44*, 1137–1166.

Bettis, R. A. (1983). Modern financial theory, corporate strategy and public policy: Three conundrums. *Academy of Management Review, 8*, 406–415.

Bharath, S. T., Dahiya, S., Saunders, A., & Srinivasan, A. (2011). Lending relationships and loan contract terms. *Review of Financial Studies, 24*, 1141–1203.

Botosan, C. A. (2000). Evidence that greater disclosure lowers the cost of equity capital. *Journal of Applied Corporate Finance, 12*(4), 60–69.

Brammer, S., & Millington, A. (2008). Does it pay to be different? An analysis of the relationship between corporate social and financial performance. *Strategic Management Journal, 29*, 1325–1343.

Buysse, K., & Verbeke, A. (2003). Proactive environmental strategies: A stakeholder management perspective. *Strategic Management Journal, 24*, 453–470.

Cai, L., Cui, J., & Jo, H. (2016). Corporate environmental responsibility and firm risk. *Journal of Business Ethics, 139*, 563–594.

Chan, M. C. C., Watson, J., & Woodliff, D. (2014). Corporate governance quality and CSR disclosures. *Journal of Business Ethics, 125*, 59–73.

Chandra, U., & Nayar, N. N. (2008). The information content of private debt placements. *Journal of Business Finance & Accounting, 35*, 1164–1195.

Chang, K., Kim, I., & Li, Y. (2014). The heterogeneous impact of corporate social responsibility activities that target different stakeholders. *Journal of Business Ethics, 125*, 211–234.

Chaplinsky, S., & Ramchand, L. (2004). The impact of SEC Rule 144A on corporate debt issuance by international firms. *The Journal of Business, 77*, 1073–1098.

Chava, S. (2014). Environmental externalities and cost of capital. *Management Science, 60*, 2223–2247.

Chou, R., & Chen, M.-J. (2014). Long-run stock return and operating performance following private debt placements. *NTU Management Review, 25*, 33–62. https://doi.org/10.6226/nturm2014.dec.r.12011

Cheng, B., Ioannou, I., & Serafeim, G. (2014). Corporate social responsibility and access to finance. *Strategic Management Journal, 35*, 1–23.

Cheung, A. W. K. (2016). Corporate social responsibility and corporate cash holdings. *Journal of Corporate Finance, 37*, 412–430.

Dang, C., Li, Z., & Yang, C. (2018). Measuring firm size in empirical corporate finance. *Journal of Banking & Finance, 86*, 159–176.

Degryse, H., & Ongena, S. (2001). Bank relationships and firm profitability. *Financial Management, 1*(Spring), 9–34.

Deng, X., Kang, J.-K., & Low, B. S. (2013). Corporate social responsibility and stakeholder value maximization: Evidence from mergers. *Journal of Financial Economics, 110*, 87–109. https://doi.org/10.1016/j.jfineco.2013.04.014

Denis, D. J., & Mihov, V. T. (2003). The choice among bank debt, non-bank private debt, and public debt: Evidence from new corporate borrowings. *Journal of Financial Economics, 70*, 3–28.

Dennis, S., Nandy, D., & Sharpe, I. G. (2000). The determinants of contract terms in bank revolving credit agreements. *Journal of Financial and Quantitative Analysis, 35*, 87–110.

Di Giuli, A., & Kostovetsky, L. (2014). Are red or blue companies more likely to go green? Politics and corporate social responsibility. *Journal of Financial Economics, 111*, 158–180. https://doi.org/10.1016/j.jfineco.2013.10.002

Dhaliwal, D. S., Li, O. Z., Tsang, A., & Yang, Y. G. (2011). Voluntary nonfinancial disclosure and the cost of equity capital: The initiation of corporate social responsibility reporting. *The Accounting Review, 86*, 59–100.

Djankov, S., Hart, O., McLiesh, C., & Shleifer, A. (2008). Debt enforcement around the world. *Journal of Political Economy, 116*, 1105–1149.

Dbouk, W., Jin, D., Wang, H., & Wang, J. (2018). Corporate social responsibility and Rule 144A debt offerings: Empirical evidence. *International Journal of Financial Studies, 6*(4), 94.

El Ghoul, S., Guedhami, O., Kwok, C. C. Y., & Mishra, D. R. (2011). Does corporate social responsibility affect the cost of capital? *Journal of Banking & Finance, 35*, 2388–2406. https://doi.org/10.1016/j.jbankfin.2011.02.007

Fama, E. F., & French, K. R. (1993). Common risk factors in the returns on stocks and bonds. *Journal of Financial Economics, 33*, 3–56.

Fenn, G. W. (2000). Speed of issuance and the adequacy of disclosure in the 144A high-yield debt market. *Journal of Financial Economics, 56*, 383–405.

Flammer, C. (2021). Corporate green bonds. *Journal of Financial Economics, 142*, 499–516.

Francis, J., LaFond, R., Olsson, P. M., & Schipper, K. (2004). Costs of equity and earnings attributes. *The Accounting Review, 79*, 967–1010.

Francis, B., Hasan, I., Liu, L., & Wang, H. (2018). Employee treatment and contracting with bank lenders: An instrumental approach for stakeholder management. *Journal of Business Ethics* (in press).

Garriga, E., & Melé, D. (2004). Corporate social responsibility theories: Mapping the territory. *Journal of Business Ethics, 53*, 51–71.

Godfrey, P. C. (2005). The relationship between corporate philanthropy and shareholder wealth: A risk management perspective. *Academy of Management Review, 30*, 777–798.

Godfrey, P. C., Merrill, C. B., & Hansen, J. M. (2009). The relationship between corporate social responsibility and shareholder value: An empirical test of the risk management hypothesis. *Strategic Management Journal, 30*, 425–445.

Goss, A., & Roberts, G. S. (2011). The impact of corporate social responsibility on the cost of bank loans. *Journal of Banking & Finance, 35*, 1794–1810. https://doi.org/10.1016/j.jbankfin.2010.12.002

Harris, M., & Raviv, A. (1996). The capital budgeting process: Incentives and information. *Journal of Finance, 51*, 1139–1174.

Harjoto, M., & Jo, H. (2015). Legal vs. normative CSR: Differential impact on analyst dispersion, stock return volatility, cost of capital, and firm value. *Journal of Business Ethics, 128*, 1–20.

Harjoto, M., & Laksmana, I. (2016). The impact of corporate social responsibility on risk taking and firm value. *Journal of Business Ethics, 151*, 353–373.

Harrison, J. S., & Bosse, D. A. (2013). How much is too much? The limits to generous treatment of stakeholders. *Business Horizons, 56*, 313–322.

Harrison, J. S., Bosse, D. A., & Phillips, R. A. (2010). Managing for stakeholders, stakeholder utility functions, and competitive advantage. *Strategic Management Journal, 31*, 58–74.

Hasan, I., Kobeissi, N., Liu, L., & Wang, H. (2018). Corporate social responsibility and firm financial performance: The mediating role of productivity. *Journal of Business Ethics, 149*, 671–688.

Hillman, A. J., & Keim, G. D. (2001). Shareholder value, stakeholder management, and social issues: What's the bottom line? *Strategic Management Journal, 22*, 125–139.

Hirshleifer, J. (1961). Risk, the discount rate, and investment decisions. *American Economic Review, 61*, 112–120.

Hsu, F. J., & Chen, Y.-C. (2015). Is a firm's financial risk associated with corporate social responsibility? *Management Decision, 53*, 2175–2199.

Huang, R., & Ramirez, G. G. (2010). Speed of issuance, lender specialization, and the rise of the 144A debt market. *Financial Management, 39*, 643–673.

Jamali, D. (2008). A stakeholder approach to corporate social responsibility: A fresh perspective into theory and practice. *Journal of Business Ethics, 82*, 213–231.

Jiraporn, P., Jiraporn, N., Boeprasert, A., & Chang, K. (2014). Does corporate social responsibility (CSR) improve credit ratings? Evidence from geographic identification. *Financial Management, 43*, 505–531.

Jo, H., & Na, H. (2012). Does CSR reduce firm risk? Evidence from controversial industry sectors. *Journal of Business Ethics, 110*, 441–456.

Kleibergen, F., & Paap, R. (2006). Generalized reduced rank tests using the singular value decomposition. *Journal of Econometrics, 133*, 97–126.

Kraus, A., & Litzenberger, R. H. (1973). A state-preference model of optimal financial leverage. *Journal of Finance, 28*, 911–922.

Kytle, B., & Ruggie, J. G. (2005). *Corporate social responsibility as risk management: A model for multinationals*. CSR Initiative Working Paper No. 10, Harvard Kennedy School.

La Porta, R., Lopez-de-Silanes, F., Shleifer, A., & Vishny, R. W. (2000). Investor protection and corporate governance. *Journal of Financial Economics, 58*, 3–27.

Lee, D. D., & Faff, R. W. (2009). Corporate sustainability performance and idiosyncratic risk. *The Financial Review, 44*, 213–237.

Li, F., Li, T., & Minor, D. (2016). CEO power, corporate social responsibility, and firm value: A test of agency theory. *International Journal of Managerial Finance, 12*, 611–628.

Lins, K. V., Servaes, H., & Tamayo, A. (2017). Social capital, trust, and firm performance: The value of corporate social responsibility during the financial crisis. *Journal of Finance, 72*, 1785–1824.

Livingston, M., & Zhou, L. (2002). The impact of Rule 144A debt offerings upon bond yields and underwriter fees. *Financial Management, 1*, 5–27.

Luo, X., & Bhattacharya, C. B. (2009). The debate over doing good: Corporate social performance, strategic marketing levers, and firm-idiosyncratic risk. *Journal of Marketing, 73*, 198–213.

Mackey, A., Mackey, T. B., & Barney, J. B. (2007). Corporate social responsibility and firm performance: Investor preferences and corporate strategies. *Academy of Management Review, 32*, 817–835.

Margolis, J., & Walsh, J. (2003). Misery loves companies: Rethinking social initiatives by business. *Administrative Science Quarterly, 48*, 268–305.

McWilliams, A., & Siegel, D. (2001). Corporate social responsibility: A theory of the firm perspective. *Academy of Management Review, 26*, 117–127.

Minor, D., & Morgan, J. (2011). CSR as reputation insurance: *Primum non nocere. California Management Review, 53*, 40–59.
Modigliani, F., & Miller, M. H. (1958). The cost of capital, corporation finance and the theory of investment. *American Economic Review, 48*, 261–297.
Myers, S. C., & Majluf, N. S. (1984). Corporate financing and investment decisions when firms have information that investors do not have. *Journal of Financial Economics, 13*, 187–221.
Oikonomou, I., Brooks, C., & Pavelin, S. (2014). The effects of corporate social performance on the cost of corporate debt and credit ratings. *Financial Review, 49*, 49–75.
Orlitzky, M., & Benjamin, J. D. (2001). Corporate social performance and firm risk: A meta-analytic review. *Business & Society, 40*, 369–396.
Petersen, M. A. (2009). Estimating standard errors in finance panel data sets: Comparing approaches. *Review of Financial Studies, 22*, 435–480.
Peterson, D. K. (2004). The relationship between perceptions of corporate citizenship and organizational commitment. *Business & Society, 43*, 296–319.
Pástor, Ľ, & Stambaugh, R. F. (2003). Liquidity risk and expected stock returns. *Journal of Political Economy, 111*, 642–685.
Rajan, R. G., & Zingales, L. (1995). What do we know about capital structure? Some evidence from international data. *Journal of Finance, 50*, 1421–1460.
Ross, S. A. (1978). A simple approach to the valuation of risky assets. *Journal of Business, 51*, 453–475.
Rubin, A. (2008). Political views and corporate decision making: The case of corporate social responsibility. *Financial Review, 43*, 337–360.
Salama, A., Anderson, K., & Toms, J. S. (2011). Does community and environmental responsibility affect firm risk? Evidence from UK panel data 1994–2006. *Business Ethics: A European Review, 20*, 192–204.
Stulz, R. M. (1996). Rethinking risk management. *Journal of Applied Corporate Finance, 9*, 8–25.
Surroca, J., Tribó, J. A., & Waddock, S. (2010). Corporate responsibility and financial performance: The role of intangible resources. *Strategic Management Journal, 31*, 463–490.
Titman, S., & Wessels, R. (1988). The determinants of capital structure choice. *Journal of Finance, 43*, 1–19.
Waddock, S., & Graves, S. (1997). The corporate social performance–financial performance link. *Strategic Management Journal, 18*, 303–319.

The Impact of ESG Initiatives During the Pandemic 8

8.1 Introduction: ESG as a Strategic Asset in Times of Crisis

The COVID-19 pandemic posed one of the most profound and unpredictable shocks to the global economy in modern history. Firms across sectors faced extraordinary disruption to supply chains, labor forces, capital markets, and consumer demand. At the same time, the crisis laid bare deep societal vulnerabilities—ranging from public health inequalities and labor precarity to the fragility of global logistics and the urgency of climate adaptation. Against this backdrop, a growing body of evidence suggests that firms with strong Environmental, Social, and Governance (ESG) foundations weathered the storm with greater resilience than their peers.

Theoretically, ESG initiatives provide firms with a multidimensional strategic buffer against exogenous shocks by embedding resilience into the very architecture of corporate decision-making. Rather than reacting to crises with ad hoc measures, ESG-oriented firms are more likely to anticipate risks and establish mechanisms for early warning, stakeholder engagement, and adaptive resource allocation. These firms often possess more transparent and accountable governance structures, enabling swift, credible responses when uncertainty escalates. Boards that prioritize ESG tend to be more diverse and independent, characteristics linked to broader perspectives, better oversight, and fewer governance failures in high-pressure environments. Moreover, ESG alignment fosters stronger and more enduring relationships with internal and external stakeholders. Employees in ESG-focused firms often report higher morale and loyalty, which can be critical in maintaining operational continuity during labor shortages or public health emergencies. Customers may demonstrate greater trust and brand attachment, making them less likely to switch providers during disruptions. Investors, particularly institutional ones, increasingly use ESG as a proxy for long-term orientation and ethical risk management, thereby offering more patient capital in turbulent times.

J. Wang, *ESG Strategies and Financial Markets*, Management for Professionals,
https://doi.org/10.1007/978-981-95-5620-5_8

From a risk management perspective, ESG frameworks also prompt firms to proactively identify and address vulnerabilities that may otherwise remain latent until triggered by a shock. This includes climate risk assessments, supply chain audits, human capital evaluations, and compliance system stress tests. These efforts not only reduce exposure to environmental and social liabilities but also enhance firms' capacity to navigate complexity and uncertainty.

Unlike traditional financial indicators, which often capture short-term performance or backward-looking metrics, ESG performance reflects a firm's forward-looking commitment to sustainable value creation. It signals to stakeholders that the firm is attuned to emerging societal and environmental expectations and is willing to invest in long-term adaptability over short-term maximization. During systemic crises such as the COVID-19 pandemic, these attributes helped firms to absorb shocks more effectively, maintain internal cohesion, and communicate credibly with markets and communities. ESG was not merely a set of reputational commitments—it became a functional toolkit for crisis response, allowing firms to preserve continuity and legitimacy when it mattered most.

Environmentally responsible firms, for instance, may already be equipped with more robust resource management systems, diversified supply chains, and environmental contingency planning. These capabilities can reduce exposure to operational breakdowns, regulatory delays, or reputational backlash linked to crisis-induced environmental hazards. Socially engaged firms tend to foster stronger employee loyalty, public trust, and community support, which are critical in managing labor continuity, safety compliance, and brand reputation under duress. Governance quality, meanwhile, ensures more effective oversight, accountability, and ethical decision-making—features that are invaluable in crisis navigation when strategic agility and stakeholder communication are tested.

The effectiveness of ESG practices during the pandemic is not an isolated phenomenon. Prior crises have shown similar patterns, offering a broader empirical foundation for understanding the resilience benefits of ESG. During the 2008–2009 global financial crisis, firms with higher CSR engagement outperformed their peers both in terms of stock returns and accounting performance. For example, Lins et al. (2017) found that firms with high social capital—measured through employee treatment, community engagement, and stakeholder relations—were better able to retain investor trust and access financing during the credit crunch. These firms suffered less reputational damage and were perceived as more trustworthy by both investors and regulators, which helped them stabilize operations during a time of extreme market volatility.

Case studies from that era also support the importance of stakeholder trust and ESG preparedness. Companies like Unilever, which had long embedded sustainability into their supply chain and employee welfare policies, managed to avoid the kinds of large-scale labor disputes and reputational backlash experienced by competitors who focused narrowly on short-term financials. Similarly, Patagonia, known for its deep-rooted environmental and social commitments, saw continued customer loyalty and brand engagement during downturns, suggesting that ESG can provide not just insurance but strategic differentiation.

Another compelling example lies in the behavior of financial institutions. In the aftermath of the financial crisis, banks with better governance scores and higher CSR engagement faced lower penalties, recovered investor confidence more quickly, and were subject to fewer regulatory sanctions. Research by Cornett et al. (2016) found that CSR-active banks had significantly stronger performance metrics during and after the financial crisis, attributed to better risk governance and reputational advantage.

Building on this foundation, the COVID-19 pandemic further exposed the financial materiality of ESG considerations. Albuquerque et al. (2020) documented that during the COVID-induced market selloff, firms with higher ESG scores experienced smaller stock price declines and faster recovery in the months that followed. They attributed this resilience to stronger investor loyalty and reduced downside risk. Similarly, Ding et al. (2020) found that ESG-intensive firms experienced smaller capital outflows and were better able to maintain their workforce and supplier relationships under severe lockdown conditions. These empirical findings align with theoretical expectations that ESG performance mitigates risk by reducing exposure to financial, operational, and reputational shocks.

At a deeper level, ESG serves as a conduit for organizational resilience. Firms that have invested in ESG infrastructures tend to develop cultures of adaptability, transparency, and long-term strategic thinking. These characteristics are crucial in managing the "rainy days"—periods of low visibility, high volatility, and constrained optionality. For example, employee-focused policies, such as enhanced sick leave, remote-work infrastructure, and mental health support, not only ensured business continuity during lockdowns but also reduced turnover and boosted morale. Similarly, companies with strong ESG disclosure practices were better positioned to communicate clearly with investors and regulators, maintaining trust in turbulent capital markets.

Moreover, the pandemic revealed the materiality of ESG factors in a way few other events could. Environmental risk, public health preparedness, supply chain fragility, and inequality—all central ESG concerns—became financial risks. This alignment elevated ESG from a peripheral consideration to a core input in financial analysis, capital allocation, and stakeholder decision-making. Institutional investors, rating agencies, and regulators began to treat ESG not merely as a qualitative indicator, but as a critical component of a firm's risk-adjusted valuation. Consequently, firms that had already integrated ESG into their operations were more agile in responding to evolving expectations from financial markets, governments, and civil society.

Another mechanism through which ESG improved firm performance during the pandemic is stakeholder alignment. Firms with ESG commitments were more likely to receive public support—both in perception and in policy—because they were viewed as contributors to social welfare rather than extractive actors. This stakeholder goodwill translated into customer loyalty, investor patience, and even more favorable treatment in government relief programs. In a crisis where trust became a currency, ESG was a reservoir.

Finally, the pandemic forced a redefinition of risk in corporate strategy. Traditional financial models failed to fully anticipate or price in pandemic risk. ESG factors—long dismissed by some as non-financial—proved to be leading indicators of firm vulnerability or resilience. As such, the crisis functioned as a natural experiment, revealing that ESG initiatives were not a luxury or a compliance obligation, but a form of strategic insurance. Firms that had already embedded ESG into their core decision-making processes were not only better positioned to survive the crisis but also emerged with enhanced reputational capital and stakeholder legitimacy.

In this chapter, we investigate these dynamics through the lens of firm-level empirical evidence. The main body of the chapter presents an academic study that examines how ESG performance influenced corporate outcomes during the COVID-19 pandemic. By analyzing a rich dataset of public firms in China, the study explores how ESG affected firm valuation, risk exposure, liquidity access, and stakeholder responses under pandemic conditions. In doing so, it contributes to the growing literature on ESG as a driver of financial and strategic resilience in times of systemic uncertainty.

8.2 Weathering the Storm: The Financial Payoff of ESG Commitment During the Pandemic

Abstract

This study examines the influence of corporate social responsibility (CSR) on firm financial performance, focusing on A-share listed companies in China between 2016 and 2020. Leveraging the exogenous shock of the COVID-19 pandemic, we investigate the CSR–performance relationship from both static and dynamic perspectives, emphasizing how abrupt changes in CSR activities shape firm outcomes under crisis conditions. In particular, the analysis considers whether CSR initiatives—such as corporate donations, employee health and safety programs, and public welfare engagement—function as strategic substitutes or complements to conventional marketing and advertising expenditures. Empirical results reveal that CSR engagement exerts a significantly positive impact on financial performance, an effect that intensifies during the pandemic period relative to normal times. Moreover, firms with higher advertising and marketing investments tend to exhibit stronger CSR commitments and superior financial outcomes, suggesting strategic alignment. Advertising investment further acts as a moderator, amplifying the positive association between CSR and firm performance. Overall, the findings underscore the strategic value of CSR in enhancing corporate resilience during systemic shocks. Rather than being a discretionary cost, CSR appears to function as a value-generating asset—especially when paired with reputational and promotional efforts. These insights provide practical implications for firms seeking to build sustainable competitive advantage and long-term stakeholder trust through integrated social responsibility strategies.

8.2.1 Introduction

The outbreak and spread of the COVID-19 pandemic has triggered unprecedented disruptions across the global social and economic landscape. From public health systems to consumer behavior, from supply chain networks to governance systems, few areas have remained untouched. Firms—the building blocks of the modern market economy—have been thrust into the eye of the storm. Confronted by profound shifts in consumption patterns, labor availability, mobility restrictions, and financial market volatility, businesses have had to swiftly adapt or face extinction. While some were unable to survive these pressures and exited the market, others demonstrated remarkable agility and resilience, undertaking significant operational risks to not only maintain business continuity but also fulfill their broader societal obligations.

In China, many enterprises actively embraced Environmental, Social, and Governance (ESG) responsibilities during the pandemic. These efforts ranged from philanthropic donations and public health campaigns to retooling production lines for medical equipment and leveraging technological infrastructure to facilitate logistics and communication. Enterprises also coordinated with local governments to support resource allocation and emergency relief. Although these socially responsible actions contributed meaningfully to pandemic mitigation efforts and reinforced public trust, they came at a cost. The financial burden of such initiatives—especially under heightened liquidity pressures—raised critical questions about the trade-offs between corporate responsibility and financial viability.

Traditionally, corporate social responsibility (CSR)—a core component of ESG—has been viewed through a cost-centric lens. Conventional economic theory suggests that allocating resources toward social initiatives may crowd out core business investment, reduce operational efficiency, and depress short-term profitability. By increasing internal costs and diverting capital from shareholder-focused objectives, CSR was often perceived as an optional expenditure, pursued mainly for reputational signaling or regulatory appeasement. However, this perspective has increasingly come under scrutiny. A growing body of scholarship argues that CSR, when integrated strategically, may enhance firm performance by strengthening intangible assets such as brand equity, customer loyalty, and investor trust.

Proponents suggest that socially responsible firms are better positioned to foster innovation, build reputational capital, and maintain strong relationships with stakeholders across the value chain. CSR engagement can help signal ethical conduct and corporate values to the public, which in turn enhances transparency and legitimacy. Voluntary ESG disclosures can reduce information asymmetry between the firm and its stakeholders, lowering transaction and monitoring costs. Firms with higher ESG ratings may benefit from easier access to financing, lower cost of capital, and improved credit terms, particularly during periods of macroeconomic instability or crisis. This is especially relevant for firms operating in high-pollution or stigmatized industries, where proactive social responsibility can partially offset public and regulatory backlash.

In the context of the COVID-19 pandemic, CSR took on renewed urgency. The crisis not only amplified the demand for corporate action in areas such as employee protection, public health, and community support, but also provided a natural experiment to test the performance implications of CSR under extreme stress. Firms were called upon to make decisions with both economic and ethical ramifications—should they continue CSR investments at the expense of liquidity, or retreat to a minimalist survival mode?

This study addresses these questions by empirically examining the relationship between corporate social responsibility and firm financial performance among A-share listed companies in China during the period 2016–2020. Excluding financial and insurance companies, ST-designated firms, and entities with missing CSR or financial data, we construct a robust panel to assess the static and dynamic effects of CSR engagement. Specifically, we explore how sudden increases in CSR activity—such as emergency donations, employee welfare initiatives, and public health-related contributions—affect corporate financial outcomes and investor sentiment during the pandemic.

Beyond the static correlation between CSR and financial performance, this study also investigates the substitutability or complementarity between CSR activities and traditional marketing investments. Many CSR efforts during the pandemic—high-visibility donations, social campaigns, and public partnerships—had public-relations value akin to advertising. Accordingly, we test whether such actions can function as substitutes for conventional advertising expenditures, or whether they reinforce the effectiveness of paid media campaigns. The results indicate that CSR investments are positively associated with improved financial performance, and this relationship becomes even stronger during the pandemic period. Moreover, advertising investment complements CSR, playing a significant moderating role that amplifies the positive effect on firm outcomes.

These findings contribute to a deeper understanding of how CSR functions as both a resilience mechanism and a strategic asset during periods of heightened uncertainty. Rather than detracting from performance, responsible behavior appears to improve stakeholder alignment, increase public trust, and support long-term value creation. The study provides empirical support for the integration of ESG principles into corporate strategy—not merely as a symbolic gesture, but as a financially material practice.

The remainder of this chapter is structured as follows. Section 8.2.2 reviews relevant theories and literature, outlining the conceptual framework and hypothesis development. Section 8.2.3 details the research design, including sample selection, data sources, and variable construction. Section 8.2.4 presents the empirical analysis, encompassing descriptive statistics, correlation matrices, and regression results. Section 8.2.5 provides robustness checks to validate the findings, and Section 8.2.6 concludes with managerial implications and policy recommendations.

8.2.2 Institutional Background and Hypotheses Development

8.2.2.1 Evolution of Corporate Social Responsibility (CSR)

The concept of corporate social responsibility (CSR) has evolved significantly over the past century, reflecting changes in economic structures, societal values, and global governance challenges. First introduced by British economist Oliver Sheldon in 1923, CSR was initially framed as a moral imperative, emphasizing the ethical duties of businesses to society. However, progress in CSR theory and practice was limited during the early twentieth century due to major global disruptions, including the Great Depression and World War II.

The 1970s marked a critical turning point. In response to accelerating environmental degradation, rising stakeholder expectations, and the shifting role of corporations in society, CSR regained scholarly and policy attention. Carroll's (1979) influential pyramid framework conceptualized CSR as comprising four hierarchical responsibilities: economic, legal, ethical, and philanthropic. At its foundation is economic responsibility—generating profits to ensure survival and competitiveness—followed by legal compliance, ethical behavior, and voluntary contributions to society. This model laid the groundwork for integrating CSR into mainstream business strategy.

Simultaneously, stakeholder theory emerged as a critical counterpoint to the traditional shareholder primacy model. Freeman (1984) and subsequent scholars emphasized that corporations must consider the interests of all parties affected by their actions—not just shareholders, but also employees, customers, suppliers, creditors, communities, and regulators. In 1997, John Elkington's "triple bottom line" theory further expanded the CSR agenda, asserting that sustainable corporate success must balance economic, social, and environmental outcomes. This framework remains foundational in contemporary ESG (Environmental, Social, and Governance) discourse.

8.2.2.2 CSR and Financial Performance: Theoretical Tensions and Empirical Evidence

CSR's relationship with financial performance has long been debated. On one hand, traditional neoclassical economists argue that CSR imposes additional costs, reducing shareholder returns and operational efficiency. Under this view, CSR spending diverts resources from core business activities and is justified only if it yields reputational or regulatory benefits. On the other hand, stakeholder theory, signaling theory, and resource-based views suggest that CSR enhances intangible assets, builds trust with key constituencies, and reduces information asymmetry—all of which contribute to sustainable value creation.

Empirical research reflects this theoretical tension. Some studies find a positive relationship between CSR and firm performance, especially when CSR initiatives align closely with stakeholder interests. For instance, Yin et al. (2014) argue that CSR enhances access to external capital and strengthens a firm's competitiveness by building institutional trust. Firms that disclose credible CSR information may enjoy lower financing costs and more stable investor support. Conversely, other scholars find that CSR's impact is not uniformly positive. Zhu and Yang (2009), based on an analysis of five CSR dimensions among Chinese listed firms, found that while responsibility to creditors and government departments enhances firm value, excessive public welfare engagement or internal employee-focused CSR may yield diminishing returns or even reduce financial performance.

Moreover, CSR-financial performance relationships may not be linear. Wang et al. (2008) found an inverted U-shaped relationship in the U.S. context: CSR contributes positively up to a point, beyond which costs outweigh benefits. Barnett and Salomon (2012) observed a U-shaped relationship, suggesting that CSR may initially depress profitability but eventually improves it as firms institutionalize stakeholder engagement. Zhang et al. (2013) noted that the relationship may be asynchronous, with CSR effects lagging behind the financial outcomes they help shape. Thus, the CSR–financial performance nexus is dynamic, context-dependent, and shaped by firm strategy, stakeholder expectations, and environmental conditions.

8.2.2.3 CSR During Systemic Crises: Lessons from the Financial Crisis and COVID-19

Periods of systemic crisis offer a natural experiment for evaluating CSR's strategic value. During crises, firms face heightened uncertainty, reputational risk, and stakeholder scrutiny. CSR activities, especially those demonstrating authentic commitment and strategic alignment, may help firms build resilience, maintain stakeholder trust, and stabilize operations.

Historical evidence supports this view. During the 2008 global financial crisis, Buchanan et al. (2018) showed that CSR-intensive firms with high institutional ownership outperformed others in terms of market value. Gangi et al.(2018) found that CSR ratings in banking positively correlated with financial performance during the crisis, especially among larger institutions. Similar dynamics have been observed during the COVID-19 pandemic. For example, Qiu et al. (2020), using data from publicly listed hotel companies in China, demonstrated that CSR activities enhanced stock returns and stakeholder attention. Yang (2020) found that proactive CSR responses—such as donations, employee support programs, and public service engagement—helped firms stabilize workforce morale, reduce reputational damage, and improve financial outcomes.

Theoretically, stakeholder theory and signaling theory offer complementary explanations. In volatile environments, stakeholders demand greater transparency and responsibility from firms. CSR engagement helps firms send credible signals about their integrity, stability, and future-oriented vision. This, in turn, reduces perceived uncertainty and strengthens stakeholder loyalty. Conversely, failure to meet societal expectations during crises can trigger backlash. For instance, Wanke's cap on employee donations during the 2008 Wenchuan earthquake sparked public outrage and a sharp drop in market valuation exceeding RMB 1.2 billion (Fu, 2011). Such cases underscore the importance of responsible behavior not only as a normative good but also as a mechanism for safeguarding firm value.

In light of this, the COVID-19 pandemic serves as a critical context to examine CSR's financial consequences. The pandemic introduced extreme liquidity constraints, operational risks, and stakeholder expectations. Firms were forced to make difficult trade-offs between cost containment and responsible engagement. In this high-stakes environment, CSR activities carried strategic and symbolic weight: they were both expressions of firm values and tools for reputation management, capital access, and stakeholder alignment.

Building on stakeholder theory, signaling theory, and empirical findings from both normal and crisis periods, this study proposes the following hypotheses:

H1 Corporate social responsibility has a positive impact on corporate financial performance.

H2 The positive impact of corporate social responsibility on corporate financial performance is more pronounced during systemic crises such as the COVID-19 pandemic.

While prior studies have often taken a static perspective on CSR, focusing on aggregate CSR scores or firm-level fixed effects, relatively little attention has been paid to the implications of changes in CSR engagement over time—especially in the context of a crisis. Firms frequently adjust their CSR strategies in response to external shocks, internal financial constraints, or evolving stakeholder expectations. Sudden increases or decreases in CSR engagement may send important signals to investors and stakeholders, triggering market responses that differ from those associated with steady-state CSR behaviors. Thus, examining the financial implications of dynamic CSR change—rather than static levels alone—can enrich our understanding of CSR's role in crisis management and capital market signaling.

In addition, CSR activities often entail public visibility, stakeholder communication, and brand enhancement. These features are shared with more traditional marketing efforts such as advertising and promotional expenditures. A growing body of literature indicates that advertising can serve not only to build brand equity but also to amplify or buffer the effects of CSR. For instance, Pan et al. (2016) report a positive correlation between advertising and corporate performance, while Skard & Thorbjørnsen(2014) finds that advertising can mitigate the reputational risks associated with CSR shortfalls.

During periods of economic disruption, firms often face trade-offs in resource allocation between marketing and CSR. The substitutability or complementarity of these expenditures becomes a strategic concern. Does advertising enhance the salience and credibility of CSR efforts, thereby strengthening financial outcomes? Or do firms need to prioritize one over the other in times of constrained liquidity? Therefore, we put forward the following hypotheses:

H3 Firms with higher levels of both corporate social responsibility engagement and advertising expenditures exhibit superior financial performance relative to firms with lower levels of such investment.

H4 Advertising expenditure positively moderates the relationship between corporate social responsibility and financial performance, such that the positive effect of CSR on financial outcomes is stronger when advertising spending is higher.

8.2.3 Data and Sample

This study examines A-share firms listed in China from 2016 to 2020. Consistent with conventions, we exclude financial and insurance firms because their reporting and regulation differ materially from nonfinancials; we also remove ST and *ST firms to avoid idiosyncratic distress effects, and drop observations with missing financial items or without disclosed CSR information. After screening, the final unbalanced panel comprises 5090 firm-year observations. Financial statement and market data are drawn from Wind and the Juchao Information Network, while annual CSR ratings are obtained from Hexun.com. To lessen the impact of extreme values, continuous variables are winsorized at the one and ninety-ninth percentiles, industries follow CSRC classifications, and monetary amounts are denominated in RMB.

Firm performance is evaluated using both accounting-based and market-based measures. Return on equity (ROE) captures profitability relative to shareholders' capital and is widely used in corporate finance. Return on assets (ROA) gauges profitability relative to the asset base and is less sensitive to leverage differences than ROE. To reflect investor expectations and market valuation, we also employ Tobin's Q, proxied by the ratio of the firm's market value (equity plus book liabilities) to total assets. Using these complementary measures allows us to assess whether CSR relates to operating efficiency, profitability, and market valuation.

The principal explanatory variable is the firm's CSR score from Hexun.com. Hexun's composite index aggregates information disclosed in CSR reports and related financials into a standardized 0–100 score covering five stakeholder dimensions—shareholders, employees, suppliers and customers, environment, and society—thus providing a broad view of a firm's social responsibility engagement. To capture dynamics in CSR behavior that may be especially salient during crisis periods, we also construct a change measure, defined as the year-over-year difference in the CSR score, which highlights abrupt increases or decreases in CSR intensity.

Because CSR initiatives are often communicated through external channels that resemble traditional promotion, we incorporate advertising intensity as a moderating variable, measured by advertising and marketing expenditures scaled by operating revenue. This measure proxies the firm's investment in reputation-building outside of CSR and enables us to test whether advertising amplifies or substitutes for the financial effects of CSR.

A standard set of firm-level controls is included to mitigate confounding. Size, measured as the natural logarithm of total assets, accounts for resource availability and scale economies that relate to both CSR capacity and performance. Firm age, proxied by years since listing, captures organizational maturity and the institutionalization of stakeholder practices. Ownership structure is represented by an SOE indicator equal to one for state-owned enterprises and zero otherwise, recognizing that public expectations and policy mandates may differentially shape SOE behavior. Leverage, calculated as total liabilities over total assets, reflects capital structure and financial constraints that influence both CSR investment and outcomes. R&D intensity, given by R&D expenditure scaled by operating revenue, controls for innovation activity that can correlate with ESG-related initiatives, especially environmental improvements and human-capital programs. Profit margin, measured as net income over operating revenue, captures slack resources and the firm's capacity to undertake discretionary CSR spending. Finally, ownership concentration is proxied by the largest shareholder's equity stake (Top1), recognizing that controlling owners may exert decisive influence on CSR priorities and financial policies.

In the empirical analysis, all right-hand-side variables are lagged one period where appropriate to temper simultaneity concerns, and the specifications include firm fixed effects to absorb time-invariant heterogeneity and year fixed effects to capture macro shocks. Standard errors are clustered by firm and year to address cross-sectional and temporal dependence. Summary definitions and descriptive statistics for all variables appear in Table 8.1, followed by correlation diagnostics and multicollinearity checks. This design permits a joint assessment of static CSR levels and CSR changes, as well as the extent to which advertising intensity conditions the link between CSR and financial performance, with particular attention to the pandemic year within our sample window.

As shown in Table 8.2, the mean CSR score is 20.805, indicating that the CSR level of the sample firms is generally low and falls short of expectations. The standard deviation is 11.661, with a minimum of −4.960 and a maximum of 75.231, showing a substantial gap between enterprises with high CSR engagement and those with low CSR performance. The average firm size is 22.471, with a standard deviation of 1.363, a minimum of 20.041, and a maximum of 26.604. This suggests that the enterprises in the sample are similar in scale, with little variation, making it more likely that their behavioral patterns and strategic choices converge. For the leverage ratio (Lev), the sample mean is 0.410, with a standard deviation of 0.191. The relatively high level of gearing implies that firms may be more cautious in undertaking CSR activities, as financial constraints could influence strategic decision-making. The average age of the sample firms (Age) is 19.483 years, with a standard deviation of 5.031. This reflects that, in general, these enterprises have not been listed for very long, although there is considerable variation in listing duration across firms. In terms of profitability (Prof), the mean profit margin is 0.160, with a standard deviation of 0.357. This suggests that most listed companies in the sample have a certain degree of profitability with relatively limited overall differences. However, the minimum value of −0.562 and the maximum of 2.802 indicate that some firms display substantial individual differences in profitability. The concentration of ownership, measured by the shareholding proportion of the largest shareholder (Top1), has a mean of 0.329 and a standard deviation of 0.144.

Table 8.1 Variable definition

	Variable	Shown in Table	Definition
Dependent	ROA	ROA	Net Income/Total Assets
	Tobin's *Q*	Tobin's *Q*	A ratio that measures how the market values a firm relative to the replacement cost of its assets
Independent Variable	CSR	CSR	CSR score from HEXUN
Moderators	Advertising expenses	Adv	Marketing Expense/Income
Controls	FirmSize	Size	Logarithm of Total asset
	FirmAge	Age	
	Ownership	SOE	Indicator variable that equals to 1 if State-owned Enterprise
	Leverage	Lev	Total debt /Total Assets
	R&D expenses	RD	R&D expenses/income
	Profit Margin	Prof	Net income/income
	Largest Shareholder (Top1) ratio	Top1	Ratio of number of shares by Largest Shareholder

This shows that the largest shareholder typically holds a relatively high proportion of shares, which generally exerts a strong influence on corporate governance and strategic decisions. With respect to ownership structure (SOE), the sample mean is 0.331, suggesting that most firms in the sample are non–state-owned enterprises. Finally, for advertising and marketing investment (Adv) and research and development expenditure (RD), the sample means are 0.082 and 0.049, with standard deviations of 0.097 and 0.047, respectively. These figures indicate that there is notable variation across firms in how they allocate resources to marketing and innovation activities, reflecting different strategic orientations.

As shown in Table 8.3, corporate social responsibility (CSR) is significantly correlated with financial performance indicators (ROA, ROE, and Tobin's *Q*) at the 1% level, suggesting a statistically significant association between CSR and firm performance and lending support to the hypothesis of this study.

8.2.4 Empirical Results

To empirically test the hypotheses proposed in the preceding section, this paper employs ordinary least squares (OLS) regression using the sample data. The results are presented in Table 8.4. Consistent with expectations, corporate social responsibility (CSR) is found to exert a significant influence on firm financial performance. Specifically, CSR is positively associated with both return on assets (ROA) and

Table 8.2 Descriptive statistics

	(1)	(2)	(3)	(4)	(5)
Variables	*N*	Mean	SD	Min	Max
ROA	5090	0.032	0.077	−0.556	0.205
ROE	5090	0.044	0.180	−1.928	0.337
Tobin's *Q*	5090	2.032	1.259	0.816	11.041
CSR	5090	20.805	11.661	−4.960	75.231
Size	5090	22.471	1.363	20.041	26.604
Lev	5090	0.410	0.191	0.057	0.891
Age	5090	19.483	5.031	8.068	34.543
Prof	5090	0.160	0.357	−0.562	2.802
Top1	5090	0.329	0.144	0.080	0.737
SOE	5090	0.331	0.471	0	1
Adv	5090	0.082	0.097	0.001	0.521
RD	5090	0.049	0.047	0.001	0.293

return on equity (ROE), with coefficients that are statistically significant at the 1% level. These findings indicate that CSR engagement enhances accounting-based measures of profitability, thereby lending strong support to Hypothesis 1. In other words, firms that allocate more resources to CSR activities tend to achieve superior financial outcomes, suggesting that socially responsible behavior creates tangible economic benefits.

A comparison of coefficients across different subsamples provides additional insights. When splitting the data between the pre-pandemic and pandemic periods, the results show that the impact of CSR on financial performance is more pronounced during the outbreak. For example, the coefficient on CSR in the ROA regression increases from 0.003 in the pre-pandemic period to 0.006 during the pandemic, while the ROE coefficient rises from 0.005 to 0.012. These larger coefficients suggest that CSR investments were particularly valuable under conditions of heightened uncertainty, supporting Hypothesis 2. The interpretation is that, during crises such as the COVID-19 pandemic, stakeholders—customers, employees, and investors—may place greater value on firms demonstrating social responsibility, which in turn strengthens firm performance. This result underscores the buffering or insurance-like role of CSR in times of external shocks.

The analysis also investigates the relationship between changes in CSR (dCSR) and market-based firm value, proxied by Tobin's *Q*. As shown in the Column (4) of Table 8.5, the coefficient on dCSR is positive but not statistically significant. This indicates that short-term fluctuations in CSR activities are not immediately capitalized into market valuations. The market appears to respond more strongly to the overall level and consistency of CSR engagement rather than to marginal year-to-year changes, which may be perceived as tactical or symbolic rather than strategic.

Table 8.3 Correlation analysis

	ROA	ROE	Tobin's *Q*	CSR	Size	Lev	Age	Growth	Top1	SOE	Sale	RD
ROA	1											
ROE	0.898***	1										
Tobin's *Q*	0.206***	0.102***	1									
CSR	0.542***	0.492***	0.083***	1								
Size	0.074***	0.144***	−0.391***	0.213***	1							
Lev	−0.264***	−0.176***	−0.329***	−0.112***	0.533***	1						
Age	0.006	0.011	−0.090***	0.001	0.177***	0.146***	1					
Growth	0.221***	0.219***	0.044***	0.134***	0.009	0.011	−0.113***	1				
Top1	0.178***	0.172***	−0.060***	0.192***	0.253***	0.058***	−0.049***	−0.009	1			
SOE	−0.006	0.041***	−0.177***	0.065***	0.415***	0.274***	0.215***	−0.093***	0.353***	1		
Sale	−0.005	−0.038***	0.154***	0.015	−0.216***	−0.252***	0.003	−0.068***	−0.133***	−0.202***	1	
RD	−0.112***	−0.122***	0.257***	−0.135***	−0.337***	−0.311***	−0.132***	−0.069***	−0.267***	−0.294***	0.233***	1

Table 8.4 The effect of CSR on firm performance

	(1)	(2)	(3)	(4)
Variables	ROA	ROE	ROA	ROE
CSR	0.003*** (30.28)	0.005*** (25.66)	0.006*** (28.48)	0.012*** (20.95)
Size	0.006*** (5.90)	0.018*** (7.72)	−0.001 (−0.65)	0.014*** (3.19)
Lev	−0.124*** (−18.97)	−0.201*** (−12.96)	−0.075*** (−7.17)	−0.247*** (−8.21)
Age	0.001*** (4.19)	0.002*** (3.46)	−0.000 (−0.18)	−0.001 (−1.28)
Prof	0.032*** (11.81)	0.073*** (11.39)	0.040*** (7.06)	0.109*** (6.71)
Top1	0.050*** (6.56)	0.093*** (5.17)	0.009 (0.69)	−0.018 (−0.50)
SOE	−0.010*** (−3.87)	−0.013** (−2.23)	0.001 (0.31)	0.016 (1.37)
Adv	−0.017 (−1.60)	−0.053** (−2.10)	−0.050*** (−3.01)	−0.128*** (−2.68)
RD	−0.145*** (−6.13)	−0.221*** (−3.95)	−0.095*** (−2.61)	−0.251** (−2.42)
Constant	−0.128*** (−6.29)	−0.437*** (−9.09)	−0.021 (−0.65)	−0.362*** (−3.95)
Observations	4072	4072	1018	1,018
R-squared	0.347	0.269	0.616	0.515
r2_a	0.345	0.267	0.613	0.511
F	239.5	165.9	179.7	118.9

Turning to Column (1) of Table 8.5, CSR is again found to be positively correlated with Tobin's Q, with statistical significance at the 1% level. This result suggests that CSR contributes not only to accounting-based profitability but also to market-based firm value. Investors may view CSR as a signal of strong corporate governance, stakeholder alignment, or long-term strategic orientation, thereby increasing the firm's valuation relative to its asset base.

The moderating role of advertising and marketing expenditures is further examined in Columns (2) and (3) of Table 8.5. When advertising and marketing investment (Adv) is included as a control variable, both CSR and Adv exhibit positive effects on Tobin's Q, significant at the 1% and 5% levels, respectively. This supports Hypothesis 3, indicating that firms engaging simultaneously in CSR and marketing activities are able to enhance financial outcomes more effectively. Moreover, the inclusion of the interaction term between CSR and Adv (csradv) in Table 8.5 yields a positive and highly significant coefficient at the 1% level. This finding confirms Hypothesis 4: advertising and marketing activities strengthen the relationship between CSR and financial performance. One interpretation is that

Table 8.5 Robustness check

	(1)	(2)	(3)	(4)
Variables	Tobin's *Q*	Tobin's *Q*	Tobin's *Q*	Tobin's *Q*
CSR	0.016*** (11.17)	0.016*** (11.03)	0.012*** (6.34)	
Adv		0.441** (2.58)	−0.570* (−1.70)	
Csradv			0.047*** (3.50)	
Size	−0.314*** (−20.40)	−0.312*** (−20.27)	−0.310*** (−20.16)	−0.190*** (−11.53)
Lev	−0.597*** (−5.77)	−0.563*** (−5.41)	−0.557*** (−5.35)	−0.918*** (−8.25)
Age	0.002 (0.56)	0.001 (0.39)	0.001 (0.39)	0.009** (2.32)
Prof	0.144*** (3.19)	0.152*** (3.36)	0.147*** (3.26)	0.274*** (5.10)
Top1	0.351*** (2.86)	0.364*** (2.97)	0.371*** (3.03)	0.558*** (4.03)
SOE	0.031 (0.78)	0.040 (1.02)	0.039 (0.99)	−0.068 (−1.53)
RD	4.053*** (10.89)	3.930*** (10.48)	4.033*** (10.74)	3.880*** (9.40)
DCSR				−0.001 (−0.42)
Constant	8.600*** (26.84)	8.521*** (26.49)	8.558*** (26.62)	6.015*** (17.03)
Observations	5090	5090	5090	4072
R-squared	0.211	0.212	0.214	0.150
r2_a	0.210	0.211	0.212	0.149
F	169.9	151.9	138.2	89.91

marketing expenditures amplify the visibility and credibility of CSR initiatives, enabling firms to reap greater reputational and financial benefits from their social engagement.

Taken together, these empirical results provide robust evidence for the positive role of CSR in shaping both accounting-based and market-based performance outcomes. They also reveal that the benefits of CSR are not static but vary with contextual conditions (e.g., during the pandemic) and can be reinforced through complementary strategic investments such as marketing. The implications are twofold: first, CSR should be viewed as an integral part of corporate strategy rather than as a peripheral or discretionary activity; second, firms can maximize the returns to CSR by combining it with communication and branding strategies that enhance stakeholder awareness and appreciation of their social responsibility efforts.

8.2.5 Robustness Tests

In order to verify the usability, reliability and stability of the findings of this study, this paper selected the independent variable CSR and the moderator variable Adv to carry out a lagged one-period regression analysis, and the results of the regression are consistent with the above, and there is no significant difference.

8.2.6 Conclusions and Implication

This paper investigates the effect of corporate social responsibility (CSR) on firm financial performance, with particular attention to the context of the COVID-19 epidemic. The analysis compares the differential impact of CSR in epidemic versus non-epidemic periods and examines the interaction between CSR and advertising and marketing investments. The empirical results reveal three core findings. First, CSR positively influences corporate financial performance, measured by both accounting-based indicators (ROA, ROE) and market-based valuation (Tobin's Q). Second, the positive effect of CSR is more pronounced during the epidemic than in normal times, suggesting that external shocks magnify the salience of responsible corporate conduct. Third, advertising and marketing expenditures not only enhance financial performance directly but also amplify the positive relationship between CSR and firm performance, indicating that visibility and stakeholder communication are critical to capturing the value of CSR.

These findings have several theoretical implications. By situating the CSR–performance relationship in a crisis context, this paper enriches the literature on strategic management, corporate governance, and marketing by highlighting how external shocks alter the payoff structure of CSR activities. The results support the view that CSR is not merely a reputational add-on but functions as an adaptive capability that strengthens resilience in volatile environments. Moreover, the moderating role of marketing demonstrates that the benefits of CSR depend not only on the substance of responsible activities but also on their communication and recognition by external stakeholders. This aligns with stakeholder theory, signaling theory, and resource-based perspectives that emphasize the importance of intangible resources in sustaining firm value.

The study also carries important managerial implications. For corporate leaders, the evidence suggests that CSR engagement should not be suspended or minimized in times of crisis. On the contrary, firms that actively fulfill social responsibilities during epidemics can gain stronger stakeholder support, enhance their reputational capital, and improve financial outcomes. However, CSR initiatives should be aligned with a firm's actual resources and capabilities to ensure credibility and avoid overstretching. In parallel, firms should design integrated marketing and communication strategies to make their CSR efforts more visible and understandable to stakeholders. Effective publicity ensures that responsible activities are recognized by customers, employees, investors, and regulators, thereby translating into measurable financial gains. Without appropriate communication, the potential value of CSR may remain latent and underappreciated.

From a policy perspective, the findings suggest that governments and regulators can encourage enterprises to sustain or even expand CSR commitments during crises by providing supportive policies, tax incentives, or recognition programs. Public policy interventions can help amplify the positive spillovers of CSR to society while reinforcing market mechanisms that reward responsible corporate conduct.

For investors and other capital-market participants, the study provides evidence that CSR is associated with both short-term financial improvements and long-term value creation, particularly during turbulent times. This underscores the importance of incorporating CSR-related metrics into investment analysis and portfolio allocation. Institutional investors, in particular, can use CSR disclosures as signals of firm resilience, stakeholder alignment, and long-run sustainability.

Finally, this paper contributes to raising awareness of CSR among firms operating in emerging markets, where responsible business practices are still evolving. The results encourage firms to view CSR not as a compliance cost but as a strategic asset that enhances competitiveness, reputation, and stakeholder trust. By embedding CSR into core strategies and coupling it with effective marketing communication, enterprises can create a virtuous cycle in which responsible practices drive financial performance, which in turn enables further investment in CSR.

Despite its contributions, this study is subject to several limitations. First, CSR is measured using a single index, which may not fully capture the multidimensional nature of environmental, social, and governance activities. Future research could adopt more granular or third-party validated CSR ratings to test the robustness of the findings. Second, the analysis is based on Chinese listed firms, which limits the generalizability of results to other institutional settings. Comparative studies across countries with different regulatory regimes and cultural expectations could provide deeper insights into how context shapes the CSR–performance nexus. Third, the empirical design primarily captures contemporaneous associations, which may not reflect the long-term dynamics of CSR investment and financial outcomes. Longitudinal or event-study approaches could shed light on whether CSR creates persistent value or primarily short-term benefits. Finally, this study focuses on advertising and marketing as moderators, but other intangible factors—such as corporate culture, board oversight, or digital engagement—could also condition the CSR–performance relationship and merit further exploration.

In summary, this study demonstrates that CSR can serve as a stabilizing and value-enhancing mechanism, particularly in periods of systemic uncertainty such as the COVID-19 epidemic. It expands the theoretical and empirical understanding of how CSR interacts with corporate strategy and marketing, and it offers actionable guidance for managers, investors, and policymakers. The broader implication is that in an era of recurring crises and heightened stakeholder expectations, CSR is not optional but integral to sustainable corporate growth.

Acknowledgement Portions of this chapter build on the empirical analyses first developed by Kai Jiang in his thesis. I am grateful to Kai Jiang for permission to adapt and extend this work for the present volume and for his contributions to data construction and empirical implementation. Any remaining errors are my own.

References

Albuquerque, R., Koskinen, Y., Yang, S., & Zhang, C. (2020). *Resiliency of environmental and social stocks: An analysis of the exogenous COVID-19 market crash* (ECGI Finance Working Paper No. 676/2020).

Barnett, M. L., & Salomon, R. M. (2012). Does it pay to be really good? Addressing the shape of the relationship between social and financial performance. *Strategic Management Journal, 33*(11), 1304–1320.

Buchanan, B., Cao, C. X., & Chen, C. (2018). Corporate social responsibility, firm value, and influential institutional ownership. *Journal of Corporate Finance, 52*, 73–95. https://doi.org/10.1016/j.jcorpfin.2018.07.004

Carroll, A. B. (1979). A three-dimensional conceptual model of corporate performance. *Academy of Management Review, 4*(4), 497–505.

Cornett, M. M., Erhemjamts, O., & Tehranian, H. (2016). Greed or good deeds: An examination of the relation between corporate social responsibility and the financial performance of U.S. commercial banks around the financial crisis. *Journal of Banking & Finance, 70*, 137–159. https://doi.org/10.1016/j.jbankfin.2016.04.024

Ding, W., Levine, R., Lin, C., & Xie, W. (2020). *Corporate immunity to the COVID-19 pandemic* (NBER Working Paper No. 27055).

Elkington, J. (1998). Cannibals with forks: The triple bottom line of 21st century business. *Environmental Quality Management, 8*(1), 37–51.

Fu, H. (2011). A review of research on the relationship between corporate social responsibility and financial performance. *Business Research, 8*, 72–77.

Gangi, F., Mustilli, M., Varrone, N., & Daniele, L. M. (2018). Corporate social responsibility and banks' financial performance. *International Business Research, 11*(10), 42–58

Lins, K. V., Servaes, H., & Tamayo, A. (2017). Social capital, trust, and firm performance: The value of corporate social responsibility during the financial crisis. *Journal of Finance, 72*(4), 1785–1824.

Pan, H.-Y., Fan, X.-Y., & Zong, Z.-C. (2016). Advertising investment and corporate performance: An empirical analysis based on listed FMCG companies. *Investment Research, 35*(1), 31–36.

Qiu, S. (C.), Jiang, J., Liu, X., Chen, M.-H., & Yuan, X. (2020). Does corporate social responsibility protect firm value during the COVID-19 pandemic? *International Journal of Hospitality Management, 93*, 102759. https://doi.org/10.1016/j.ijhm.2020.102759

Skard, S., & Thorbjørnsen, H. (2014). Is publicity always better than advertising? The role of brand reputation in communicating corporate social responsibility. *Journal of Business Ethics, 124*(1), 149–160.

Wang, H., Choi, J., & Li, J. (2008). Too little or too much? Untangling the relationship between corporate philanthropy and firm financial performance. *Organization Science, 19*(1), 143–159.

Yang, R. (2020). *Analysis of influencing factors and effectiveness of corporate adoption of social responsibility behavior in crisis situations* (Master's thesis). University of Science and Technology of China.

Yin, K., Liu, X., & Chen, H. (2014). CSR and financial performance based on endogeneity: Evidence from Chinese listed firms. *China Soft Science, 6*, 98–108.

Zhang, Z., Jin, X., & Li, G. (2013). An empirical study of the cross-period interaction between corporate social responsibility and financial performance. *Accounting Research, 8*, 32–39.

Zhu, J., & Yang, P. (2009). An empirical test of the relationship between corporate social responsibility and financial performance. *Statistics and Decision, 7*, 135–137.

Part III

Discussions and Conclusions

Conclusion and Contributions 9

9.1 Summary and Conclusion

This book shows how ESG moves from a slogan to a system that reallocates risk, capital, and corporate attention. It connects antecedents, governance mechanisms, and market consequences into one empirical and theoretical frame. The throughline is simple: firms face heterogeneous constraints and opportunities; institutions set the feasible set; managers translate constraints into choices; markets price the consequences. ESG matters when it shifts that chain in measurable ways.

ESG is not window dressing. It is a testable set of capabilities with microfoundations in established theory. Agency theory explains why risk-sensitive incentives such as inside debt, clawbacks, and deferred equity push managers toward investments in safety, reliability, and compliance systems that reduce downside variance. Instrumental stakeholder theory predicts cooperation rents when firms credibly invest in employees, suppliers, customers, and communities; these rents appear as lower disruption probability, faster recovery, and higher repeat business. The resource-based view and dynamic capabilities show how ESG-aligned routines—process safety, supply-chain traceability, data governance, eco-efficiency—become hard-to-imitate operational assets that scale across plants and time. Real-options theory values these routines as flexibility under uncertainty: they keep growth options alive and truncate the left tail in bad states. Incomplete-contracts and transaction-cost economics clarify why verifiable ESG policies substitute for missing contingencies and reduce haggling costs with counterparties. Signaling and information-economics show how auditable ESG disclosures lower asymmetry, broaden investor participation, and improve screening in private placements. These foundations yield clear, falsifiable predictions about cash flows, risks, and financing.

Value creation is concrete. On cash flows, credible ESG raises process yields through quality and safety programs, cuts input costs via energy and water efficiency, and improves talent acquisition and retention. It expands revenue by

J. Wang, *ESG Strategies and Financial Markets*, Management for Professionals,
https://doi.org/10.1007/978-981-95-5620-5_9

aligning products with material customer preferences and by winning procurement where sustainability is a threshold requirement. On risk, ESG compresses the loss distribution's left tail by lowering the frequency and severity of environmental, safety, and conduct incidents; it stabilizes working capital through stronger supplier and customer ties; it narrows liquidity risk by sustaining stakeholder cooperation and preserving access to funding in stress. On strategy, ESG becomes capital budgeting discipline. Internal carbon prices, science-based targets, and scenario-consistent hurdle rates guide make-or-buy, site selection, reshoring, and product redesign. Governance integrates these choices through board oversight, risk committees, and disclosure controls that link operational metrics to financial outcomes. These statements are not rhetorical; they are testable with data that firms and markets already generate.

Empirical designs implement the tests. Cash-flow channels can be identified with plant- or line-level productivity, defect, and downtime data linked to ESG process adoption dates. Risk effects can be estimated with hazard models of incident occurrence, insurance premia, catastrophe exposure maps, and distributional measures of realized losses. Financing effects can be measured with offering outcomes—spreads, fees, covenants, pricing grids, and acceptance rates—across public bonds, bank loans, and Rule 144A placements. Information channels can be isolated with event studies on ESG disclosure shocks, rating methodology changes, and regulatory announcements, combined with cross-sectional moderators for financial materiality and data assurance. Causal identification leverages staggered policy adoption across China, the United States, and Europe; issuer fixed effects in repeated financings; instrumented exposure to exogenous hazards; mediation tests that place CSR between incentives and risk outcomes; and text measures from reports, calls, and supplier audits to reduce rater disagreement. Boundary conditions are explicit and testable: effects concentrate where issues are financially material, verification credible, operations hazard-exposed, and institutions enforceable; symbolic programs should fail these tests and should not price.

The book's chapters operationalize this program. Social capital complements ESG by lowering counterparty risk and easing coordination, which improves access and terms in private placements such as Rule 144A. Liquidity risk narrows where ESG strengthens operating reliability and disclosure credibility. The cost of capital falls where ESG reduces idiosyncratic volatility, shifts transition-risk exposures, and improves screening by debt and equity investors. The pandemic provides an exogenous stress test: firms with well-implemented ESG sustained supply continuity, protected human capital, and preserved financing flexibility, with effects strongest in jurisdictions and sectors where hazards were binding and verification feasible. Across these settings the payoff is asymmetric: modest in normal times, large in bad states—consistent with insurance and real-options interpretations.

The book establishes the baseline. We trace the evolution from shareholder primacy to a stakeholder-aware finance that remains valuation-driven. CSR provides the conceptual bridge to ESG by moving from broad social obligations to measurable, decision-relevant pillars. We clarify what ESG is, why firms invest in it, how the E-S-G pillars transmit to value, and why measurement divergence persists. We map regulatory geographies across China, the United States, and Europe, and derive implications for multinationals facing multi-regime compliance. We position four corporate approaches—compliance minimum, strategy for upside, insurance against tail risk, and misrepresentation—and explain cross-firm heterogeneity using incentives, frictions, and regulatory exposure. The synthesis previews an empirical agenda: study ESG not as virtue but as an allocative technology that shifts cash flows, discount rates, tail distributions, and access to financing.

Then this book moves from description to mechanism. We anchor ESG in standard incentive theory by showing how governance shape real choices. We find that in the M&A deals, acquiring firms with better governance structure experience higher announcement returns and exhibit superior post-merger market and operating performance. We then embed social capital into the ESG production function. Social capital eases coordination, reduces counterparty risk, and increases informal enforcement. In the private debt market, especially Rule 144A issuances, stronger community and network ties complement formal disclosure by reducing information asymmetry and expected contracting costs. The result is better access and improved terms when sustainability signals are credible and locally embedded.

In the end, this bookquantifies real effects in risk and financing channels and tests ESG in a crisis lab. We show that ESG relates to lower liquidity risk through operating reliability, stakeholder cooperation, and reporting quality. We link ESG to the cost of capital and the probability and terms of market access, again with private placements as a clean setting. Finally, the pandemic provides an exogenous shock. Firms with stronger, well-implemented ESG programs maintained supply continuity, protected human capital, and preserved financing flexibility. The performance differential concentrates where ESG is financially material, governance is credible, and local institutions reward cooperative behavior. Across these studies, the payoffs are asymmetric: ESG is most valuable in adverse states and in tight funding markets, which is consistent with the insurance interpretation and with option-like payoffs to operational resilience.

The book therefore closes four loops. First, a conceptual loop from purpose to policy to price. Second, a governance loop from contracts to choices to outcomes. Third, a market loop from disclosure to beliefs to spreads and quantities. Fourth, a crisis loop where the previous three are stress-tested. ESG affects firms when and because it passes through these loops with discipline, data, and institutional reinforcement.

9.2 Theoretical Contributions

We recast ESG as a set of contingent, priced organizational capabilities rather than a diffuse moral stance. In this view, ESG consists of repeatable routines, controls, and relational assets that alter cash flows, risk distributions, and financing terms under identifiable states of the world. The logic is sequential and testable: institutions define the feasible set; governance translates constraints into choices;

counterparties update beliefs in light of credible information; markets reprice exposures. ESG matters only when it predictably shifts that chain and leaves observable traces in operations, contracts, and prices.

Within this architecture, three levers interact inside the firm. Compliance sets the legal floor and the information baseline by reducing expected penalties, shrinking disclosure uncertainty, and standardizing measurement; in incomplete-contract environments, credible compliance substitutes for missing contingencies and lowers transaction costs with regulators, lenders, and supply-chain partners. Strategy embeds sustainability into product design, process engineering, and capital allocation so that efficiency gains, quality improvements, and demand alignment raise operating cash flows while preserving growth options in carbon-, safety-, and data-sensitive markets; under resource-based and dynamic-capabilities logics these routines are path-dependent, costly to imitate, and therefore rent-producing. Insurance compresses the left tail by investing in safety systems, supply-chain transparency, data governance, and community relations that stabilize cooperation during stress, reduce incident frequency and severity, and keep financing windows open; real-options logic values this as flexible capacity that truncates downside while preserving upside. Misrepresentation lies outside the feasible set because it destroys trust capital and increases expected litigation, enforcement, and adverse-selection premia.

The foundations are grounded in established theory and lead to falsifiable predictions. Agency theory explains why risk-sensitive incentives—inside debt, clawbacks, and deferred equity—shift managerial preferences toward downside control; the implied test is that higher inside-debt intensity is associated with greater CSR process investment and lower realized risk, with CSR mediating the relationship. Instrumental stakeholder theory predicts cooperation rents when firms invest credibly in employees, suppliers, customers, and communities; the empirical signature is higher throughput stability and lower working-capital volatility where ESG targets financially material frictions. The resource-based view and dynamic-capabilities framework imply persistence and learning spillovers; plants that adopt ESG process controls should exhibit rising yields and falling defect rates relative to peers over time. Real-options theory predicts convex payoffs; ESG effects should be modest in benign periods and large during shocks, visible in smaller drawdowns and faster recoveries. Information economics and signaling theory imply that assured, decision-relevant ESG disclosure broadens investor participation and improves screening, especially in private placements; spreads, covenants, and acceptance rates should improve with assurance depth and pillar-specific metrics. Transaction-cost and incomplete-contract theories imply fewer renegotiations and faster dispute resolution when verifiable ESG substitutes for missing clauses; large supplier contracts should close faster and require fewer post-shock modifications. Industrial-organization and "regulatory geography" perspectives predict that multinationals adjust disclosure menus, organizational forms, and financing venues as exposure to stricter regimes rises; early harmonizers should face lower disclosure-related discount penalties across markets.

These levers map to priced quantities in cash flows, risk, and financing. On cash flows, compliance reduces expected outflows from penalties, strategy raises margins through resource efficiency and product fit, and insurance protects utilization rates when conditions deteriorate. On risk, insurance reduces variance and fat tails in operational loss distributions, strategy dampens demand volatility where customers price sustainability attributes, and compliance lowers legal and regulatory jump risk. On financing, credible ESG lowers required returns when it reduces expected losses or information asymmetry; primary-market spreads, fees, pricing grids, covenant intensity, and acceptance rates across bonds, loans, and private placements reflect this mechanism, as do secondary-market depth and volatility around disclosure events. Each channel can be measured with existing corporate and market data: line-level yields, defect minutes, energy and water intensity, incident and downtime records, churn and on-time delivery, bid–ask behavior under stress, loss-severity distributions, and issuance outcomes in Rule 144A and bank debt.

The framework is explicit about boundary conditions and comparative statics. Effects concentrate where issues are financially material, verification is credible, hazard exposure is high, and institutions enforce rules. Assurance strengthens signals and should dominate narrative claims in pricing power. Social capital complements formal controls by lowering the cost of establishing credibility, amplifying the financing and shock-absorption benefits of ESG in opaque settings and accelerated placements. Substitution and complementarity across levers are observable: for example, stronger compliance and assurance can raise the marginal payoff to strategy by converting process metrics into priced information, while robust community ties can magnify the insurance value of safety and supply-chain programs.

Placing ESG inside the theory of the firm clarifies roles and limits. In capital budgeting, ESG enters project NPV through internal carbon prices, failure-cost curves, and business-interruption models that affect both cash-flow forecasts and discount rates; managers should map each initiative to a cash-flow or discount-rate lever and require scenario-consistent hurdle rates. In financing policy, verifiable ESG reshapes the feasible set for covenant design, step-ups, and security choice, particularly in private markets where screening dominates pooling. In governance, boards allocate attention across compliance, strategy, and insurance, ensure assurance quality, and align pay so that the left tail is protected without starving innovation. Misrepresentation is modeled as value destruction through elevated legal and reputational jump risk; in equilibrium it dilutes signal quality and raises industry-wide required returns.

9.3 Empirical Contributions

This book provides an integrated empirical program across chapters and settings to identify how ESG affects cash flows, risk, and financing. The designs triangulate mechanisms rather than rely on single-context correlations, and they standardize variables and identification choices so evidence can cumulate. We first test the incentive channel that links managerial contracts to corporate behavior and then to realized risk. Using inside-debt intensity as a risk-sensitive incentive, we estimate a mediation pathway in which higher inside debt increases CSR process investment and CSR in turn lowers firm risk. The tests condition on environmental munificence and dynamism to separate prudence from foregone growth. The estimates isolate a micro-mechanism, not a halo effect that conflates "good management" and "good outcomes."

We next examine financing frictions where screening and bilateral information are central. In private placements, with emphasis on Rule 144A issuances, we show that locally embedded social capital interacts with ESG quality to improve market access and pricing terms. This isolates a financing channel distinct from broad equity sentiment and public-market liquidity. The cross-sectional gradients are strongest where disclosure opacity is high and relationship enforcement matters, consistent with ESG operating as a credibility technology that reduces expected contracting costs.

We then link ESG to liquidity risk and operating resilience. Firms with stronger, process-level ESG exhibit narrower liquidity premia, smaller spread blowouts in stress, and more stable depth. The mechanism runs through inventory discipline, supplier reliability, customer retention, and disclosure credibility that reduces adverse selection when markets seize up. Working-capital metrics and stress-period microstructure confirm that the channel is operational, not only narrative.

We quantify effects on the cost of capital. Where financial materiality is high and data are verifiable, credible ESG programs associate with lower required returns. The reduction operates through both systematic and idiosyncratic components. Transition-risk exposures shift beta-like terms, while process reliability reduces firm-specific volatility. Primary-market outcomes—spreads, fees, acceptance rates, and covenant intensity in bonds, loans, and 144A deals—match secondary-market evidence on volatility and depth around disclosure events, reinforcing the pricing result.

We finally test convexity under shock. The COVID-19 pandemic serves as an exogenous stressor. ESG-intensive firms retained employees, coordinated with suppliers and customers, and maintained access to funding. Return and cash-flow differentials concentrate where mobility restrictions and operational hazards were binding, which is consistent with an insurance value that is small in normal times and large in bad times. Recovery speed and drawdown profiles show the same asymmetry.

Across studies we implement a common measurement discipline. We operationalize ESG with decision-relevant constructs tied to mechanisms, including supply continuity, safety and training, disclosure credibility, and community embeddedness. We address rater disagreement by triangulating data providers and by constructing pillar-level measures aligned with hypothesized channels rather than relying on opaque composites. Variable definitions are harmonized, and robustness includes alternative data sources, placebo timings, and sensitivity to rating weights, ensuring that results are not artifacts of a single vendor or score.

Methodologically, the work emphasizes identification that matches theory. Mediation analyses pin the incentive pathway from inside debt to CSR to risk. Within-issuer comparisons in private placements separate issuer quality from issue-level screening. Tests condition on financial materiality to avoid false positives in immaterial domains. Stress-period estimation identifies left-tail effects that would be attenuated in pooled samples. Event designs around disclosure shocks, rater methodology changes, and regulatory announcements isolate information channels. We formalize "regulatory geography" as a treatment intensity that uses jurisdictional exposure and venue choice to compare firms facing different enforcement and disclosure regimes, enabling cross-regime inference without assuming global homogeneity.

The breadth of contexts—managerial contracts, private debt markets, market microstructure in stress, asset-pricing decompositions, and crisis performance—supports external validity and clarifies boundary conditions. Effects are strongest where hazards are real, materiality is high, and verification is credible. By keeping constructs, measures, and identification aligned with theory across chapters, the evidence traces a coherent map from ESG inputs to priced outputs that can be replicated, extended, and challenged in future work.

9.4 Implications

9.4.1 Policy Implications

Regulation raises welfare when it improves signal quality, reduces coordination failures, and preserves room for innovation. Priorities follow directly from the evidence. Authorities should establish clear baselines and a limited set of decision-relevant metrics so disclosures map to priced risks and cash-flow levers. Core items should be digitally tagged with audit trails and machine-readable schemas so investors can aggregate and compare across issuers and time. Greenwashing must be deterred through a mix of ex-ante standardization and ex-post enforcement: calculation methods, boundary conditions, and materiality thresholds should be specified up front, while sanctions for misstatement and omission must be strong enough to maintain deterrence without chilling bona fide experimentation. Sector-specific materiality keeps reporting proportional to hazard and impact; prescriptive items belong where externalities and incident severity are large, while lower-hazard sectors should retain flexibility to innovate. Assurance markets need clear scope, qualifications, and liability rules. Limited assurance can be the floor and ramp to reasonable assurance on metrics tied to financing and compensation, supported by safe harbors for forward-looking analysis that adheres to stated methods.

Jurisdictional design should match institutional strengths. In China, policy complementarities are decisive. Coordinated industrial upgrading, IP protection, and disclosure regimes can channel ESG toward real capability building in energy efficiency, safety, and quality systems. Credit guidance and taxonomy alignment should steer bank lending and bond issuance to SMEs that adopt verifiable controls, while specialized IP adjudication reduces appropriation risk that would otherwise discourage process innovation. Provincial pilots in data standards, digital tagging, and third-party assurance can scale nationally once measurement noise falls. In the United States, a market-led system works when anti-fraud enforcement is credible and materiality guidance is specific. Clear definitions of financially material ESG topics, safe harbors for scenario analysis, and coordination among securities, banking, and justice authorities reduce ambiguity and litigation overhang. Private markets—Rule 144A placements, direct lending, sustainability-linked loans—transmit discipline when covenants reference auditable metrics and step-ups are enforced. In Europe, ambitious reporting and taxonomy frameworks already shape global practice through supply chains and capital markets. Implementation quality now dominates: proportionality for SMEs, usability of the EU Taxonomy beyond niche assets, interoperability with international standards, and pragmatic assurance timelines will determine whether the regime lowers capital costs for credible transition plans rather than only for already-green issuers.

Cross-regime spillovers argue for partial harmonization rather than full convergence. A common core of definitions, units, and machine-readable tags lowers fixed compliance costs and improves comparability for global investors, while optional extensions let jurisdictions pursue local policy aims. Mutual recognition of assurance standards and shared registries for auditors and methodologies would prevent races to the bottom on credibility. Data infrastructure has public-good properties. Open repositories for activity- and location-based hazard data, standardized event logs for environmental, safety, and conduct incidents, and reference datasets for emissions factors and supply-chain maps reduce measurement error at the source. Transition finance requires clear labels and pathway tests. "Use-of-proceeds," "performance-linked," and "transition" instruments should be distinguished, with pathway credibility tied to sectoral feasibility curves rather than generic pledges. Supervisors should integrate climate and conduct risks into stress testing without conflating prudential and industrial policy. Evaluation must be built in. Periodic reviews of reporting burdens, assurance yields, and pricing responsiveness should sunset low-value disclosures and elevate high-signal metrics that demonstrably tighten the link between information and capital allocation.

9.4.2 Managerial Implications

Managers approach ESG as capital allocation under uncertainty. Every initiative links to a cash-flow or discount-rate channel with quantified, state-dependent payoffs. Internal carbon pricing, failure-cost curves, and business-interruption modeling translate environmental, safety, and conduct exposures into expected-value and tail-risk estimates suitable for project appraisal. Working-capital policy incorporates supplier concentration, geographic risk, and audit outcomes, with buffers and dual-sourcing justified by explicit outage-cost modeling rather than broad resilience claims. Product strategy aligns willingness-to-pay for sustainability attributes with design and capacity decisions through revealed-preference data and structured market analysis. Financing decisions connect to verifiable controls. Sustainability-linked loans and bonds depend on auditable, management-controlled indicators; pricing adjustments and covenants operate above measurement noise and enforce contract credibility. Investor communication integrates operational data with risk and cash-flow sensitivity, enabling direct input to valuation models—unsubstantiated narrative remains unpriced.

Governance translates intent into discipline. Boards define mandates across compliance, strategy, and insurance, including explicit risk appetite and escalation protocols. Compensation structures penalize left-tail outcomes while supporting innovation via budgets anchored in science-based targets and observable progress, avoiding scoring systems that encourage manipulation. Data stewardship sits with primary operating units; operations, procurement, and IT jointly generate metrics, with internal audit providing independent challenge and assurance readiness. Data systems prioritize origin-level capture, version control, and immutable audit trails, supporting external verification. Scenario analysis centers on a small set of plausible states, predefined triggers and responses, and rehearsed operational adjustments such as supplier substitution and inventory scaling. M&A and capital-project reviews extend to operational maturity, incident records, and regulatory history, with contingent pricing and earn-outs distributing transition risk. Crisis management maintains established communication with workforce, community, supply chain, customers, and creditors to sustain coordination under stress. Misrepresentation erodes value through litigation, regulatory action, and reputation loss; as assurance and traceability expand, the cost of exaggeration increases, making verifiable modesty the prevailing approach.

Limitations and Future Research Directions

10

10.1 Limitations

The current evidence on ESG is shaped by a range of persistent limitations that hinder both causal inference and generalizability. A primary obstacle is the incomplete and uneven observation of operational data at the granular level required for robust analysis. Ideally, assessing the real impact of ESG adoption would rely on detailed microdata—such as plant-level records of throughput, defect rates, downtime, maintenance activities, workforce composition, and time-stamped incident logs. In practice, such information remains scarce, inconsistently collected, and often locked behind confidentiality barriers. Where available, these datasets typically lack standardization in collection methods and vary widely in quality. Without consistent access to operational data at the line or site level, researchers must depend on aggregated firm-level indicators that conflate multiple processes, technologies, and managerial practices. This aggregation attenuates estimated effects and impedes precise mapping of ESG process improvements to outcomes like yield, learning-curve gains, bottleneck relief, or recovery from disruption. The challenges are compounded in supply networks, where information on upstream risk exposure, input substitutability, switching frictions, and shock propagation is rarely accessible beyond direct suppliers. Multi-tiered supply networks remain largely opaque, forcing researchers to impute network dynamics from partial or public data, which raises concerns about the external validity and causal interpretation of resilience models.

Similar data constraints appear in the study of ESG's role in financing. Contract terms for loans and bonds—such as covenant definitions, measurement periods, remediation procedures, audit clauses, and events of default—are infrequently disclosed, especially for private placements and customized sustainability-linked instruments. Even for public instruments, important details may be contained in confidential side letters or omitted altogether. Consequently, researchers rely on proxies like spreads, maturities, and covenant counts that blur distinctions

J. Wang, *ESG Strategies and Financial Markets*, Management for Professionals,
https://doi.org/10.1007/978-981-95-5620-5_10

between firm characteristics and contract design, making it difficult to disentangle the specific influence of ESG on financial outcomes. Further complicating inference, practices differ widely among agent banks, calculation agents, and assurance providers, introducing additional variability that is difficult to observe or control.

Cross-country and cross-regime analysis faces endogeneity from firms' strategic choices and heterogeneity in regulatory enforcement. Firms actively select their listing venues, legal structures, supply-chain footprints, and disclosure practices in response to regulation, taxation, and investor expectations. These choices introduce selection bias, as policy exposure becomes confounded with firm-level adaptation and anticipatory behavior. Enforcement itself is inconsistent, with jurisdictions varying in audit depth, liability standards, and regulatory resources. These differences make it challenging to draw valid comparisons or to generalize findings from treated to untreated firms, especially in studies relying on difference-in-differences or event-study frameworks.

Measurement error permeates the ESG data ecosystem. Definitions of ESG remain multi-dimensional and contested, with rating agencies and data providers employing divergent taxonomies, weighting, and aggregation methods. Ratings often rely more on the frequency and quality of disclosure than on underlying operational outcomes, creating mechanical correlations between transparency and assessed "quality." The adoption of alternative data—such as text analytics on sustainability reports, satellite imagery, and local news—adds new layers of risk, including model drift, sectoral and geographic domain shifts, and non-transparent feature attribution, all of which complicate replication and auditability. The absence of standardized corpora and documented model evolution further impedes systematic validation across firms, periods, or jurisdictions.

Endogeneity and selection bias persist despite attempts at careful research design. Firms with superior management, stronger data systems, and more advanced operational capabilities are more likely to implement credible ESG practices and attract favorable financing, making it difficult to isolate the effect of ESG from the underlying quality of the firm. Efforts to use regulatory timing or geographic hazard as instruments are only partially effective, as anticipatory actions and strategic disclosures often undermine exclusion restrictions. Dynamic selection, where weaker firms exit or merge, further skews samples and introduces survivorship bias, while unobserved factors like organizational culture or governance can still drive both ESG adoption and firm outcomes.

External validity is bounded by industry structure, risk profile, audit capacity, and supply-chain architecture. Findings from capital-intensive, high-hazard sectors with strong assurance infrastructure may not apply to service industries or digital firms, where risks and controls differ fundamentally. Practices effective in jurisdictions with robust audit markets or enforcement may lose impact where such ecosystems are weak. Differences in supplier concentration, logistics, customs, and capital controls limit the generalizability of mechanisms that presume flexible contracting or dual sourcing. Temporal instability presents another boundary: operational benefits of ESG adoption accumulate slowly through learning and supply development, while market perceptions can change rapidly in response to new information, technological advances, or regulatory resets, rendering effect estimates highly sensitive to the period studied.

Transparency and replicability are hampered by access barriers to the most valuable data. Information such as supplier evaluations, corrective-action logs, incident reports, compliance records, and assurance files is often proprietary or covered by non-disclosure agreements. Publicly available data are noisier and can reflect strategic reporting behavior, making robust replication and multi-team validation challenging. These frictions slow the development of stable effect estimates and the emergence of common measurement standards.

Attribution of ESG effects in the face of shocks is further complicated by overlapping policy interventions and measurement noise. The pandemic, for example, coincided with broad fiscal and monetary measures, sectoral shutdowns, and staggered reopening schedules, making it difficult to separate the effects of ESG from those of concurrent policy supports or demand shocks. Weather-related studies face similar attribution challenges due to overlapping events, delays in damage assessment, and incomplete operational records. These factors increase the risk of misattribution—either overstating or understating the real benefits of ESG during tail events.

The timing of information flow and market response also imposes limits. ESG information typically diffuses gradually through channels such as supplier audits, regulatory filings, NGO reports, and media coverage before it appears in official corporate disclosures. Assurance scopes vary widely and may not cover metrics most relevant to investors. Event-study windows can capture unrelated news or macroeconomic developments, and varied reporting calendars weaken the alignment needed for clean identification of market reactions. This asynchrony further raises uncertainty about when and how markets incorporate ESG information into prices or expectations.

Overcoming these limitations will require substantial investment in data infrastructure, movement toward standardized definitions and taxonomies, and deeper transparency from both firms and financial intermediaries. Advances in digital traceability, open-data efforts, and rigorous validation protocols may gradually reduce some of these constraints. However, the complexity and evolving nature of ESG ensure that no single empirical approach will suffice. Continued vigilance, methodological innovation, and clear communication of uncertainty remain essential for researchers and practitioners seeking reliable insight and actionable guidance in the ESG domain.

10.2 Future Research Direction

A natural next step is to move from firm-level averages to explicitly networked analyses. Production, finance, and information circulate through multi-tier buyer–supplier structures, syndicated lending constellations, and ownership webs, not isolated units. Mapping these graphs at scale would allow identification of how ESG practices propagate across input–output links, how bottlenecks amplify or dampen operational shocks, and which nodes generate disproportionate real and financial externalities. Designs that integrate supplier hierarchies, logistics corridors, and location-specific hazard maps can trace spillovers from a focal firm's investments in safety and traceability to upstream defect rates, on-time delivery, and downstream inventory buffers. Financial networks merit comparable attention. Syndicate composition, common lenders, benchmark index membership, and cross-holdings create channels through which assurance gains or controversies at one issuer reprice peers via covenant tightening, collateral haircuts, and reweighting. A credible empirical program will model these systems dynamically, allowing for endogenous rewiring as suppliers switch, banks retrench, and funds rebalance, and will separate transmission from selection by exploiting plausibly exogenous shocks to nodes and edges.

Progress will also depend on turning unstructured, multilingual evidence into analysis-ready data with transparent, replicable pipelines. Large language models can be deployed to parse contracts and extract covenant definitions, calculation-agent roles, cure periods, and step-up triggers; to align these terms across issuers and years; and to link them to realized enforcement in amendments and waivers. The same tools can harvest plant-level indicators from inspection reports, permits, incident narratives, and earnings-call transcripts; reconcile entities across languages and scripts; and co-reference facilities with geospatial registries. Multimodal models extend coverage to images and tables by inferring flaring and stockpiles from satellite imagery, heat exposure and flood risk from remote sensing, and safety findings from scanned audit PDFs. To make such pipelines scientific rather than artisanal, future work should adopt versioned model cards, fixed prompts and schemas, documented preprocessing, and validation against hand-labeled benchmarks and ground truth from sensors, meters, and supervisory control systems. Privacy-preserving computation—federated learning, secure enclaves, and differential privacy—should be normalized so that researchers can learn from sensitive microdata without bulk transfers.

Methodologically, machine learning should be brought to bear for both prediction and identification. Predictive models can rank facilities by incident risk, forecast supplier non-performance under hazard scenarios, and anticipate spread changes conditional on process controls. Causal machine learning—orthogonalization, double machine learning, generalized random forests, targeted maximum likelihood, and conformal inference—can estimate heterogeneous treatment effects by sector, hazard, and verification depth, while reducing model dependence. Sequence models can capture lag structures between operational changes and financial outcomes. Graph neural networks provide a principled way to learn propagation on supply chains and credit webs. Active-learning loops can prioritize audits, document requests, or facility visits where expected information gain is highest. Critically, these methods should be embedded in designs that respect identification requirements, with pre-analysis plans, holdout verification, and sensitivity analyses to plausible violations of assumptions.

Artificial intelligence is itself an object of ESG analysis and should be studied as such. The resource footprint of AI systems—energy use by workload and geography, water consumption for cooling, and lifecycle emissions of hardware—should be measured with facility-level resolution and priced into cost of capital, procurement, and location choice. Governance of AI—fairness, privacy, security, and model risk—creates new control systems analogous to environment, health, and safety, and warrants assurance and incident disclosure with comparable rigor. Organizationally, AI alters decision processes: predictive maintenance changes failure distributions and spare-parts policy; anomaly detection modifies quality control and scrap rates; supply-chain copilots influence contracting, inventory, and compliance. Markets may also price AI-enabled ESG differently from traditional practices if AI improves verification and reduces measurement error; event studies around adoption of continuous emissions monitoring, digital assurance, or AI-based safety analytics can isolate these information effects.

Finally, future work should adopt decision-grade stress testing that links physical and transition risks to operations, working capital, and financing. High-resolution climate and catastrophe models can be combined with precise plant coordinates, supplier graphs, and covenant maps to generate Monte Carlo scenarios in which ESG programs are evaluated as portfolios of state-contingent hedges and growth options rather than static scores. Internal prices for carbon, water scarcity, outage minutes, and legal penalties should be integrated into capital budgeting with explicit checks on calibration error over time. The field would benefit from open, versioned benchmarks that allow cumulative learning: shared tasks for extracting contract terms, classifying incidents, mapping facilities, predicting supplier failure, and estimating tail risks; standardized corpora for multilingual reporting; and replication packages that tie code to data with immutable identifiers. A network-aware, spillover-sensitive, AI-enabled empirical agenda of this kind is the most direct path to testing at scale when and how ESG changes cash flows, compresses downside risk, and lowers financing frictions.

ESG is not a moral add-on. It is a contingent, priced capability that reshapes cash flows, risk, and financing under identifiable mechanisms and institutions. When embedded in governance, aligned with incentives, supported by social capital, and verified by credible rules, ESG improves resilience, lowers financing frictions, and preserves option value in bad states. That is the book's core contribution: a disciplined, testable map from ESG inputs to financial outputs that managers, investors, and policymakers can use to make better decisions.

Appendix

A1 Variable Definition in Chapter 4

Variable	Definitions
Yield spreads	Natural logarithm of yield spreads, which is the difference in basis points between the original yield of Rule 144A bond and that of a U.S. Treasury bond with comparable maturity
Years to maturity	Number of years to maturity of a debt contract
Issue size	Total amount of a debt (in $millions) obtained by a firm in year t
Debt rating	The categorical variable capturing S&P senior debt rating for a firm in year t
Firm size	Natural logarithm of the book value of firm assets
Tobin's Q	Ratio of the market value of the asset to book value of the asset
ROA	Return on asset. Net income divided by total assets
Market leverage	Total debt divided by the market value of equity, which is the product of stock price times the number of shares outstanding
Investment	Common equity divided by the invested capital
Tax avoidance	Tax expense divided by pre-tax income
Dividend payment	Common and preferred dividends divided by income before extraordinary items
Cash holding	Cash and marketable securities divided by total assets
Tangibility	Net property, plant, and equipment divided by total assets
MTOB	Ratio of market value to asset to book value of asset
DEBT	Ratio of total debt to total asset
EBITDA	EBITDA divided by total asset
CASH	Total cash divided by total asset
Social capital	The first principal component of a PCA based on NRCRD data
Ln (POP)	Natural logarithm of the population size of a county
County population growth	The rate at which the number of individuals in a county increases in one year
Ln (Income)	Natural logarithm of the median household income per capita in a county

Variable	Definitions
Institutional ownership	The percentage of the holding by firm's top five institutional investors
Religiosity	The adherence rate, which is the fraction of a county's population that claims affiliation with an organized religion
FC_Dummy	A dummy variable which equals to 1 if issuing year is after 2009 and 0 otherwise
Border distance	Natural logarithm of the distance between a county and the Canadian border
Trust Score	The first principal component of a PCA based on World Value Survey (WVS)

A2 Stata Scripts Used to Construct Control Variables Using Financial and Accounting Data from Compustat

```
/**The purpose is to generate control variables***/
   clear
   use funda, clear
   set more off
   ****************************************************************
   //Check data quality //
   ****************************************************************
   duplicates report gvkey fyear //examine the panel data fiscal
year
   duplicates example gvkey fyear //
   duplicates drop gvkey fyear, force //drop duplicated
observations

   joinby gvkey fyear using " sic5015.dta",unm(master)
   drop _merge
   save as funda,replace

   ****************************************************************
   //Check data quality //
   ****************************************************************
   duplicates report gvkey fyear //examine the panel data fiscal
year
```

```
   duplicates example gvkey fyear //
   duplicates drop gvkey fyear, force //drop duplicated
observations

   ***************************************
   ***Step 1. clean data***
   ***************************************
   /*exclude firm-years if total asset is not positive,follow
khan&watt 2009*/
   drop if at<=0
   /*exclude firms-years price per share is less than $1, follow
khan&watt 2009*/
   drop if ceq<=0 //

   /*exclude firm-years if sales is not positive*/
drop if sale <=0

   /*exclude ceq (book value of equity) that is not positive*/
 drop if ceq<=0


   /**Excluding financial firms and utility firms depends on the
project**/
   /*exclude financial firms*/
   drop if sic_int>=6000 & sic_int<7000
   /*exclude utility firms*/
   drop if sic_int>=4900 & sic_int<5000

   /**not sure whether it's appropriate to drop all the missing
data**/
   /* exclude missing data*/
   //ni:net income; dp:Depreciation and Amortization;
rect:Receivables - Total
   //revt: Inventories - Total;csho: Common Shares Outstanding;
ceq:common equity-total
   //ap:account payable; txp:Income Taxes Payablexpp:Prepaid
Expense;

   drop if ni>=. | rect>=. | revt>=. | xpp>=. | ap >=.
   drop if at>=. | csho>=. | ceq>=.

   /*If some variables have missing value, they can be set to be
0*/
   replace act=0 if missing(act)
   replace dlc=0 if missing(dlc)
```

```
replace che=0 if missing(che)
replace txp=0 if missing(txp)
replace dltt=0 if missing(dltt)
replace pstk=0 if missing(pstk)
replace dp=0 if missing(dp)
replace lct=0 if missing(lct) //lct:current liability

//*Generate market equity value* //
gen be_comp=ceq
gen be = teq+txditc-pstk //BE = Stockholders Equity + Deferred
Taxes + Investment Tax Credit - Preferred Stock
gen me_comp=mkvalt
gen me =csho*prcc_f //calculate the the market value of
equity at the fiscal year-end

/*exclude firms if maket value is less than 10 milion, follow
callen&hope 2010*/
//Why not keep if me > 10

drop if me<10
//gen drop_flag = me<10
//egen drop_flag_for_firm = total(drop_flag),by(gvkey_int)
//drop if drop_flag_for_firm >=1
//drop drop_flag drop_flag_for_firm

/*exclude ADR*/
/*follow the code from: http://www.mit.edu/~rverdi/acct-
comp_2013.sas*/

**Generate calendar year and begin&end date for the fiscal
year**
gen cyear=fyear
replace cyear=fyear+1 if fyr<=5 //change fiscal year to calen-
dar year

gen date1= mdy( fyr, 1, cyear)
gen endfyr= datadate //define the end date of fiscal year
gen begfyr=mdy(month(endfyr-364),1,year(endfyr-364)) //define
the begin date of each fiscal year
format %td begfyr
format %td endfyr

*************************************************************
// Step 2. Generate variables that are often used in the
project
*************************************************************
```

```
// Firm Size

gen logasset=ln(at)
gen logsale=ln(sale)
gen logemp=ln(emp)
gen logmktve_f=ln(me) //

//Liquidity JFE 1999 Cash Holding Paper
gen liquidasset=che/at //Cash and short term investment(Item 1) / Total Asset(Item 6 )
gen liquidsale=che/sale //cash to sale
gen wkcapital= (act - dlc)/at
gen currentratio=act/lct //current ratio=current asset/current liability

//Levarage
gen leverage_tot= dt / at // total book leverage
gen firm_debt=dltt+dlc //calculate firm's debt= total long-term debt+total debt in current liabilities used by jfe cash holding
gen mktlev=firm_debt/me //market-debt ratio used by jfe 1999 cash holding
gen bklev=firm_debt/at //book-debt ratio

gen LEVERAGE= dltt/[(at[_n-1]+at[_n]+at[_n+1])/3]
label var LEVERAGE "Total long-term liabilities divided by average total assets"

//operation condition
gen RDtoSale=xrd/sale //r&d ratio JFE 1999 CASH HOLDING_a measure of the potential for financial distress costs.
gen RDintensity_1=xrd/emp //
gen RDintensity_2=xrd/revt //used by "The Effect of Mandatory Financial Statement Disclosures of Tax Uncertainty on Tax Reporting and Collections"//
gen tangibility=ppent/at //ppent:Property, Plant and Equipment - Total (Net)
gen tangibility_2=(0.715*rect+0.547*invt+0.535*ppent+che)/at

gen intangibility_at =( xrd+xad)/at
gen intaginility_sale=( xrd+xad)/sale
gen capxratio=capx/at //capital expenditure JFE 1999 cash holding


gen saletoasset=sale/at
```

```
gen altman_z= 3.3*ebit/at +0.99*sale/at +0.6*me/dltt +1.2*act/at +1.4*re/at

//Profitability
sort gvkey fyear
by gvkey: gen lagsale=sale[_n-1]
by gvkey:gen lagsale_2 =logsale[_n-1]
gen salegrowth=sale/lagsale-1
gen salegrowth_2 = logsale/lagsale_2 -1 //Sales Growth is the natural log of sales in year t, minus the natural log of sales in year t-1 (JFE1999 CASH HOLDING)
label var salegrowth_2 "natural log of sales in year t, minus the natural log of sales in year t-1"

//control for sales growth**
/*followed by Ahmed et al. 2007 JAE*/
gen SaleGrowth=(sale[_n]-sale[_n-1])/sale[_n-1]
label var SaleGrowth "Percentage of annual growth in total sales"

gen grossprofit=(revt-cogs)/at //JFE2013 the other side of value gross profit=(revenue-cost of goods sold)/asset
gen profitability=ebitda/at

gen freecashflow_1=(ni+dp-wcapch-capx)/be
gen freecashflow_2= (ni+dp-wcapch-capx)/be_comp

gen roa1=ib/at //ib is Income Before Extraordinary Items
gen roa2=ibcom/at //ibcom is Income Before Extraordinary Items - Available for Common
gen roa3=ebitda/at //roa=EBITDA/at JF 2007 Inside debt and its role in managerial compensation

gen roe1=ebitda/be
gen roe2=ebitda/be_comp

gen tobin_q1=(at+me-be)/at
gen tobin_q2=(at+me_comp-be_comp)/at

gen CFO_TA=oancf/[(at[_n-1]+at[_n]+at[_n+1])/3]/*followed by Ahmed et al. 2007 JAE*/
label var CFO_TA "Cash flow from operations divided by average total assets"
gen cfo_at=oancf/at
// oancf:Operating Activities - Net Cash Flow (Statement of Cash Flows)
```

```
//JFE 1999 cash holding measures the likelihood that a firm will have positive net present value (NPV) projects in the future
gen MtB1=me_comp/be_comp // market to book ratio;
gen MtB2=me/be

//gen MBRatio= (data6-data60+data199*data25)/data6
//label var MBRatio "the ratio of market value to book value in the fiscal year t"

//Control for the effect of bondholder-shareholder conflicts over dividend policy **
/*followed by Jerry Sun, 2011 MF*/
gen DIV= (dvpsp_f *csho)/at //dvpsp_f:dividends per share-fiscal
label var DIV "common dividends divided by total assets"

//gen DEBT=data9/data6
//label var DEBT "long-term debt divided by total assets"

gen AstGROWTH=(at[_n]-at[_n-1])/at[_n-1]
label var AstGROWTH "growth in assets"

//control for growth opportunities**
**rdip:in process R&D Expense**
**xad:Advertising expense**
gen RD_ADV=(rdip+xad)/sale
label var RD_ADV "Research and Development costs plus advertising expense divided by sales"

//control for firms with high litigation risk**

destring sic, replace
gen highlitRisk=0
replace highlitRisk=1 if (sic>2833 & sic<2836) | (sic>3570 & sic<3577) | (sic>5200 & sic<5961) | (sic<7374 & sic>7370)
label var highlitRisk "High Litigation Risk firms"

//From Liuling's file, need to check the definition and citation
gen equityissue=(sstk-prstkc)/at //sstk:sale of Common and Preferred Stock; prstkc:Purchase of Common and Preferred Stock
gen debtissue=(dltis-dltr)/at //dltis: Long-Term Debt Issuance; dltr: Long-Term Debt Reduction
gen externalfinancing=((sstk-prstkc)+(dltis-dltr))/at
gen equityissize=equityissue-debtissue
```

```
gen equityfin = (equityissize>=0.05)
gen debtfin=(equityissize<0.05)

***************************************************************
// Step 3. Join with Geographic data
***************************************************************
*****
//create 2-digit SIC code

tostring sic, replace
sort sic
browse sic

gen sic2=substr(sic,1,2) if length(sic)==4
replace sic2=substr(sic, 1,1) if missing(sic2)
sort sic2
browse sic2

destring sic sic2, replace

//create 3-digit SIC code

tostring sic, replace
sort sic
browse sic

gen sic3=substr(sic,1,3) if length(sic)==4
replace sic3=substr(sic, 1,1) if missing(sic3)
sort sic3
browse sic3
```

A3: Stata Scripts Used to Generate Firm-Level Risk Measures

```
// This code estimates idio. risk using weekly data.
// The market models here include
      // Capm
      // Mkt + Industry
      // Mkt + Lagged Mkt
      // Mkt + Lagged Mkt + Industry
      // Mkt + Lagged Mkt + Industry + Lagged Industry
      // Fama-French three-factor
```

```
//  Industry  return  is  specified  using  Fama-French  49
classification
// For each week each stock, an industry return is estimated as
the vw & ew average
      // industry return excluding this stock.
// VW industry returns use both same period and previous period
mkt cap.
// Idio. risk is estimated using the same method as with daily
return.
      // Sample std
      // sum( residuals^2 + 2*residual*lagged residual)
// Both total return and ex-div returns are used
// All the volatility is annualized, scalling by the num of
within-year obs.

use ab72df043a1deb9a, clear
drop if missing(prc)
drop if missing(retx)
replace prc = -prc if prc < 0
gen cap = prc * shrout
merge m:1 date using weeknum
drop if _merge == 2
drop _merge permno prc shr* weekday
replace ret = ln(1+ret)
replace retx = ln(1+retx)
collapse (sum) rd = ret rx = retx ///
    (lastnm) sic = siccd capw = cap , by(cusip weeknum) cw // t
= 579.60s
replace rd = exp(rd) - 1
replace rx = exp(rx) - 1
save ret_wk, replace
sort cusip weeknum
by cusip: gen capwL = capw[_n-1]

if 1 > 0 {
gen ind = 49
//01 Agric
replace ind = 1 if sic >= 100 & sic <= 199
replace ind = 1 if sic >= 200 & sic <= 299
replace ind = 1 if sic >= 700 & sic <= 799
replace ind = 1 if sic >= 910 & sic <= 919
replace ind = 1 if sic >= 2048 & sic <= 2048
```

```
//02 Food
replace ind = 2 if sic >= 2000 & sic <= 2009
replace ind = 2 if sic >= 2010 & sic <= 2019
replace ind = 2 if sic >= 2020 & sic <= 2029
replace ind = 2 if sic >= 2030 & sic <= 2039
replace ind = 2 if sic >= 2040 & sic <= 2046
replace ind = 2 if sic >= 2050 & sic <= 2059
replace ind = 2 if sic >= 2060 & sic <= 2063
replace ind = 2 if sic >= 2070 & sic <= 2079
replace ind = 2 if sic >= 2090 & sic <= 2092
replace ind = 2 if sic >= 2095 & sic <= 2095
replace ind = 2 if sic >= 2098 & sic <= 2099

//03 Soda
replace ind = 3 if sic >= 2064 & sic <= 2068
replace ind = 3 if sic >= 2086 & sic <= 2086
replace ind = 3 if sic >= 2087 & sic <= 2087
replace ind = 3 if sic >= 2096 & sic <= 2096
replace ind = 3 if sic >= 2097 & sic <= 2097

//04 Beer
replace ind = 4 if sic >= 2080 & sic <= 2080
replace ind = 4 if sic >= 2082 & sic <= 2082
replace ind = 4 if sic >= 2083 & sic <= 2083
replace ind = 4 if sic >= 2084 & sic <= 2084
replace ind = 4 if sic >= 2085 & sic <= 2085

//05 Smoke
replace ind = 5 if sic >= 2100 & sic <= 2199

//06 Toys
replace ind = 6 if sic >= 920 & sic <= 999
replace ind = 6 if sic >= 3650 & sic <= 3651
replace ind = 6 if sic >= 3652 & sic <= 3652
replace ind = 6 if sic >= 3732 & sic <= 3732
replace ind = 6 if sic >= 3930 & sic <= 3931
replace ind = 6 if sic >= 3940 & sic <= 3949

//07 Fun
replace ind = 7 if sic >= 7800 & sic <= 7829
replace ind = 7 if sic >= 7830 & sic <= 7833
replace ind = 7 if sic >= 7840 & sic <= 7841
replace ind = 7 if sic >= 7900 & sic <= 7900
replace ind = 7 if sic >= 7910 & sic <= 7911
```

```
replace ind = 7 if sic >= 7920 & sic <= 7929
replace ind = 7 if sic >= 7930 & sic <= 7933
replace ind = 7 if sic >= 7940 & sic <= 7949
replace ind = 7 if sic >= 7980 & sic <= 7980
replace ind = 7 if sic >= 7990 & sic <= 7999

//08 Books
replace ind = 8 if sic >= 2700 & sic <= 2709
replace ind = 8 if sic >= 2710 & sic <= 2719
replace ind = 8 if sic >= 2720 & sic <= 2729
replace ind = 8 if sic >= 2730 & sic <= 2739
replace ind = 8 if sic >= 2740 & sic <= 2749
replace ind = 8 if sic >= 2770 & sic <= 2771
replace ind = 8 if sic >= 2780 & sic <= 2789
replace ind = 8 if sic >= 2790 & sic <= 2799

//09 Hshld
replace ind = 9 if sic >= 2047 & sic <= 2047
replace ind = 9 if sic >= 2391 & sic <= 2392
replace ind = 9 if sic >= 2510 & sic <= 2519
replace ind = 9 if sic >= 2590 & sic <= 2599
replace ind = 9 if sic >= 2840 & sic <= 2843
replace ind = 9 if sic >= 2844 & sic <= 2844
replace ind = 9 if sic >= 3160 & sic <= 3161
replace ind = 9 if sic >= 3170 & sic <= 3171
replace ind = 9 if sic >= 3172 & sic <= 3172
replace ind = 9 if sic >= 3190 & sic <= 3199
replace ind = 9 if sic >= 3229 & sic <= 3229
replace ind = 9 if sic >= 3260 & sic <= 3260
replace ind = 9 if sic >= 3262 & sic <= 3263
replace ind = 9 if sic >= 3269 & sic <= 3269
replace ind = 9 if sic >= 3230 & sic <= 3231
replace ind = 9 if sic >= 3630 & sic <= 3639
replace ind = 9 if sic >= 3750 & sic <= 3751
replace ind = 9 if sic >= 3800 & sic <= 3800
replace ind = 9 if sic >= 3860 & sic <= 3861
replace ind = 9 if sic >= 3870 & sic <= 3873
replace ind = 9 if sic >= 3910 & sic <= 3911
replace ind = 9 if sic >= 3914 & sic <= 3914
replace ind = 9 if sic >= 3915 & sic <= 3915
replace ind = 9 if sic >= 3960 & sic <= 3962
replace ind = 9 if sic >= 3991 & sic <= 3991
replace ind = 9 if sic >= 3995 & sic <= 3995
```

```
//10 Clths
replace ind = 10 if sic >= 2300 & sic <= 2390
replace ind = 10 if sic >= 3020 & sic <= 3021
replace ind = 10 if sic >= 3100 & sic <= 3111
replace ind = 10 if sic >= 3130 & sic <= 3131
replace ind = 10 if sic >= 3140 & sic <= 3149
replace ind = 10 if sic >= 3150 & sic <= 3151
replace ind = 10 if sic >= 3963 & sic <= 3965

//11 Hlth
replace ind = 11 if sic >= 8000 & sic <= 8099

//12 MedEq
replace ind = 12 if sic >= 3693 & sic <= 3693
replace ind = 12 if sic >= 3840 & sic <= 3849
replace ind = 12 if sic >= 3850 & sic <= 3851

//13 Drugs
replace ind = 13 if sic >= 2830 & sic <= 2830
replace ind = 13 if sic >= 2831 & sic <= 2831
replace ind = 13 if sic >= 2833 & sic <= 2833
replace ind = 13 if sic >= 2834 & sic <= 2834
replace ind = 13 if sic >= 2835 & sic <= 2835
replace ind = 13 if sic >= 2836 & sic <= 2836

//14 Chems
replace ind = 14 if sic >= 2800 & sic <= 2809
replace ind = 14 if sic >= 2810 & sic <= 2819
replace ind = 14 if sic >= 2820 & sic <= 2829
replace ind = 14 if sic >= 2850 & sic <= 2859
replace ind = 14 if sic >= 2860 & sic <= 2869
replace ind = 14 if sic >= 2870 & sic <= 2879
replace ind = 14 if sic >= 2890 & sic <= 2899

//15 Rubbr
replace ind = 15 if sic >= 3031 & sic <= 3031
replace ind = 15 if sic >= 3041 & sic <= 3041
replace ind = 15 if sic >= 3050 & sic <= 3053
replace ind = 15 if sic >= 3060 & sic <= 3069
replace ind = 15 if sic >= 3070 & sic <= 3079
replace ind = 15 if sic >= 3080 & sic <= 3089
replace ind = 15 if sic >= 3090 & sic <= 3099
```

```
//16 Txtls
replace ind = 16 if sic >= 2200 & sic <= 2269
replace ind = 16 if sic >= 2270 & sic <= 2279
replace ind = 16 if sic >= 2280 & sic <= 2284
replace ind = 16 if sic >= 2290 & sic <= 2295
replace ind = 16 if sic >= 2297 & sic <= 2297
replace ind = 16 if sic >= 2298 & sic <= 2298
replace ind = 16 if sic >= 2299 & sic <= 2299
replace ind = 16 if sic >= 2393 & sic <= 2395
replace ind = 16 if sic >= 2397 & sic <= 2399

//17 BldMt
replace ind = 17 if sic >= 800 & sic <= 899
replace ind = 17 if sic >= 2400 & sic <= 2439
replace ind = 17 if sic >= 2450 & sic <= 2459
replace ind = 17 if sic >= 2490 & sic <= 2499
replace ind = 17 if sic >= 2660 & sic <= 2661
replace ind = 17 if sic >= 2950 & sic <= 2952
replace ind = 17 if sic >= 3200 & sic <= 3200
replace ind = 17 if sic >= 3210 & sic <= 3211
replace ind = 17 if sic >= 3240 & sic <= 3241
replace ind = 17 if sic >= 3250 & sic <= 3259
replace ind = 17 if sic >= 3261 & sic <= 3261
replace ind = 17 if sic >= 3264 & sic <= 3264
replace ind = 17 if sic >= 3270 & sic <= 3275
replace ind = 17 if sic >= 3280 & sic <= 3281
replace ind = 17 if sic >= 3290 & sic <= 3293
replace ind = 17 if sic >= 3295 & sic <= 3299
replace ind = 17 if sic >= 3420 & sic <= 3429
replace ind = 17 if sic >= 3430 & sic <= 3433
replace ind = 17 if sic >= 3440 & sic <= 3441
replace ind = 17 if sic >= 3442 & sic <= 3442
replace ind = 17 if sic >= 3446 & sic <= 3446
replace ind = 17 if sic >= 3448 & sic <= 3448
replace ind = 17 if sic >= 3449 & sic <= 3449
replace ind = 17 if sic >= 3450 & sic <= 3451
replace ind = 17 if sic >= 3452 & sic <= 3452
replace ind = 17 if sic >= 3490 & sic <= 3499
replace ind = 17 if sic >= 3996 & sic <= 3996

//18 Cnstr
replace ind = 18 if sic >= 1500 & sic <= 1511
replace ind = 18 if sic >= 1520 & sic <= 1529
replace ind = 18 if sic >= 1530 & sic <= 1539
replace ind = 18 if sic >= 1540 & sic <= 1549
```

```
replace ind = 18 if sic >= 1600 & sic <= 1699
replace ind = 18 if sic >= 1700 & sic <= 1799

//19 Steel
replace ind = 19 if sic >= 3300 & sic <= 3300
replace ind = 19 if sic >= 3310 & sic <= 3317
replace ind = 19 if sic >= 3320 & sic <= 3325
replace ind = 19 if sic >= 3330 & sic <= 3339
replace ind = 19 if sic >= 3340 & sic <= 3341
replace ind = 19 if sic >= 3350 & sic <= 3357
replace ind = 19 if sic >= 3360 & sic <= 3369
replace ind = 19 if sic >= 3370 & sic <= 3379
replace ind = 19 if sic >= 3390 & sic <= 3399

//20 FabPr
replace ind = 20 if sic >= 3400 & sic <= 3400
replace ind = 20 if sic >= 3443 & sic <= 3443
replace ind = 20 if sic >= 3444 & sic <= 3444
replace ind = 20 if sic >= 3460 & sic <= 3469
replace ind = 20 if sic >= 3470 & sic <= 3479

//21 Mach
replace ind = 21 if sic >= 3510 & sic <= 3519
replace ind = 21 if sic >= 3520 & sic <= 3529
replace ind = 21 if sic >= 3530 & sic <= 3530
replace ind = 21 if sic >= 3531 & sic <= 3531
replace ind = 21 if sic >= 3532 & sic <= 3532
replace ind = 21 if sic >= 3533 & sic <= 3533
replace ind = 21 if sic >= 3534 & sic <= 3534
replace ind = 21 if sic >= 3535 & sic <= 3535
replace ind = 21 if sic >= 3536 & sic <= 3536
replace ind = 21 if sic >= 3538 & sic <= 3538
replace ind = 21 if sic >= 3540 & sic <= 3549
replace ind = 21 if sic >= 3550 & sic <= 3559
replace ind = 21 if sic >= 3560 & sic <= 3569
replace ind = 21 if sic >= 3580 & sic <= 3580
replace ind = 21 if sic >= 3581 & sic <= 3581
replace ind = 21 if sic >= 3582 & sic <= 3582
replace ind = 21 if sic >= 3585 & sic <= 3585
replace ind = 21 if sic >= 3586 & sic <= 3586
replace ind = 21 if sic >= 3589 & sic <= 3589
replace ind = 21 if sic >= 3590 & sic <= 3599
```

```
//22 ElcEq
replace ind = 22 if sic >= 3600 & sic <= 3600
replace ind = 22 if sic >= 3610 & sic <= 3613
replace ind = 22 if sic >= 3620 & sic <= 3621
replace ind = 22 if sic >= 3623 & sic <= 3629
replace ind = 22 if sic >= 3640 & sic <= 3644
replace ind = 22 if sic >= 3645 & sic <= 3645
replace ind = 22 if sic >= 3646 & sic <= 3646
replace ind = 22 if sic >= 3648 & sic <= 3649
replace ind = 22 if sic >= 3660 & sic <= 3660
replace ind = 22 if sic >= 3690 & sic <= 3690
replace ind = 22 if sic >= 3691 & sic <= 3692
replace ind = 22 if sic >= 3699 & sic <= 3699

//23 Autos
replace ind = 23 if sic >= 2296 & sic <= 2296
replace ind = 23 if sic >= 2396 & sic <= 2396
replace ind = 23 if sic >= 3010 & sic <= 3011
replace ind = 23 if sic >= 3537 & sic <= 3537
replace ind = 23 if sic >= 3647 & sic <= 3647
replace ind = 23 if sic >= 3694 & sic <= 3694
replace ind = 23 if sic >= 3700 & sic <= 3700
replace ind = 23 if sic >= 3710 & sic <= 3710
replace ind = 23 if sic >= 3711 & sic <= 3711
replace ind = 23 if sic >= 3713 & sic <= 3713
replace ind = 23 if sic >= 3714 & sic <= 3714
replace ind = 23 if sic >= 3715 & sic <= 3715
replace ind = 23 if sic >= 3716 & sic <= 3716
replace ind = 23 if sic >= 3792 & sic <= 3792
replace ind = 23 if sic >= 3790 & sic <= 3791
replace ind = 23 if sic >= 3799 & sic <= 3799

//24 Aero
replace ind = 24 if sic >= 3720 & sic <= 3720
replace ind = 24 if sic >= 3721 & sic <= 3721
replace ind = 24 if sic >= 3723 & sic <= 3724
replace ind = 24 if sic >= 3725 & sic <= 3725
replace ind = 24 if sic >= 3728 & sic <= 3729

//25 Ships
replace ind = 25 if sic >= 3730 & sic <= 3731
replace ind = 25 if sic >= 3740 & sic <= 3743
```

```
//26 Guns
replace ind = 26 if sic >= 3760 & sic <= 3769
replace ind = 26 if sic >= 3795 & sic <= 3795
replace ind = 26 if sic >= 3480 & sic <= 3489

//27 Gold
replace ind = 27 if sic >= 1040 & sic <= 1049

//28 Mines
replace ind = 28 if sic >= 1000 & sic <= 1009
replace ind = 28 if sic >= 1010 & sic <= 1019
replace ind = 28 if sic >= 1020 & sic <= 1029
replace ind = 28 if sic >= 1030 & sic <= 1039
replace ind = 28 if sic >= 1050 & sic <= 1059
replace ind = 28 if sic >= 1060 & sic <= 1069
replace ind = 28 if sic >= 1070 & sic <= 1079
replace ind = 28 if sic >= 1080 & sic <= 1089
replace ind = 28 if sic >= 1090 & sic <= 1099
replace ind = 28 if sic >= 1100 & sic <= 1119
replace ind = 28 if sic >= 1400 & sic <= 1499

//29 Coal
replace ind = 29 if sic >= 1200 & sic <= 1299

//30 Oil
replace ind = 30 if sic >= 1300 & sic <= 1300
replace ind = 30 if sic >= 1310 & sic <= 1319
replace ind = 30 if sic >= 1320 & sic <= 1329
replace ind = 30 if sic >= 1330 & sic <= 1339
replace ind = 30 if sic >= 1370 & sic <= 1379
replace ind = 30 if sic >= 1380 & sic <= 1380
replace ind = 30 if sic >= 1381 & sic <= 1381
replace ind = 30 if sic >= 1382 & sic <= 1382
replace ind = 30 if sic >= 1389 & sic <= 1389
replace ind = 30 if sic >= 2900 & sic <= 2912
replace ind = 30 if sic >= 2990 & sic <= 2999

//31 Util
replace ind = 31 if sic >= 4900 & sic <= 4900
replace ind = 31 if sic >= 4910 & sic <= 4911
replace ind = 31 if sic >= 4920 & sic <= 4922
replace ind = 31 if sic >= 4923 & sic <= 4923
replace ind = 31 if sic >= 4924 & sic <= 4925
replace ind = 31 if sic >= 4930 & sic <= 4931
replace ind = 31 if sic >= 4932 & sic <= 4932
```

```
replace ind = 31 if sic >= 4939 & sic <= 4939
replace ind = 31 if sic >= 4940 & sic <= 4942

//32 Telcm
replace ind = 32 if sic >= 4800 & sic <= 4800
replace ind = 32 if sic >= 4810 & sic <= 4813
replace ind = 32 if sic >= 4820 & sic <= 4822
replace ind = 32 if sic >= 4830 & sic <= 4839
replace ind = 32 if sic >= 4840 & sic <= 4841
replace ind = 32 if sic >= 4880 & sic <= 4889
replace ind = 32 if sic >= 4890 & sic <= 4890
replace ind = 32 if sic >= 4891 & sic <= 4891
replace ind = 32 if sic >= 4892 & sic <= 4892
replace ind = 32 if sic >= 4899 & sic <= 4899

//33 PerSv
replace ind = 33 if sic >= 7020 & sic <= 7021
replace ind = 33 if sic >= 7030 & sic <= 7033
replace ind = 33 if sic >= 7200 & sic <= 7200
replace ind = 33 if sic >= 7210 & sic <= 7212
replace ind = 33 if sic >= 7214 & sic <= 7214
replace ind = 33 if sic >= 7215 & sic <= 7216
replace ind = 33 if sic >= 7217 & sic <= 7217
replace ind = 33 if sic >= 7219 & sic <= 7219
replace ind = 33 if sic >= 7220 & sic <= 7221
replace ind = 33 if sic >= 7230 & sic <= 7231
replace ind = 33 if sic >= 7240 & sic <= 7241
replace ind = 33 if sic >= 7250 & sic <= 7251
replace ind = 33 if sic >= 7260 & sic <= 7269
replace ind = 33 if sic >= 7270 & sic <= 7290
replace ind = 33 if sic >= 7291 & sic <= 7291
replace ind = 33 if sic >= 7292 & sic <= 7299
replace ind = 33 if sic >= 7395 & sic <= 7395
replace ind = 33 if sic >= 7500 & sic <= 7500
replace ind = 33 if sic >= 7520 & sic <= 7529
replace ind = 33 if sic >= 7530 & sic <= 7539
replace ind = 33 if sic >= 7540 & sic <= 7549
replace ind = 33 if sic >= 7600 & sic <= 7600
replace ind = 33 if sic >= 7620 & sic <= 7620
replace ind = 33 if sic >= 7622 & sic <= 7622
replace ind = 33 if sic >= 7623 & sic <= 7623
replace ind = 33 if sic >= 7629 & sic <= 7629
replace ind = 33 if sic >= 7630 & sic <= 7631
replace ind = 33 if sic >= 7640 & sic <= 7641
replace ind = 33 if sic >= 7690 & sic <= 7699
```

```
replace ind = 33 if sic >= 8100 & sic <= 8199
replace ind = 33 if sic >= 8200 & sic <= 8299
replace ind = 33 if sic >= 8300 & sic <= 8399
replace ind = 33 if sic >= 8400 & sic <= 8499
replace ind = 33 if sic >= 8600 & sic <= 8699
replace ind = 33 if sic >= 8800 & sic <= 8899
replace ind = 33 if sic >= 7510 & sic <= 7515

//34 BusSv
replace ind = 34 if sic >= 2750 & sic <= 2759
replace ind = 34 if sic >= 3993 & sic <= 3993
replace ind = 34 if sic >= 7218 & sic <= 7218
replace ind = 34 if sic >= 7300 & sic <= 7300
replace ind = 34 if sic >= 7310 & sic <= 7319
replace ind = 34 if sic >= 7320 & sic <= 7329
replace ind = 34 if sic >= 7330 & sic <= 7339
replace ind = 34 if sic >= 7340 & sic <= 7342
replace ind = 34 if sic >= 7349 & sic <= 7349
replace ind = 34 if sic >= 7350 & sic <= 7351
replace ind = 34 if sic >= 7352 & sic <= 7352
replace ind = 34 if sic >= 7353 & sic <= 7353
replace ind = 34 if sic >= 7359 & sic <= 7359
replace ind = 34 if sic >= 7360 & sic <= 7369
replace ind = 34 if sic >= 7370 & sic <= 7372
replace ind = 34 if sic >= 7374 & sic <= 7374
replace ind = 34 if sic >= 7375 & sic <= 7375
replace ind = 34 if sic >= 7376 & sic <= 7376
replace ind = 34 if sic >= 7377 & sic <= 7377
replace ind = 34 if sic >= 7378 & sic <= 7378
replace ind = 34 if sic >= 7379 & sic <= 7379
replace ind = 34 if sic >= 7380 & sic <= 7380
replace ind = 34 if sic >= 7381 & sic <= 7382
replace ind = 34 if sic >= 7383 & sic <= 7383
replace ind = 34 if sic >= 7384 & sic <= 7384
replace ind = 34 if sic >= 7385 & sic <= 7385
replace ind = 34 if sic >= 7389 & sic <= 7390
replace ind = 34 if sic >= 7391 & sic <= 7391
replace ind = 34 if sic >= 7392 & sic <= 7392
replace ind = 34 if sic >= 7393 & sic <= 7393
replace ind = 34 if sic >= 7394 & sic <= 7394
replace ind = 34 if sic >= 7396 & sic <= 7396
replace ind = 34 if sic >= 7397 & sic <= 7397
replace ind = 34 if sic >= 7399 & sic <= 7399
replace ind = 34 if sic >= 7519 & sic <= 7519
replace ind = 34 if sic >= 8700 & sic <= 8700
```

```
replace ind = 34 if sic >= 8710 & sic <= 8713
replace ind = 34 if sic >= 8720 & sic <= 8721
replace ind = 34 if sic >= 8730 & sic <= 8734
replace ind = 34 if sic >= 8740 & sic <= 8748
replace ind = 34 if sic >= 8900 & sic <= 8910
replace ind = 34 if sic >= 8911 & sic <= 8911
replace ind = 34 if sic >= 8920 & sic <= 8999
replace ind = 34 if sic >= 4220 & sic <= 4229

//35 Comps
replace ind = 35 if sic >= 3570 & sic <= 3579
replace ind = 35 if sic >= 3680 & sic <= 3680
replace ind = 35 if sic >= 3681 & sic <= 3681
replace ind = 35 if sic >= 3682 & sic <= 3682
replace ind = 35 if sic >= 3683 & sic <= 3683
replace ind = 35 if sic >= 3684 & sic <= 3684
replace ind = 35 if sic >= 3685 & sic <= 3685
replace ind = 35 if sic >= 3686 & sic <= 3686
replace ind = 35 if sic >= 3687 & sic <= 3687
replace ind = 35 if sic >= 3688 & sic <= 3688
replace ind = 35 if sic >= 3689 & sic <= 3689
replace ind = 35 if sic >= 3695 & sic <= 3695
replace ind = 35 if sic >= 7373 & sic <= 7373

//36 Chips
replace ind = 36 if sic >= 3622 & sic <= 3622
replace ind = 36 if sic >= 3661 & sic <= 3661
replace ind = 36 if sic >= 3662 & sic <= 3662
replace ind = 36 if sic >= 3663 & sic <= 3663
replace ind = 36 if sic >= 3664 & sic <= 3664
replace ind = 36 if sic >= 3665 & sic <= 3665
replace ind = 36 if sic >= 3666 & sic <= 3666
replace ind = 36 if sic >= 3669 & sic <= 3669
replace ind = 36 if sic >= 3670 & sic <= 3679
replace ind = 36 if sic >= 3810 & sic <= 3810
replace ind = 36 if sic >= 3812 & sic <= 3812

//37 LabEq
replace ind = 37 if sic >= 3811 & sic <= 3811
replace ind = 37 if sic >= 3820 & sic <= 3820
replace ind = 37 if sic >= 3821 & sic <= 3821
replace ind = 37 if sic >= 3822 & sic <= 3822
replace ind = 37 if sic >= 3823 & sic <= 3823
replace ind = 37 if sic >= 3824 & sic <= 3824
replace ind = 37 if sic >= 3825 & sic <= 3825
```

```
replace ind = 37 if sic >= 3826 & sic <= 3826
replace ind = 37 if sic >= 3827 & sic <= 3827
replace ind = 37 if sic >= 3829 & sic <= 3829
replace ind = 37 if sic >= 3830 & sic <= 3839

//38 Paper
replace ind = 38 if sic >= 2520 & sic <= 2549
replace ind = 38 if sic >= 2600 & sic <= 2639
replace ind = 38 if sic >= 2670 & sic <= 2699
replace ind = 38 if sic >= 2760 & sic <= 2761
replace ind = 38 if sic >= 3950 & sic <= 3955

//39 Boxes
replace ind = 39 if sic >= 2440 & sic <= 2449
replace ind = 39 if sic >= 2640 & sic <= 2659
replace ind = 39 if sic >= 3220 & sic <= 3221
replace ind = 39 if sic >= 3410 & sic <= 3412

//40 Trans
replace ind = 40 if sic >= 4000 & sic <= 4013
replace ind = 40 if sic >= 4040 & sic <= 4049
replace ind = 40 if sic >= 4100 & sic <= 4100
replace ind = 40 if sic >= 4110 & sic <= 4119
replace ind = 40 if sic >= 4120 & sic <= 4121
replace ind = 40 if sic >= 4130 & sic <= 4131
replace ind = 40 if sic >= 4140 & sic <= 4142
replace ind = 40 if sic >= 4150 & sic <= 4151
replace ind = 40 if sic >= 4170 & sic <= 4173
replace ind = 40 if sic >= 4190 & sic <= 4199
replace ind = 40 if sic >= 4200 & sic <= 4200
replace ind = 40 if sic >= 4210 & sic <= 4219
replace ind = 40 if sic >= 4230 & sic <= 4231
replace ind = 40 if sic >= 4240 & sic <= 4249
replace ind = 40 if sic >= 4400 & sic <= 4499
replace ind = 40 if sic >= 4500 & sic <= 4599
replace ind = 40 if sic >= 4600 & sic <= 4699
replace ind = 40 if sic >= 4700 & sic <= 4700
replace ind = 40 if sic >= 4710 & sic <= 4712
replace ind = 40 if sic >= 4720 & sic <= 4729
replace ind = 40 if sic >= 4730 & sic <= 4739
replace ind = 40 if sic >= 4740 & sic <= 4749
replace ind = 40 if sic >= 4780 & sic <= 4780
replace ind = 40 if sic >= 4782 & sic <= 4782
replace ind = 40 if sic >= 4783 & sic <= 4783
```

```
replace ind = 40 if sic >= 4784 & sic <= 4784
replace ind = 40 if sic >= 4785 & sic <= 4785
replace ind = 40 if sic >= 4789 & sic <= 4789

//41 Whlsl
replace ind = 41 if sic >= 5000 & sic <= 5000
replace ind = 41 if sic >= 5010 & sic <= 5015
replace ind = 41 if sic >= 5020 & sic <= 5023
replace ind = 41 if sic >= 5030 & sic <= 5039
replace ind = 41 if sic >= 5040 & sic <= 5042
replace ind = 41 if sic >= 5043 & sic <= 5043
replace ind = 41 if sic >= 5044 & sic <= 5044
replace ind = 41 if sic >= 5045 & sic <= 5045
replace ind = 41 if sic >= 5046 & sic <= 5046
replace ind = 41 if sic >= 5047 & sic <= 5047
replace ind = 41 if sic >= 5048 & sic <= 5048
replace ind = 41 if sic >= 5049 & sic <= 5049
replace ind = 41 if sic >= 5050 & sic <= 5059
replace ind = 41 if sic >= 5060 & sic <= 5060
replace ind = 41 if sic >= 5063 & sic <= 5063
replace ind = 41 if sic >= 5064 & sic <= 5064
replace ind = 41 if sic >= 5065 & sic <= 5065
replace ind = 41 if sic >= 5070 & sic <= 5078
replace ind = 41 if sic >= 5080 & sic <= 5080
replace ind = 41 if sic >= 5081 & sic <= 5081
replace ind = 41 if sic >= 5082 & sic <= 5082
replace ind = 41 if sic >= 5083 & sic <= 5083
replace ind = 41 if sic >= 5084 & sic <= 5084
replace ind = 41 if sic >= 5085 & sic <= 5085
replace ind = 41 if sic >= 5086 & sic <= 5087
replace ind = 41 if sic >= 5088 & sic <= 5088
replace ind = 41 if sic >= 5090 & sic <= 5090
replace ind = 41 if sic >= 5091 & sic <= 5092
replace ind = 41 if sic >= 5093 & sic <= 5093
replace ind = 41 if sic >= 5094 & sic <= 5094
replace ind = 41 if sic >= 5099 & sic <= 5099
replace ind = 41 if sic >= 5100 & sic <= 5100
replace ind = 41 if sic >= 5110 & sic <= 5113
replace ind = 41 if sic >= 5120 & sic <= 5122
replace ind = 41 if sic >= 5130 & sic <= 5139
replace ind = 41 if sic >= 5140 & sic <= 5149
replace ind = 41 if sic >= 5150 & sic <= 5159
replace ind = 41 if sic >= 5160 & sic <= 5169
replace ind = 41 if sic >= 5170 & sic <= 5172
```

```
replace ind = 41 if sic >= 5180 & sic <= 5182
replace ind = 41 if sic >= 5190 & sic <= 5199

//42 Rtail
replace ind = 42 if sic >= 5200 & sic <= 5200
replace ind = 42 if sic >= 5210 & sic <= 5219
replace ind = 42 if sic >= 5220 & sic <= 5229
replace ind = 42 if sic >= 5230 & sic <= 5231
replace ind = 42 if sic >= 5250 & sic <= 5251
replace ind = 42 if sic >= 5260 & sic <= 5261
replace ind = 42 if sic >= 5270 & sic <= 5271
replace ind = 42 if sic >= 5300 & sic <= 5300
replace ind = 42 if sic >= 5310 & sic <= 5311
replace ind = 42 if sic >= 5320 & sic <= 5320
replace ind = 42 if sic >= 5330 & sic <= 5331
replace ind = 42 if sic >= 5334 & sic <= 5334
replace ind = 42 if sic >= 5340 & sic <= 5349
replace ind = 42 if sic >= 5390 & sic <= 5399
replace ind = 42 if sic >= 5400 & sic <= 5400
replace ind = 42 if sic >= 5410 & sic <= 5411
replace ind = 42 if sic >= 5412 & sic <= 5412
replace ind = 42 if sic >= 5420 & sic <= 5429
replace ind = 42 if sic >= 5430 & sic <= 5439
replace ind = 42 if sic >= 5440 & sic <= 5449
replace ind = 42 if sic >= 5450 & sic <= 5459
replace ind = 42 if sic >= 5460 & sic <= 5469
replace ind = 42 if sic >= 5490 & sic <= 5499
replace ind = 42 if sic >= 5500 & sic <= 5500
replace ind = 42 if sic >= 5510 & sic <= 5529
replace ind = 42 if sic >= 5530 & sic <= 5539
replace ind = 42 if sic >= 5540 & sic <= 5549
replace ind = 42 if sic >= 5550 & sic <= 5559
replace ind = 42 if sic >= 5560 & sic <= 5569
replace ind = 42 if sic >= 5570 & sic <= 5579
replace ind = 42 if sic >= 5590 & sic <= 5599
replace ind = 42 if sic >= 5600 & sic <= 5699
replace ind = 42 if sic >= 5700 & sic <= 5700
replace ind = 42 if sic >= 5710 & sic <= 5719
replace ind = 42 if sic >= 5720 & sic <= 5722
replace ind = 42 if sic >= 5730 & sic <= 5733
replace ind = 42 if sic >= 5734 & sic <= 5734
replace ind = 42 if sic >= 5735 & sic <= 5735
replace ind = 42 if sic >= 5736 & sic <= 5736
replace ind = 42 if sic >= 5750 & sic <= 5799
replace ind = 42 if sic >= 5900 & sic <= 5900
```

```
replace ind = 42 if sic >= 5910 & sic <= 5912
replace ind = 42 if sic >= 5920 & sic <= 5929
replace ind = 42 if sic >= 5930 & sic <= 5932
replace ind = 42 if sic >= 5940 & sic <= 5940
replace ind = 42 if sic >= 5941 & sic <= 5941
replace ind = 42 if sic >= 5942 & sic <= 5942
replace ind = 42 if sic >= 5943 & sic <= 5943
replace ind = 42 if sic >= 5944 & sic <= 5944
replace ind = 42 if sic >= 5945 & sic <= 5945
replace ind = 42 if sic >= 5946 & sic <= 5946
replace ind = 42 if sic >= 5947 & sic <= 5947
replace ind = 42 if sic >= 5948 & sic <= 5948
replace ind = 42 if sic >= 5949 & sic <= 5949
replace ind = 42 if sic >= 5950 & sic <= 5959
replace ind = 42 if sic >= 5960 & sic <= 5969
replace ind = 42 if sic >= 5970 & sic <= 5979
replace ind = 42 if sic >= 5980 & sic <= 5989
replace ind = 42 if sic >= 5990 & sic <= 5990
replace ind = 42 if sic >= 5992 & sic <= 5992
replace ind = 42 if sic >= 5993 & sic <= 5993
replace ind = 42 if sic >= 5994 & sic <= 5994
replace ind = 42 if sic >= 5995 & sic <= 5995
replace ind = 42 if sic >= 5999 & sic <= 5999

//43 Meals
replace ind = 43 if sic >= 5800 & sic <= 5819
replace ind = 43 if sic >= 5820 & sic <= 5829
replace ind = 43 if sic >= 5890 & sic <= 5899
replace ind = 43 if sic >= 7000 & sic <= 7000
replace ind = 43 if sic >= 7010 & sic <= 7019
replace ind = 43 if sic >= 7040 & sic <= 7049
replace ind = 43 if sic >= 7213 & sic <= 7213

//44 Banks
replace ind = 44 if sic >= 6000 & sic <= 6000
replace ind = 44 if sic >= 6010 & sic <= 6019
replace ind = 44 if sic >= 6020 & sic <= 6020
replace ind = 44 if sic >= 6021 & sic <= 6021
replace ind = 44 if sic >= 6022 & sic <= 6022
replace ind = 44 if sic >= 6023 & sic <= 6024
replace ind = 44 if sic >= 6025 & sic <= 6025
replace ind = 44 if sic >= 6026 & sic <= 6026
replace ind = 44 if sic >= 6027 & sic <= 6027
replace ind = 44 if sic >= 6028 & sic <= 6029
replace ind = 44 if sic >= 6030 & sic <= 6036
```

```
replace ind = 44 if sic >= 6040 & sic <= 6059
replace ind = 44 if sic >= 6060 & sic <= 6062
replace ind = 44 if sic >= 6080 & sic <= 6082
replace ind = 44 if sic >= 6090 & sic <= 6099
replace ind = 44 if sic >= 6100 & sic <= 6100
replace ind = 44 if sic >= 6110 & sic <= 6111
replace ind = 44 if sic >= 6112 & sic <= 6113
replace ind = 44 if sic >= 6120 & sic <= 6129
replace ind = 44 if sic >= 6130 & sic <= 6139
replace ind = 44 if sic >= 6140 & sic <= 6149
replace ind = 44 if sic >= 6150 & sic <= 6159
replace ind = 44 if sic >= 6160 & sic <= 6169
replace ind = 44 if sic >= 6170 & sic <= 6179
replace ind = 44 if sic >= 6190 & sic <= 6199

//45 Insur
replace ind = 45 if sic >= 6300 & sic <= 6300
replace ind = 45 if sic >= 6310 & sic <= 6319
replace ind = 45 if sic >= 6320 & sic <= 6329
replace ind = 45 if sic >= 6330 & sic <= 6331
replace ind = 45 if sic >= 6350 & sic <= 6351
replace ind = 45 if sic >= 6360 & sic <= 6361
replace ind = 45 if sic >= 6370 & sic <= 6379
replace ind = 45 if sic >= 6390 & sic <= 6399
replace ind = 45 if sic >= 6400 & sic <= 6411

//46 RlEst
replace ind = 46 if sic >= 6500 & sic <= 6500
replace ind = 46 if sic >= 6510 & sic <= 6510
replace ind = 46 if sic >= 6512 & sic <= 6512
replace ind = 46 if sic >= 6513 & sic <= 6513
replace ind = 46 if sic >= 6514 & sic <= 6514
replace ind = 46 if sic >= 6515 & sic <= 6515
replace ind = 46 if sic >= 6517 & sic <= 6519
replace ind = 46 if sic >= 6520 & sic <= 6529
replace ind = 46 if sic >= 6530 & sic <= 6531
replace ind = 46 if sic >= 6532 & sic <= 6532
replace ind = 46 if sic >= 6540 & sic <= 6541
replace ind = 46 if sic >= 6550 & sic <= 6553
replace ind = 46 if sic >= 6590 & sic <= 6599
replace ind = 46 if sic >= 6610 & sic <= 6611

//47 Fin
replace ind = 47 if sic >= 6200 & sic <= 6299
replace ind = 47 if sic >= 6700 & sic <= 6700
```

```
replace ind = 47 if sic >= 6710 & sic <= 6719
replace ind = 47 if sic >= 6720 & sic <= 6722
replace ind = 47 if sic >= 6723 & sic <= 6723
replace ind = 47 if sic >= 6724 & sic <= 6724
replace ind = 47 if sic >= 6725 & sic <= 6725
replace ind = 47 if sic >= 6726 & sic <= 6726
replace ind = 47 if sic >= 6730 & sic <= 6733
replace ind = 47 if sic >= 6740 & sic <= 6779
replace ind = 47 if sic >= 6790 & sic <= 6791
replace ind = 47 if sic >= 6792 & sic <= 6792
replace ind = 47 if sic >= 6793 & sic <= 6793
replace ind = 47 if sic >= 6794 & sic <= 6794
replace ind = 47 if sic >= 6795 & sic <= 6795
replace ind = 47 if sic >= 6798 & sic <= 6798
replace ind = 47 if sic >= 6799 & sic <= 6799

//48 Other
replace ind = 48 if sic >= 4950 & sic <= 4959
replace ind = 48 if sic >= 4960 & sic <= 4961
replace ind = 48 if sic >= 4970 & sic <= 4971
replace ind = 48 if sic >= 4990 & sic <= 4991

}


keep cusip weeknum rd rx capw capwL ind
sort ind weeknum cusip
by ind weeknum: gen obs = _N
by ind weeknum: egen obs2 = count(capwL)
by ind weeknum : gen id_firm = _n
egen id_wk = group(weeknum)
gen indxw_ew = .
gen inddw_ew = .
gen indxw_vw = .
gen inddw_vw = .
gen indxw_vwL = .
gen inddw_vwL = .
save temp_str_02, replace
*/

forval i = 1/49 {
     use temp_str_02, clear
     qui: keep if ind == `i'
     save ind_`i'
}
```

```
forval k = 1/49 {

      use ind_`k', clear
      local fn = id_wk[_N]

      forval i = 1/`fn' {    //

            use ind_`k', clear
            display "~~~~~~  Ind  "  `k'  "  &  week  :  "  `i'
            " ~~~~~~"
            qui: keep if id_wk == `i'
            local A = obs[1]

            forval j = 1/`A' {

                  su rx if id_firm != `j', meanonly
                  local B1 = r(mean)
                  qui: replace indxw_ew = `B1' if id_firm ==
                  `j'

                  su rd if id_firm != `j', meanonly
                  local B2 = r(mean)
                  qui: replace inddw_ew = `B2' if id_firm ==
                  `j'

                  su  rx  if  id_firm  !=  `j'  [iw  =  capw],
                  meanonly
                  local B3 = r(mean)
                  qui: replace indxw_vw = `B3' if id_firm ==
                  `j'

                  su  rd  if  id_firm  !=  `j'  [iw  =  capw],
                  meanonly
                  local B4 = r(mean)
                  qui: replace inddw_vw = `B4' if id_firm ==
                  `j'

                  su obs2, meanonly
                  local cc = r(mean)

                  if `cc'>4 & obs2[`j']>0 {

                        su  rx  if  id_firm  !=  `j'  [iw  =
                        capwL], meanonly
                        local B5 = r(mean)
                        qui: replace indxw_vwL = `B5' if
                        id_firm == `j'
```

```
                                        su rd if id_firm != `j' [iw =
                                        capwL], meanonly
                                        local B6 = r(mean)
                                        qui: replace inddw_vwL = `B6' if
                                        id_firm == `j'

                              }

                  }
                  qui: drop rx* rd* id_* obs*
                  qui: save z_ind_`k'_wk_`i'
            }
}

forval k = 1/49 {
      use ind_`k', clear
      local fn = id_wk[_N]
      use z_ind_`k'_wk_1, clear
      forval i = 2/`fn' {
                append using z_ind_`k'_wk_`i'
      }
      save done_ind_`k'
}


use done_ind_1, clear
forval i = 2/49 {
       append using done_ind_`i'
}

save ind_wk_new, replace

/*
use Market.Daily.dta, clear // calculate weekly market index
keep vw* ew* date
merge m:1 date using weeknum
keep if _merge == 3
drop weekday _merge*
drop if year(date) < 1970
replace vwretd = ln(1+vwretd)
replace vwretx = ln(1+vwretx)
replace ewretd = ln(1+ewretd)
replace ewretx = ln(1+ewretx)
collapse (sum) md_vw=vwretd mx_vw=vwretx ///
        md_ew=ewretd mx_ew=ewretx ///
              , by(weeknum) cw // t =
replace md_vw = exp(md_vw) - 1
```

```
replace mx_vw = exp(mx_vw) - 1
replace md_ew = exp(md_ew) - 1
replace mx_ew = exp(mx_ew) - 1
save mkt_wk, replace

use FF_3_weekly, clear // recreate week num of Fama-French weekly
data
merge m:1 date using weeknum
keep if _merge == 3
drop weekday _merge*
save ff_wk, replace

use temp_str_02, clear // merge weekly ret w/ mkt, FF, and index
data
drop ind* cap* obs id_*
merge 1:1 cusip weeknum using ind_wk_new, nogen
merge m:1 weeknum using mkt_wk
keep if _merge == 3
drop _merge
merge m:1 weeknum using ff_wk
keep if _merge == 3
drop _merge obs2
replace smb = smb / 100
replace hml = hml / 100
replace mktrf = mktrf / 100
replace rf = rf / 100
rename smb ff_smb
rename hml ff_hml
rename mktrf ff_mkt
replace rd = rd - rf
replace rx = rx - rf
replace md_vw = md_vw - rf
replace md_ew = md_ew - rf
replace mx_vw = mx_vw - rf
replace mx_ew = mx_ew - rf
replace indxw_ew = indxw_ew - rf
replace inddw_ew = inddw_ew - rf
replace indxw_vw = indxw_vw - rf
replace inddw_vw = inddw_vw - rf
replace indxw_vwL = indxw_vwL - rf
replace inddw_vwL = inddw_vwL - rf
gen year = year(date)
sort cusip year
egen id_firm = group(cusip)
*drop if missing(rd)
```

```
*drop if missing(rx)
*drop if missing(inddw_ew)
*drop if missing(inddw_vw)
*drop if missing(indxw_ew)
*drop if missing(indxw_vw)
by cusip: gen id_year = sum(year != year[_n-1])
by cusip : gen indxw_ew_L = indxw_ew[_n-1]
by cusip : gen inddw_ew_L = inddw_ew[_n-1]
by cusip : gen indxw_vw_L = indxw_vw[_n-1]
by cusip : gen inddw_vw_L = inddw_vw[_n-1]
by cusip : gen indxw_vwL_L = indxw_vwL[_n-1]
by cusip : gen inddw_vwL_L = inddw_vwL[_n-1]
by cusip : gen md_ewL = md_ew[_n-1]
by cusip : gen md_vwL = md_vw[_n-1]
by cusip : gen mx_ewL = mx_ew[_n-1]
by cusip : gen mx_vwL = mx_vw[_n-1]
by cusip year: egen obs = count(rx)
by cusip year: egen obs2 = count(inddw_vwL)
by cusip year: egen obs3 = count(indxw_vw_L)
by cusip year: egen obs4 = count(inddw_vwL_L)
drop date rf
save freg_wk, replace
*/

/*


program split // spliting the total data file into 31 smaller files
     args filename num // less the time of reading dta in the for
     loop
     use `filename', clear
     local N = id_firm[_N]
     local step = (`N' - mod(`N', `num'))/`num'
     display `N'
     display `step'
     forval i = 1/`num'{
             local s1 = 1 + `step'*(`i'-1)
             local s2 = `s1' + `step' - 1
             use `filename', clear
             keep if id_firm >= `s1' & id_firm <= `s2'
             save tmp_`i', replace
     }
     display `s2'
     local fin = `num' + 1
     use `filename', clear
```

```
     keep if id_firm > `s2'
     save tmp_`fin', replace
end
split freg_wk 50
program drop split
*/

local thre = 11 // take 5-day a month to 12 weeks a year

forval j = 1/51 { //51
    use tmp_`j', clear
    local s1 = id_firm[1]
    local s2 = id_firm[_N]

    forval i = `s1'/`s2' { //
            use tmp_`j', clear
            display "~~~~~~ " "Firm: " `i' " ~~~~~~"
            qui: keep if id_firm == `i'
            local t2 = id_year[_N]

            forval h = 1/14 {
                    qui: gen err_x`h' = .
                    qui: gen r2_x`h' = .
                    qui: gen err_d`h' = .
                    qui: gen r2_d`h' = .
             }

             forval k = 1/`t2' {
             //display " ~~~~~~ Firm " `i' " & Year " `k' " of "
             `t2' " ~~~~~~ "
             // ~~~ <I> obs = count(rt)
                     su obs if id_year == `k', meanonly // get
                     num of obs
                     local p1 = r(mean)
                     if `p1'> `thre' {
                     // ~~~ (1) total return
                             // CAPM & equally weigted mkt index
                             reg rd md_ew if id_year == `k',
                             noheader notable
                             qui: predict tmp if id_year ==
                             `k', residuals
                             qui: replace err_d1 = tmp if id_
                             year == `k'
                             qui: replace r2_d1 = e(r2) if id_
                             year == `k'
                             qui: drop tmp
```

```
// CAPM & value weigted mkt index
reg rd md_vw if id_year == `k',
noheader notable
qui: predict tmp if id_year ==
`k', residuals
qui: replace err_d2 = tmp if id_
year == `k'
qui: replace r2_d2 = e(r2) if id_
year == `k'
qui: drop tmp

// Fama-French
reg rd ff_mkt ff_smb ff_hml if id_
year == `k', noheader notable
qui: predict tmp if id_year ==
`k', residuals
qui: replace err_d3 = tmp if id_
year == `k'
qui: replace r2_d3 = e(r2) if id_
year == `k'
qui: drop tmp

// mkt + index ew
reg rd md_ew inddw_ew if id_year
== `k', noheader notable
qui: predict tmp if id_year ==
`k', residuals
qui: replace err_d4 = tmp if id_
year == `k'
qui: replace r2_d4 = e(r2) if id_
year == `k'
qui: drop tmp

// mkt + index vw (same preiod mkt
cap)
reg rd md_vw inddw_vw if id_year
== `k', noheader notable
qui: predict tmp if id_year ==
`k', residuals
qui: replace err_d5 = tmp if id_
year == `k'
qui: replace r2_d5 = e(r2) if id_
year == `k'
qui: drop tmp
```

```
// ~~~ (2) ex-div return
        // CAPM & equally weigted mkt index
        reg rx mx_ew if id_year == `k',
        noheader notable
        qui: predict tmp if id_year ==
        `k', residuals
        qui: replace err_x1 = tmp if id_
        year == `k'
        qui: replace r2_x1 = e(r2) if id_
        year == `k'
        qui: drop tmp

        // CAPM & value weigted mkt index
        reg rx mx_vw if id_year == `k',
        noheader notable
        qui: predict tmp if id_year ==
        `k', residuals
        qui: replace err_x2 = tmp if id_
        year == `k'
        qui: replace r2_x2 = e(r2) if id_
        year == `k'
        qui: drop tmp

        // Fama-French
        reg rx ff_mkt ff_smb ff_hml if id_
        year == `k', noheader notable
        qui: predict tmp if id_year ==
        `k', residuals
        qui: replace err_x3 = tmp if id_
        year == `k'
        qui: replace r2_x3 = e(r2) if id_
        year == `k'
        qui: drop tmp

        // mkt + index ew
        reg rx mx_ew indxw_ew if id_year
        == `k', noheader notable
        qui: predict tmp if id_year ==
        `k', residuals
        qui: replace err_x4 = tmp if id_
        year == `k'
        qui: replace r2_x4 = e(r2) if id_
        year == `k'
        qui: drop tmp
```

```
            // mkt + index vwv (same preiod mkt
            cap)
            reg rx mx_vw indxw_vw if id_year
            == `k', noheader notable
            qui: predict tmp if id_year ==
            `k', residuals
            qui: replace err_x5 = tmp if id_
            year == `k'
            qui: replace r2_x5 = e(r2) if id_
            year == `k'
            qui: drop tmp

    }

// ~~~ <II> obs2 = count(lagged mkt) =
count(lagged ind) ind vw (same preiod)
su obs2 if id_year == `k', meanonly
local p2 = r(mean)
if `p2' > `thre' {

// ~~~ (1) total return
            reg rd md_ew md_ewL if id_year ==
            `k', noheader notable
            qui: predict tmp if id_year ==
            `k', residuals
            qui: replace err_d6 = tmp if id_
            year == `k'
            qui: replace r2_d6 = e(r2) if id_
            year == `k'
            qui: drop tmp

            reg rd md_vw md_vwL if id_year ==
            `k', noheader notable
            qui: predict tmp if id_year ==
            `k', residuals
            qui: replace err_d7 = tmp if id_
            year == `k'
            qui: replace r2_d7 = e(r2) if id_
            year == `k'
            qui: drop tmp

            reg rd md_ew md_ewL inddw_ew if id_
            year == `k', noheader notable
            qui: predict tmp if id_year ==
            `k', residuals
            qui: replace err_d8 = tmp if id_
            year == `k'
```

```
                                        qui: replace r2_d8 = e(r2) if id_
                                        year == `k'
                                        qui: drop tmp

                                        reg rd md_vw md_vwL inddw_vw if id_
year == `k', noheader notable
                                        qui: predict tmp if id_year ==
                                        `k', residuals
                                        qui: replace err_d9 = tmp if id_
                                        year == `k'
                                        qui: replace r2_d9 = e(r2) if id_
                                        year == `k'
                                        qui: drop tmp

                                        reg rd md_ew md_ewL inddw_ew inddw_
ew_L if id_year == `k', noheader notable
                                        qui: predict tmp if id_year ==
                                        `k', residuals
                                        qui: replace err_d10 = tmp if id_
                                        year == `k'
                                        qui: replace r2_d10 = e(r2) if id_
                                        year == `k'
                                        qui: drop tmp

                                        reg rd md_vw md_vwL inddw_vw inddw_
vw_L if id_year == `k', noheader notable
                                        qui: predict tmp if id_year ==
                                        `k', residuals
                                        qui: replace err_d11 = tmp if id_
                                        year == `k'
                                        qui: replace r2_d11 = e(r2) if id_
                                        year == `k'
                                        qui: drop tmp

                                // ~~~ (2) ex-div return
                                        reg rx mx_ew mx_ewL if id_year ==
                                        `k', noheader notable
                                        qui: predict tmp if id_year ==
                                        `k', residuals
                                        qui: replace err_x6 = tmp if id_
                                        year == `k'
                                        qui: replace r2_x6 = e(r2) if id_
                                        year == `k'
                                        qui: drop tmp
```

```
                              reg rx mx_vw mx_vwL if id_year ==
                              `k', noheader notable
                              qui: predict tmp if id_year ==
                              `k', residuals
                              qui: replace err_x7 = tmp if id_
                              year == `k'
                              qui: replace r2_x7 = e(r2) if id_
                              year == `k'
                              qui: drop tmp

                              reg rx mx_ew mx_ewL indxw_ew if id_
                              year == `k', noheader notable
                              qui: predict tmp if id_year ==
                              `k', residuals
                              qui: replace err_x8 = tmp if id_
                              year == `k'
                              qui: replace r2_x8 = e(r2) if id_
                              year == `k'
                              qui: drop tmp

                              reg rx mx_vw mx_vwL indxw_vw if id_
                              year == `k', noheader notable
                              qui: predict tmp if id_year ==
                              `k', residuals
                              qui: replace err_x9 = tmp if id_
                              year == `k'
                              qui: replace r2_x9 = e(r2) if id_
                              year == `k'
                              qui: drop tmp

                              reg rx mx_ew mx_ewL indxw_ew indxw_
ew_L if id_year == `k', noheader notable
                              qui: predict tmp if id_year ==
                              `k', residuals
                              qui: replace err_x10 = tmp if id_
                              year == `k'
                              qui: replace r2_x10 = e(r2) if id_
                              year == `k'
                              qui: drop tmp

                              reg rx mx_vw mx_vwL indxw_vw indxw_
vw_L if id_year == `k', noheader notable
                              qui: predict tmp if id_year ==
                              `k', residuals
```

```
            qui: replace err_x11 = tmp if id_
            year == `k'
            qui: replace r2_x11 = e(r2) if id_
            year == `k'
            qui: drop tmp
      }

// ~~~ <III> obs3 = count(ind_vw_L) ind vw
(last preiod)
su obs3 if id_year == `k', meanonly
local p3 = r(mean)
if `p3' > `thre' {

            reg rd md_vw inddw_vwL if id_year
            == `k', noheader notable
            qui: predict tmp if id_year ==
            `k', residuals
            qui: replace err_d12 = tmp if id_
            year == `k'
            qui: replace r2_d12 = e(r2) if id_
            year == `k'
            qui: drop tmp

            reg rx mx_vw indxw_vwL if id_year
            == `k', noheader notable
            qui: predict tmp if id_year ==
            `k', residuals
            qui: replace err_x12 = tmp if id_
            year == `k'
            qui: replace r2_x12 = e(r2) if id_
            year == `k'
            qui: drop tmp

            reg rd md_vw md_vwL inddw_vwL if
            id_year == `k', noheader notable
            qui: predict tmp if id_year ==
            `k', residuals
            qui: replace err_d13 = tmp if id_
            year == `k'
            qui: replace r2_d13 = e(r2) if id_
            year == `k'
            qui: drop tmp
```

```
                    reg rx mx_vw mx_vwL indxw_vwL if
                    id_year == `k', noheader notable
                    qui: predict tmp if id_year ==
                    `k', residuals
                    qui: replace err_x13 = tmp if id_
                    year == `k'
                    qui: replace r2_x13 = e(r2) if id_
                    year == `k'
                    qui: drop tmp

                }

            // ~~~ <IV> obs4 = count(ind_vw_L lagged)
            ind vw (last preiod)
            su obs4 if id_year == `k', meanonly
            local p4 = r(mean)
            if `p4' > `thre' {

                    reg rd md_vw md_vwL inddw_vwL
inddw_vwL_L if id_year == `k', noheader notable
                    qui: predict tmp if id_year ==
                    `k', residuals
                    qui: replace err_d14 = tmp if id_
                    year == `k'
                    qui: replace r2_d14 = e(r2) if id_
                    year == `k'
                    qui: drop tmp

                    reg rx mx_vw mx_vwL indxw_vwL
indxw_vwL_L if id_year == `k', noheader notable

                    qui: predict tmp if id_year ==
                    `k', residuals
                    qui: replace err_x14 = tmp if id_
                    year == `k'
                    qui: replace r2_x14 = e(r2) if id_
                    year == `k'
                    qui: drop tmp

                }

        }
        qui: keep cusip year err* r2* weeknum obs*
        qui: save z_firm_`i'
  }
} // t = 5562.94s
```

```
use z_firm_1, clear
forval i = 2/26372 {
     append using z_firm_`i'
}
save done_wk_err, replace

use done_wk_err, clear
drop obs*
sort cusip year weeknum
forval i = 1/14 {
     display " ~~~~~~ " `i'
     by cusip year: egen ivxw_`i'_J1 = sd(err_x`i')
     by cusip year: egen ivdw_`i'_J1 = sd(err_d`i')
     by cusip year: egen num = count(ivxw_`i'_J1)
     replace ivxw_`i'_J1 = ivxw_`i'_J1*sqrt(num) // annualized
     replace ivdw_`i'_J1 = ivdw_`i'_J1*sqrt(num)
     by cusip year: gen tmpx = err_x`i'[_n-1]
     by cusip year: gen tmpd = err_d`i'[_n-1]
     gen tmpx2 = err_x`i'^2 + 2*err_x`i'*tmpx
     gen tmpd2 = err_d`i'^2 + 2*err_d`i'*tmpd
     replace tmpx2 = err_x`i'^2 if tmpx2 <= 0
     replace tmpd2 = err_d`i'^2 if tmpd2 <= 0
     by cusip year: egen ivxw_`i'_J3 = sum(tmpx2)
     by cusip year: egen ivdw_`i'_J3 = sum(tmpd2)
     replace ivxw_`i'_J3 = sqrt(ivxw_`i'_J3) // take sqrt
     replace ivdw_`i'_J3 = sqrt(ivdw_`i'_J3)
     drop tmp* err_x`i' err_d`i' num
}
drop weeknum
duplicates drop cusip year, force

forval i = 1/14 {
     replace ivxw_`i'_J1 = . if ivxw_`i'_J1 == 0
     replace ivdw_`i'_J1 = . if ivdw_`i'_J1 == 0
     replace ivxw_`i'_J3 = . if ivxw_`i'_J3 == 0
     replace ivdw_`i'_J3 = . if ivdw_`i'_J3 == 0
     }

correl iv*
tabstat iv* , stat( count mean sd min ///
                              p5 p25 p50 p75 p90 p95 max) c(s)
save v_id_w, replace
```

```
use ret_wk, clear
sort cusip year
by cusip year: egen obs = count(rd)
replace rd = rd*sqrt(obs)
replace rx = rx*sqrt(obs)
drop if obs<11
drop obs
collapse (sd) tvxw=rx tvdw=rd, by(cusip year) cw
save v_tot_w, replace
```

MIX
Papier aus verantwortungsvollen Quellen
Paper from responsible sources
FSC® C105338

If you have any concerns about our products,
you can contact us on
ProductSafety@springernature.com

In case Publisher is established outside the EU,
the EU authorized representative is:
Springer Nature Customer Service Center GmbH
Europaplatz 3, 69115 Heidelberg, Germany

Printed by Libri Plureos GmbH
in Hamburg, Germany